IMAGES
of America

OGEMAW COUNTY

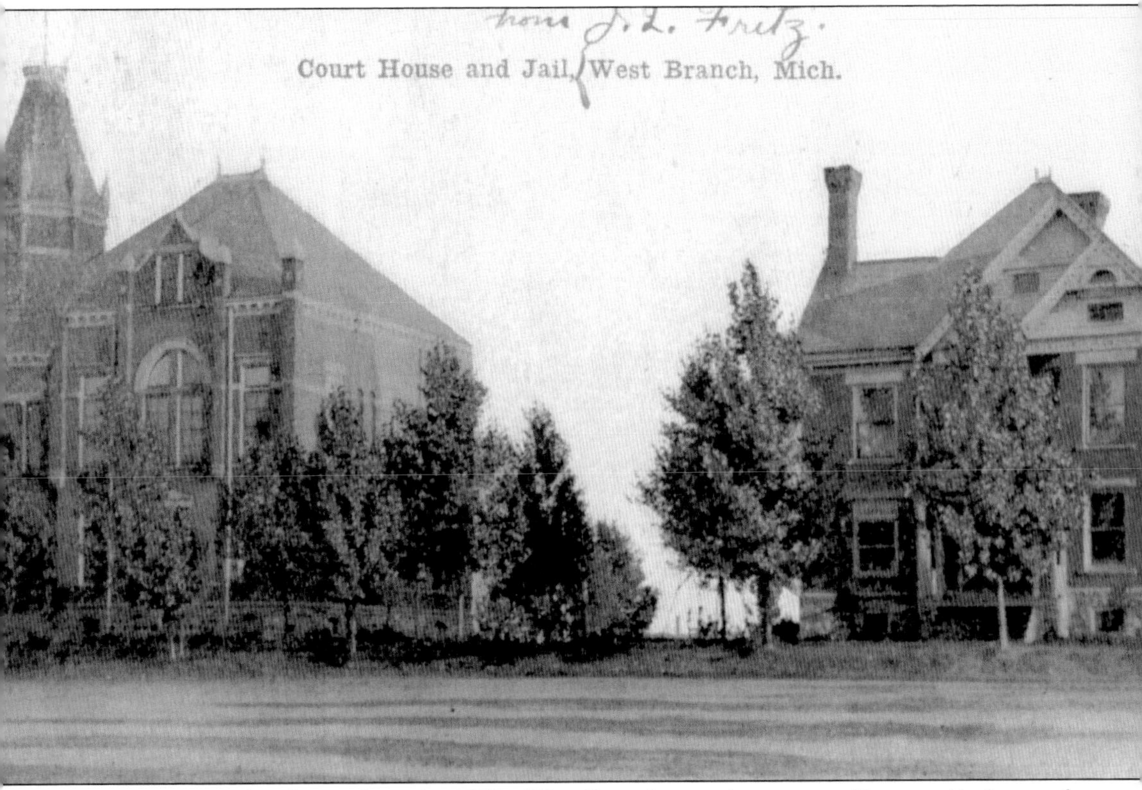

According to local record, in the 1870s, West Branch was chosen over Ogemaw Springs to be the Ogemaw County seat by one vote in a hotly debated race. (Courtesy of the Rose City Area Historical Society.)

On the cover: Shown is one of the many lumber camps in Ogemaw County. The majestic white pines brought people to this area. (Courtesy of the Rose City Area Historical Society.)

IMAGES
of America

OGEMAW COUNTY

Rose City Area Historical Society

ARCADIA
PUBLISHING

ISBN 978-0-7385-6145-5

Published by Arcadia Publishing
Charleston, South Carolina

Printed in the United States of America

Library of Congress Control Number: 2008932835

For all general information contact Arcadia Publishing at:
Telephone 843-853-2070
Fax 843-853-0044
E-mail sales@arcadiapublishing.com
For customer service and orders:
Toll-Free 1-888-313-2665

Visit us on the Internet at www.arcadiapublishing.com

This book is dedicated to all the historians and genealogists who have preserved the beginnings and to those who will preserve the future.

Contents

ACKNOWLEDGMENTS

The Rose City Area Historical Society wishes to thank all the people, past and present, who have worked to make the Ogemaw County area such a wonderful place to live. Without their determination to tame a wilderness, this rich history could not exist.

The society's members, under the guidance and leadership of current president Cathy Snider, have compiled this publication for your enjoyment. Cathy's perseverance and tireless work on this project will be seen in the pages that follow. The photographs used, unless otherwise noted, are from the archives of the Rose City Area Historical Society.

As with any group endeavor, it will be impossible to name all those who assisted in the collection of data and photographs, but special acknowledgment goes to members of the Rose City Area Historical Society: Sharon Alderton, Janet Arnott, Dora Jean Babcock, Evelyn Berry, Melvin and Pam Conway, Lugene Daniels, Gene and Mary Densmore, Richard and Grace Dooley, Glendora Fitzgerald, Lottie McGregor, John and Vivian Mellon, Marilyn Pachota, Cliff Parent, John Reetz, David Rice, Cathy Snider, Lou Wilebski, and many others who dedicated time and energy to this book.

A special thank-you to photographer Tony Brent, the Friends Church of Lupton, Beulah Huebner, Ron McCarthy, the Ogemaw County Herald, the Ogemaw District Libraries in Rose City, Prescott, and Skidway, the Ogemaw Genealogical and Historical Society and Museum, Beverly Scott, Steve Steinhauser, the West Branch Library, and LuAnn Zettle.

Moreover, the Rose City Area Historical Society is grateful for the personal contributions from community members all over the county that have made this story of Ogemaw County more complete.

INTRODUCTION

Ogemaw County is said to have taken its name from Ogemaw Ke-Ke-To, chief speaker of the Chippewa Indians. In 1819, Chief Ke-Ke-To eloquently opposed the proposals tendered by Gen. Lewis Cass at the Saginaw Conference and asked General Cass, "Shall we sell from under them [woman and children] the spot where they spread their blankets?" When he was not able to defend against the firewater, a case of whiskey, or the silver offered, the rest of the tribe voted to sell their land. In 1819, the Treaty of Saginaw was signed by Ke-Ke-To.

Among Ogemaw County's greatest treasures are four very old American Indian earthworks located near Selkirk along the Rifle River. In 1931, Cranbrook Institute of Science authorized Fred Dustin and assistant William E. Parkin to survey these mounds. The mounds were found to be somewhat circular and are 186 to 314 feet across with several gateways crossing them and surrounded by ditches from five to seven feet deep. The walls on top of the mounds are two and one-half feet higher than the floors. The mounds are strategically located near the river, where old American Indian trails followed the river. A few pieces of pottery unearthed indicate Algonquian Indian culture.

Three old Chippewa footpaths converged in the county becoming the basis for highways M-76, M-30, and M-55. After the footpaths, the first roads to come into the county were tote roads, used for hauling settlers and supplies through the forest.

On April 1, 1840, Ogemaw County was designated by the state legislature and encompassed 595 square miles. The county was later organized with 16 townships. The townships were Edwards and Ogemaw in 1873, Rose in 1876, Klacking and Cummings in 1878, Foster and Richland in 1879, West Branch and Damon in 1881, Hill and Horton in 1883, Mills in 1884, Logan and Churchill in 1887, Goodar in 1888, and Beaver Lake. Beaver Lake is now part of Foster Township, and Damon is now part of Foster and Rose Townships.

Speculators and land barons began buying up large tracts of land as early as 1852–1853. The first recorded land patents were by Eber Ward of Detroit, Volney A. Ripley of St. Clair, and Joseph Copeland of Pontiac in 1856.

Government surveyors in 1856 said, "The only tenants of the towering pine and hardwood forests were deer, bear, and other wild game." In 1871, the county was a wilderness of huge majestic white pine, with very few inhabitants. George Sherman came to the Peach Lake area hunting and fishing for four months in 1869 and did not see a single person the entire time.

In 1867, William Edwards built a log cabin in Edwards Township and cleared a small area for his lumber operations. In 1871, the company of Weidmann and Wright built its log cabin and lumber camp near West Branch. The Houghton Lumber Camp was located near Rose City. Between 1867 and 1909, there were 30 or more settlements established in Ogemaw County.

The earliest lumbermen in the county had worked their way north from Saginaw and Bay City. Millions of feet of white pine and Norway pine were harvested in Ogemaw County. In 1870, the *Saginaw Daily Courier* reported that 15 camps along the Rifle River employed approximately 1,500 men and hundreds of horses and oxen. The year 1871 is considered to be the real beginning of lumbering operations in Ogemaw County. The coming of the railroads is closely tied to the lumber operations. In 1872, the Jackson, Lansing and Saginaw Railroad extended its Michigan Central track north from Bay City, through Alger, West Branch, and Ogemaw Springs, thus opening up the lumber boom. Around 1872, as the lumber companies harvested most of the pine and sold the land or let it go back to the state for taxes, the farmers and other more permanent residents began to arrive in the county as did other lumbermen who harvested the hardwoods. Log cabins were replaced by sawed-lumber homes. Committees and township boards were formed to build roads and provide other services to the communities.

Among those newly arrived farmers were John Klacking, Christopher Reetz, and Horace Sherman, who settled an area north of Campbell Corners. Others settled near Damon and in Rose Township. Henry Craner came to Richland Township in 1869 to hunt and decided to stay and farm the land there. William Rose, Scott White, Sherman T. and Decatur A. Neal, James Campbell, and George Sherman homesteaded and also became prosperous farmers in the county. Many others, including John Tolfree, came to harvest the timber and stayed to farm the land. Farming is still very much a part of this county today. Agriculture is now the county's leading industry.

During the 1930s, Ogemaw County experienced an oil boom. Many oil wells were built, and to this day new wells are being drilled. By 1936, there were 128 wells, producing 2,300 barrels a day. Producers Refining, Incorporated, built a refinery in West Branch in 1936 that operated until 1953. In 1954, the refinery was sold to the United Refining Company of Warren, Pennsylvania.

As early as 1911, newspaper articles listed good fishing in our lakes, streams, and the Rifle River. Since the 1920s, the tourist industry has grown continuously. Ogemaw County is a mecca for the sports enthusiast. The Rifle River begins in northern Ogemaw County near Lupton and runs the entire length of the county. The Tittabawassee River runs out of Edwards Township in the southwestern corner of the county. The county is said to have about 119 lakes, both private and public. Canoeing, kayaking, tubing, and fishing are a great asset to this community. Winter sports abound as several large and connecting snowmobile trails traverse the county. During the summer many of these trails double as all-terrain vehicle trails.

Ogemaw County maintains a country charm admired by many. The rolling landscapes encompass babbling brooks and scenic rivers that attract residents and tourists alike. Tranquil lakes reflect sunrises and sunsets to those seeking the serenity of the water. Fertile farmland and a pleasant growing season yield bountiful harvests that promote area agriculture. Small-town atmospheres remain, where locals and tourists blend together as friends. And, above all, the faith and deep heritage of the people of Ogemaw County provide the area with a spirit that continues to flourish.

One

UNFORGETTABLE

Throughout the history of the area, many strong and unusual people created the legacy left to those who followed. Some people left the area to make a mark on the world. Others stayed and gave this community all that they had to give. In this chapter, some of the more special citizens are honored, but certainly not all of them. Some of the things that make the area unique are also celebrated. Ogemaw County is a strong, caring, and giving community. Volunteerism is a way of life for many. It is a community that draws strength from one another, while protecting and nurturing its own.

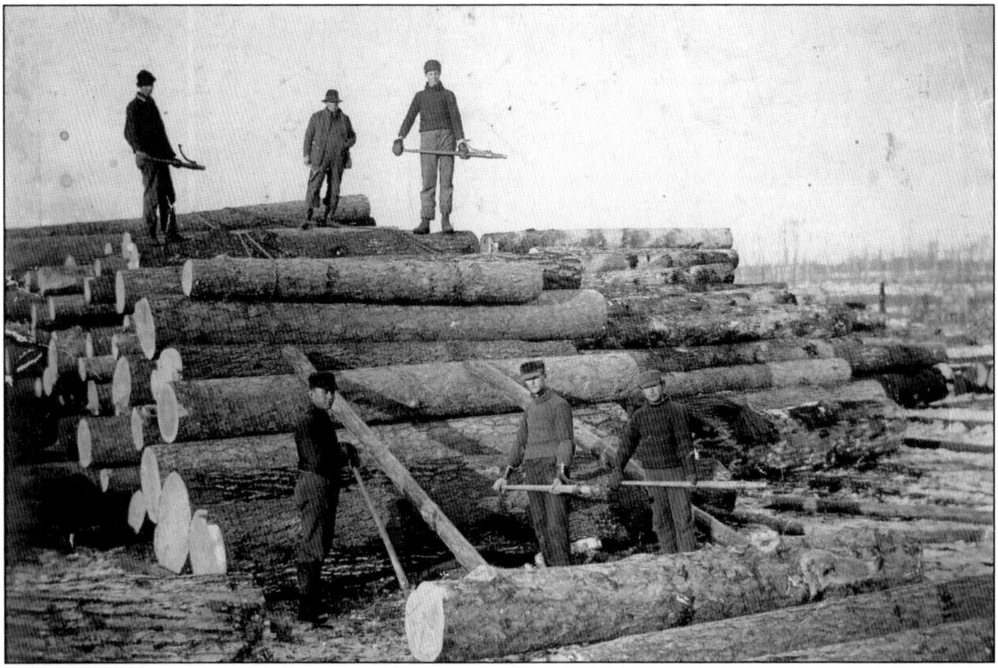

In 1872, the Jackson, Lansing and Saginaw Railroad extended its Michigan Central tracks north from Bay City through Alger, West Branch, and Ogemaw Springs to Beaver Lake. Logging crews began to arrive and sawmills and lumber camps were established overnight. The first buildings were built from logs but soon were replaced by sawed lumber covered with tar paper. The light, sandy soil of Ogemaw County produced some of the straightest, largest, and tallest trees in the country. The rivers were used to float logs down to the Saginaw Bay, where they were lashed together and taken to the large mills in the cities.

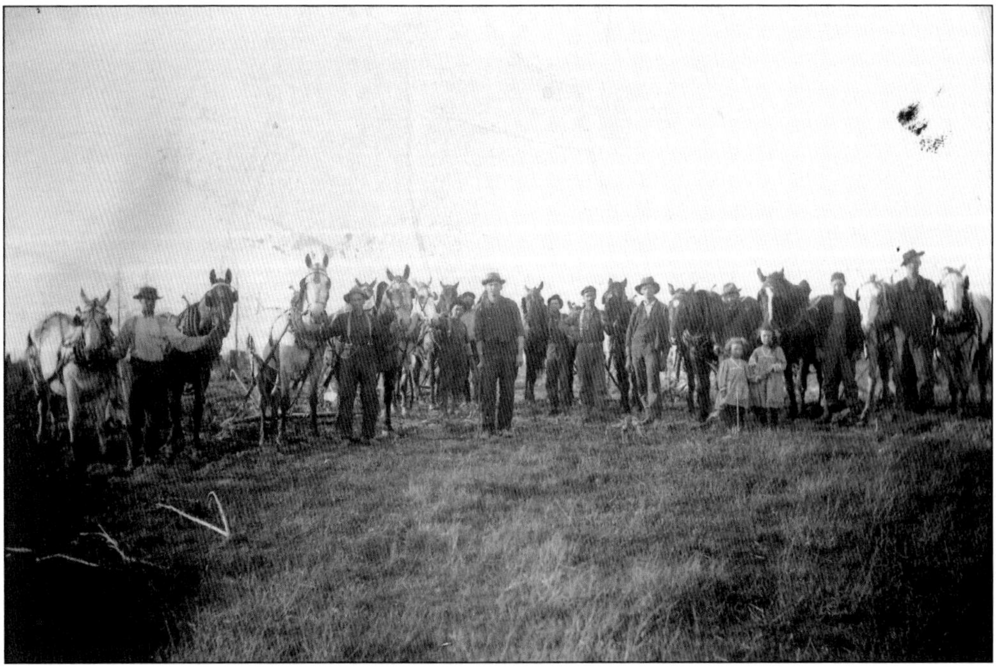

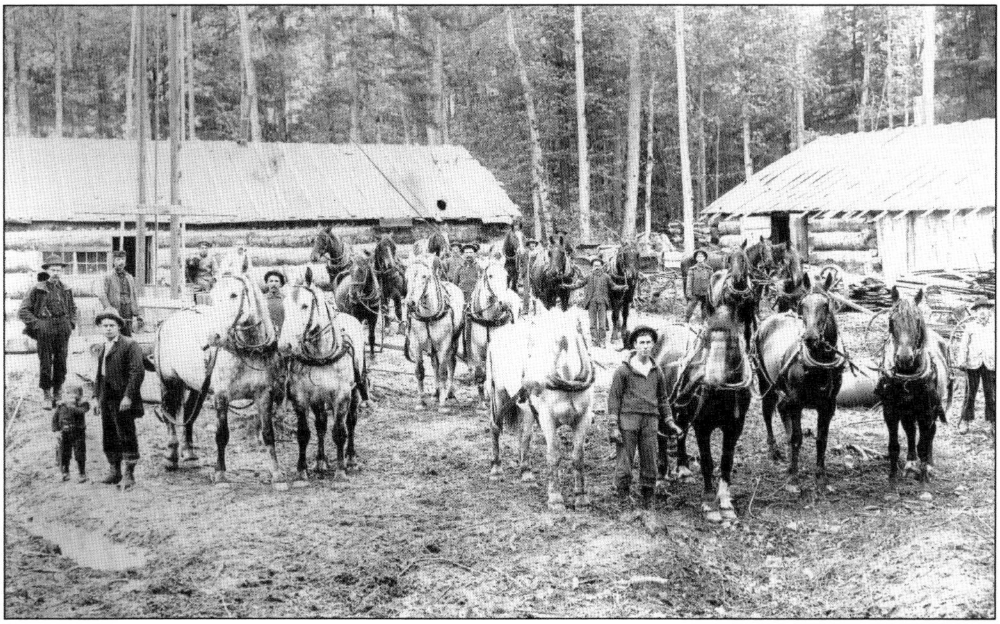

Logs were stored or staged at various areas along the rivers through the winter. In the spring, when the water ran high, these logs were skidded into the river. Teams of horses and oxen dragged the logs from the woods to these areas. Usually the staging area was close to where the logs were cut, perhaps only a mile or two. This is why many small settlements developed. As the lumber was cut and the lumbermen moved, many of these small settlements disappeared.

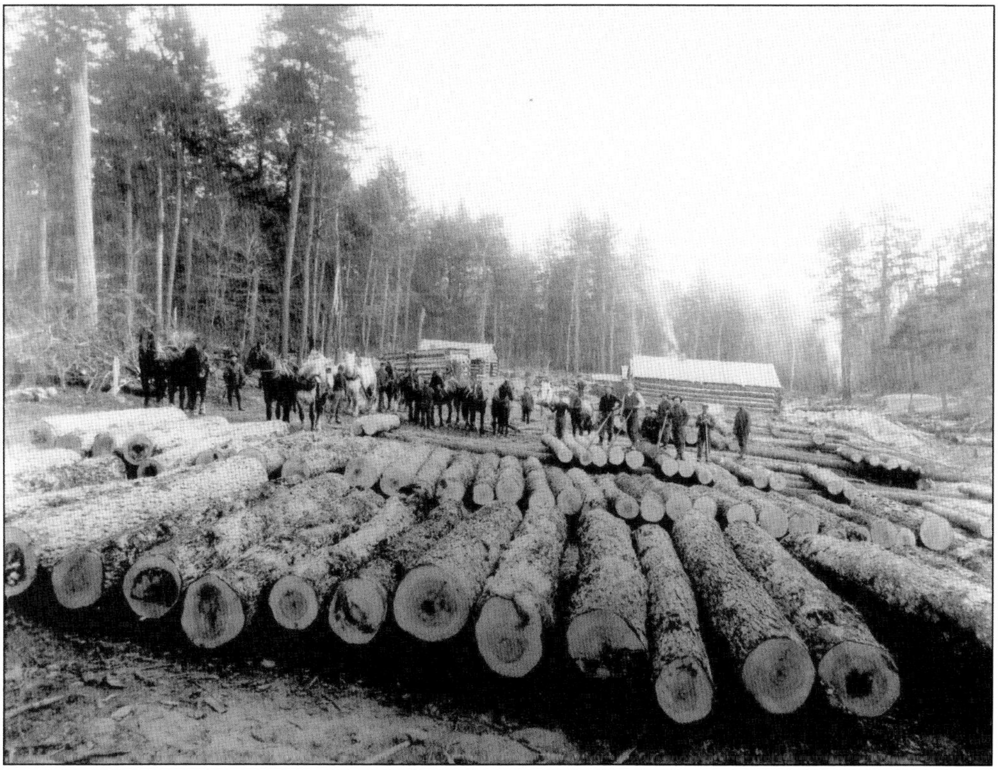

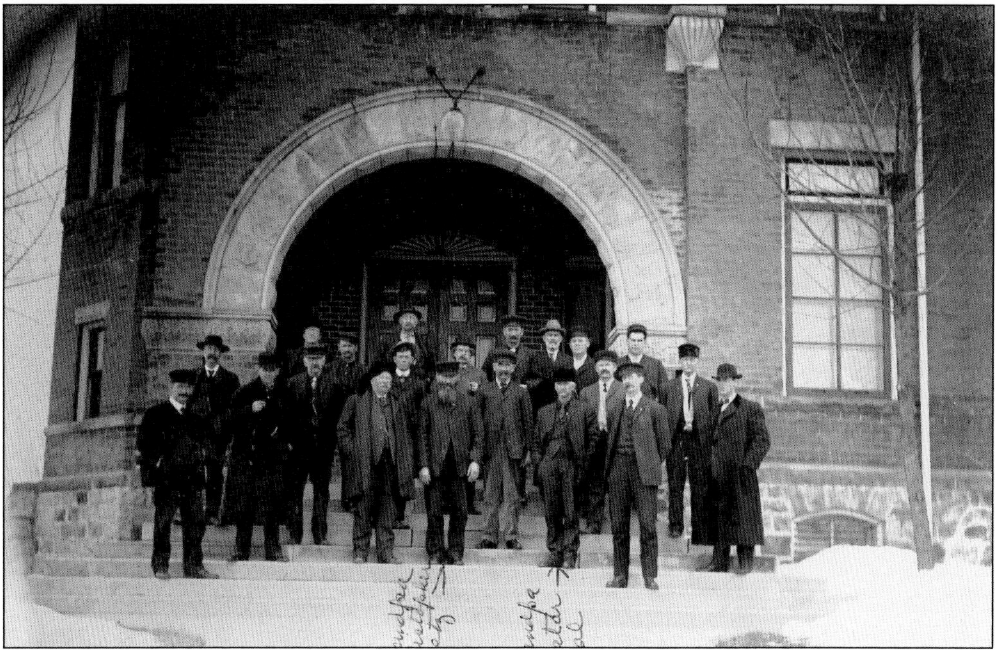

The founding fathers of the area, mostly unidentified, stand in front of the courthouse. Identified are first row, fourth from left, Christopher Reetz from Klacking Township and, sixth from left, Decatur Neal from Damon Township. These men, and more, came to this county with hopes and dreams of living free and raising their families.

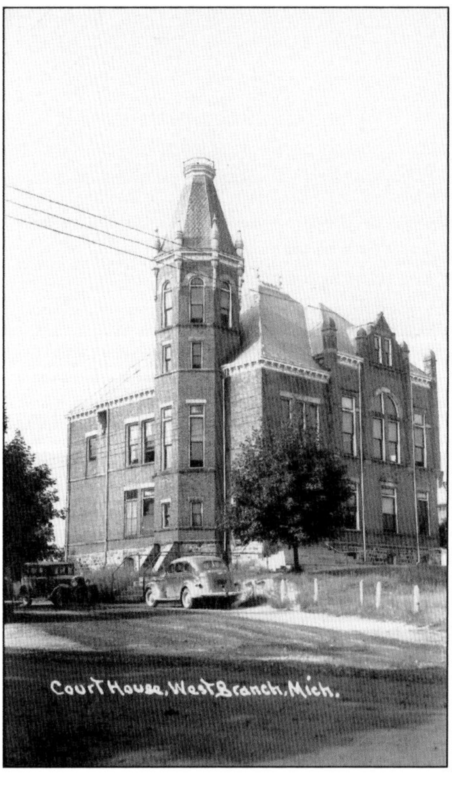

In the 1870s, an election determined the county seat. Voters chose between Ogemaw Springs and West Branch. West Branch won by one vote, although Ogemaw Springs was larger at the time. The first courthouse was built in 1876. This courthouse burned in 1887. Pictured here is the new courthouse that was erected on the original foundations in 1888. (Courtesy of Glendora Fitzgerald.)

Millie "the Chiseler" Miller (1912–1998) was a local sculptress. Miller's impression of Chief Ke-Ke-To was made the official insignia of the county in 1964. Her totem poles stand at the fairgrounds. She helped create the county flag, the West Branch and Rose City coats of arms, and the emblem for the Boy Scouts at Northwood Reservation. She also has a sculpture on display at the 4-H Center in Washington, D.C.

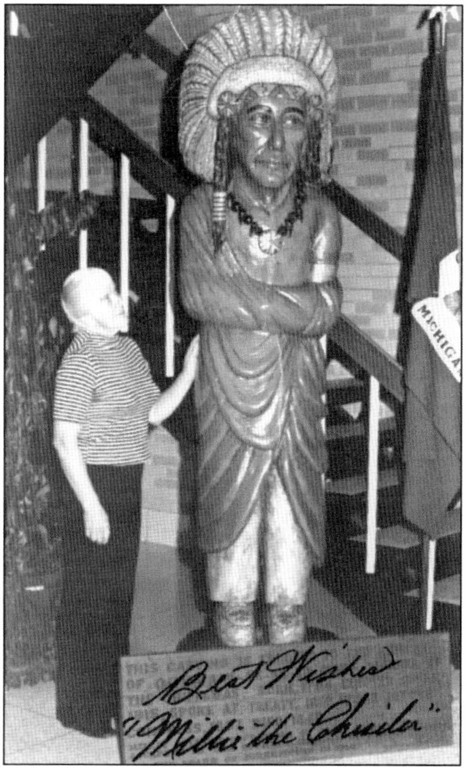

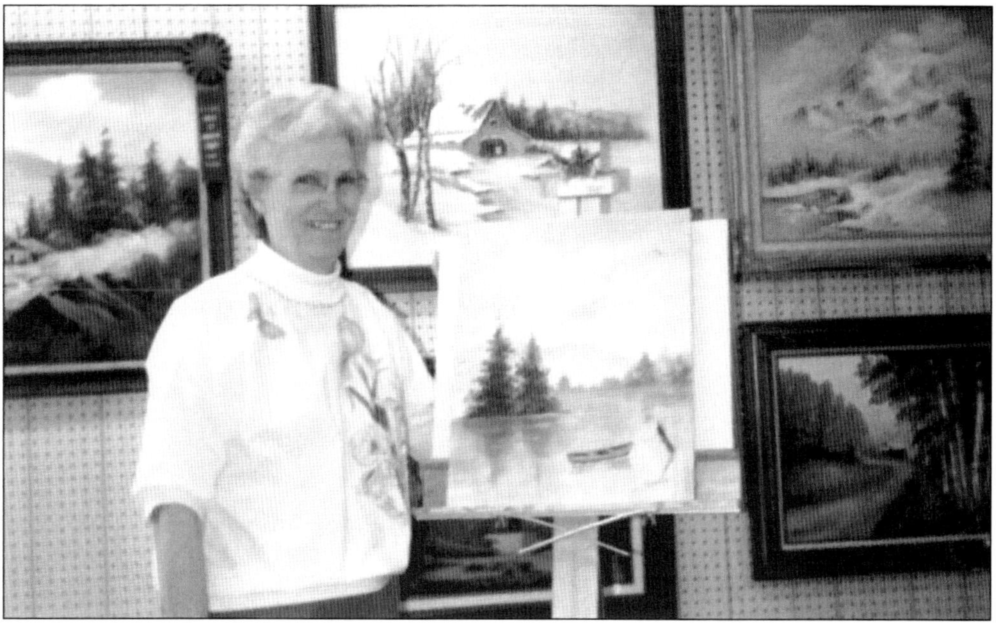

Bernie (Sullivan) Banghart (1928–1997) was a longtime resident of Ogemaw County. She is a self-taught artist who began painting during her family's years of military travel to keep herself busy. As a member of the West Branch Art Association, Banghart donated many of her paintings to area businesses. She is a descendent of the Borden family, who were early pioneers in the county. (Courtesy of Dora Jean Babcock.)

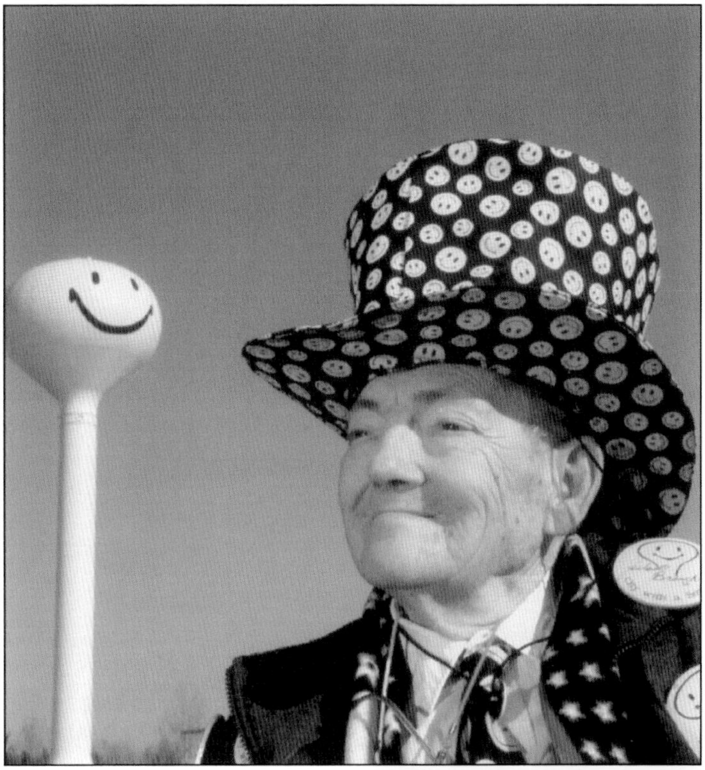

When the West Branch water tower was built in 1974, Ralph "Steinie" Steinhauser (1922–2003) raised money in less than a month to pay for the smiley face to be painted on the tower. In 1999, the tower needed repair, and wheelchair-bound Ralph "Smiley" again began a crusade to save Smiley. His determination was a success. Now the tower greets travelers with its friendly smile. (Courtesy of Steve Steinhauser.)

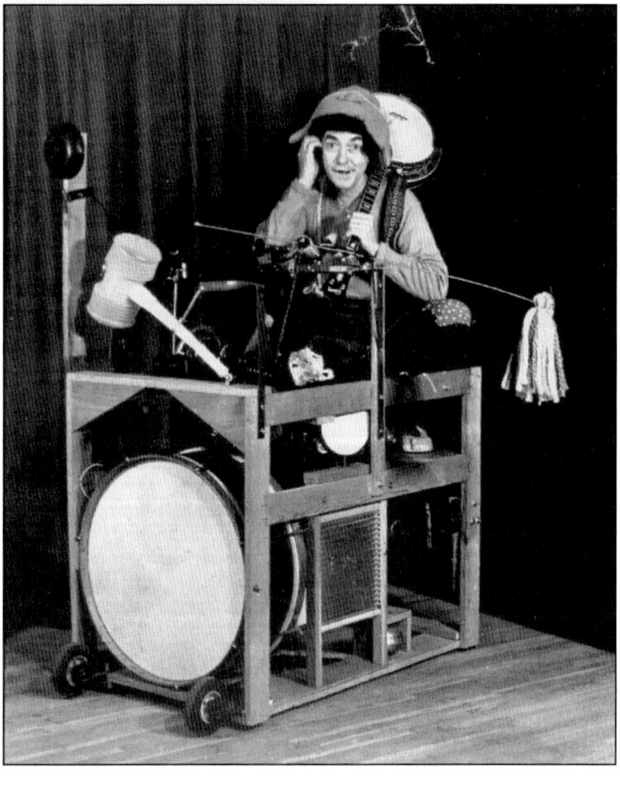

Ernie Tripp (1920–1992) grew up in Shepard. As a U.S. Army captain during World War II, his men called him Wilful Stumble, a label he later used to identify his one-man-band routine. In 1969, after Tripp retired from dairy farming near Prescott, Wilful Stumble and His Whazat emerged, and during the 1980s, he performed on *Hee Haw*, the popular country music and comedy television show.

Alfred W. Ebelt (1904–1978) was known as the poet of the North Country. Ebelt published two books of northern Michigan poetry: *Shoulder the Sky* and *Back Through Many Doors*. He was a member of the Ogemaw County Board of Supervisors from 1953 to 1968 and headed the county commissioners from 1960 to 1974. His inspirations often came from his home on Grass Lake, just west of Clear Lake. (Courtesy of the Ebelt family.)

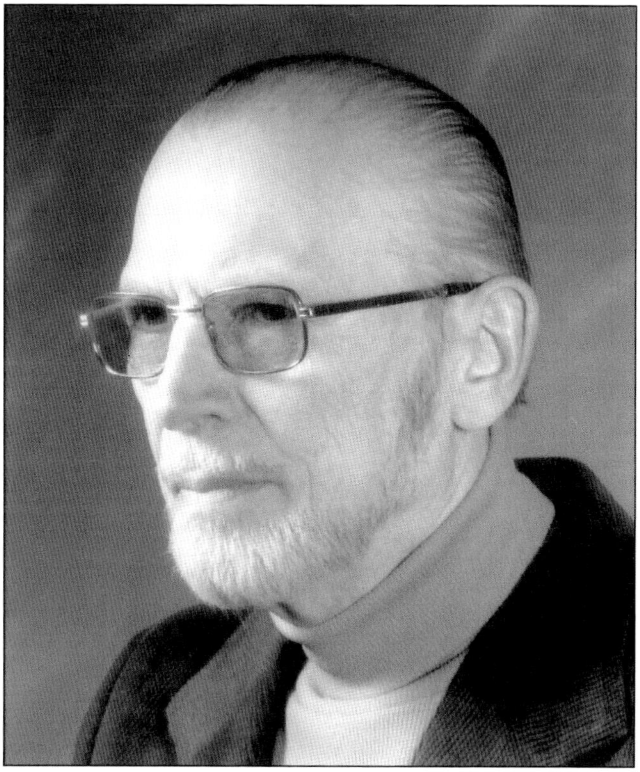

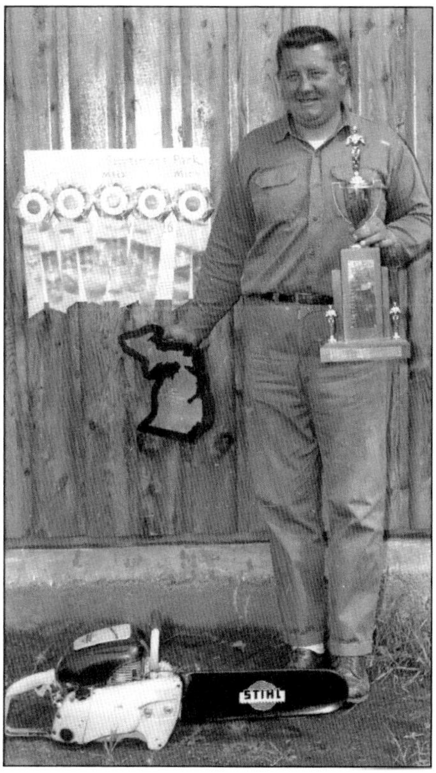

Russell Mason (1932–2001), descendant of the Rose family of Rose City, was an outstanding member of the community. Mason helped organize the Rose City Ambulance Service and the Ogemaw District Library and served on the Ogemaw County Board of Commissioners, AuSable Mental Health Board, and Ogemaw Zoning Board. He taught school and coached sports. He was a logger and held the State Logging Championship title for 17 years.

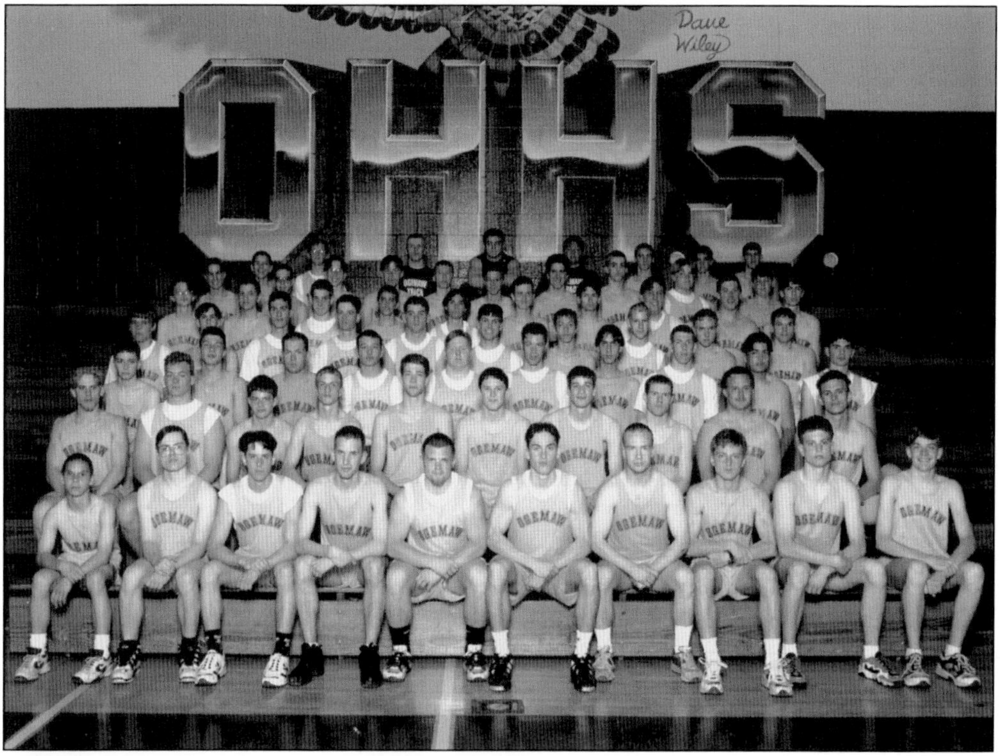

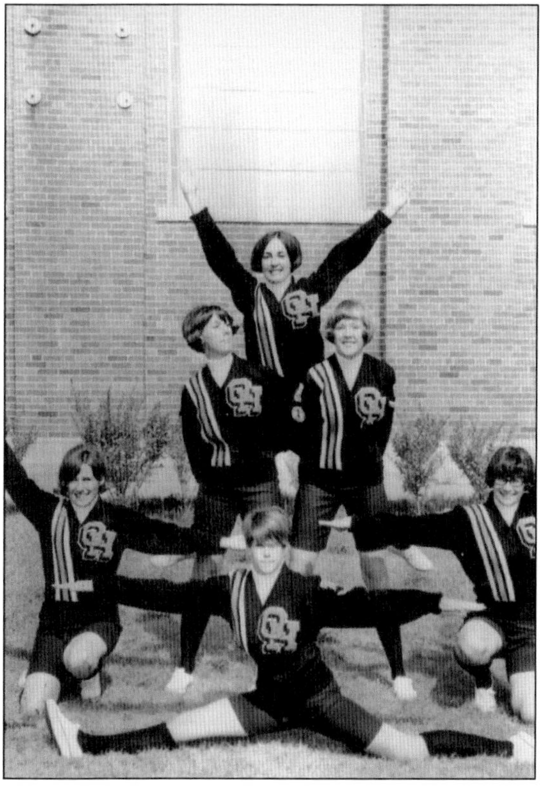

In 1965, the Rose City and West Branch schools consolidated. From 1965 to 1969, students were bused to schools out of their neighborhoods as the one-room schools closed. The buses from Rose City and West Branch met at the Klacking Creek Church parking lot and exchanged students. In 1968, Ogemaw Heights High School was officially named and the new school was opened in 1968–1969. Pictured above is a 1980s Ogemaw Heights basketball team and at left are the 1968 Ogemaw Heights football cheerleaders: Patty Brindley, Linda Hendriks, Julie VanOosten, Karen Atherton, Patti Short, and Karen Bell.

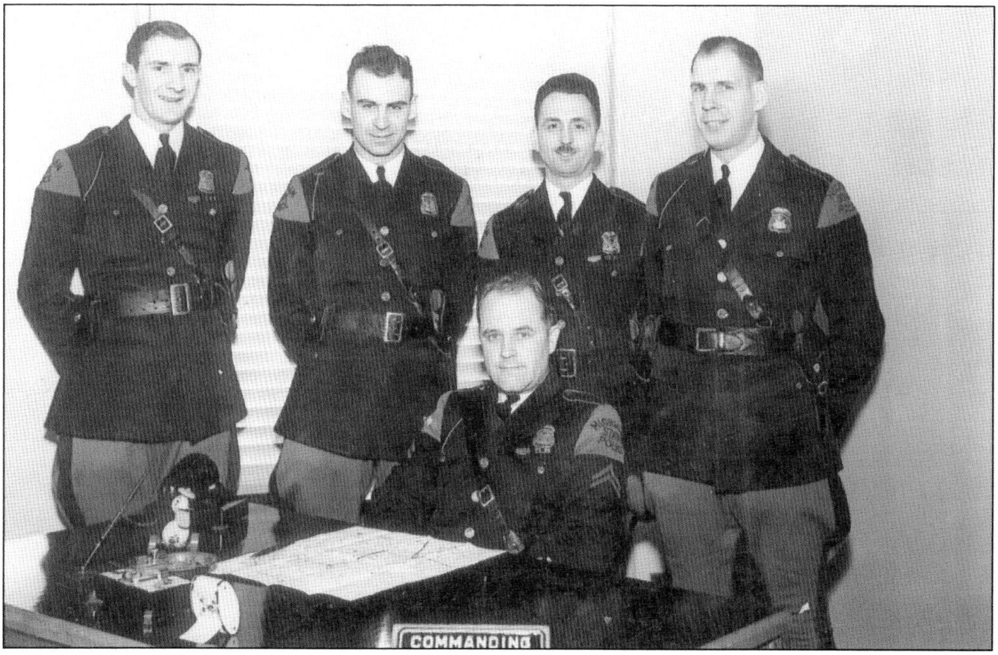

In the 1930s, the West Branch Chamber of Commerce formed a committee to secure a state police post in Ogemaw County. On December 8, 1931, the post was officially established at the Steuernol House on North First Street. The troopers pictured here, from left to right, are Vic Beck, Fred Buschell, Lynn Smith, Claude Cook, and Wright Needham (seated).

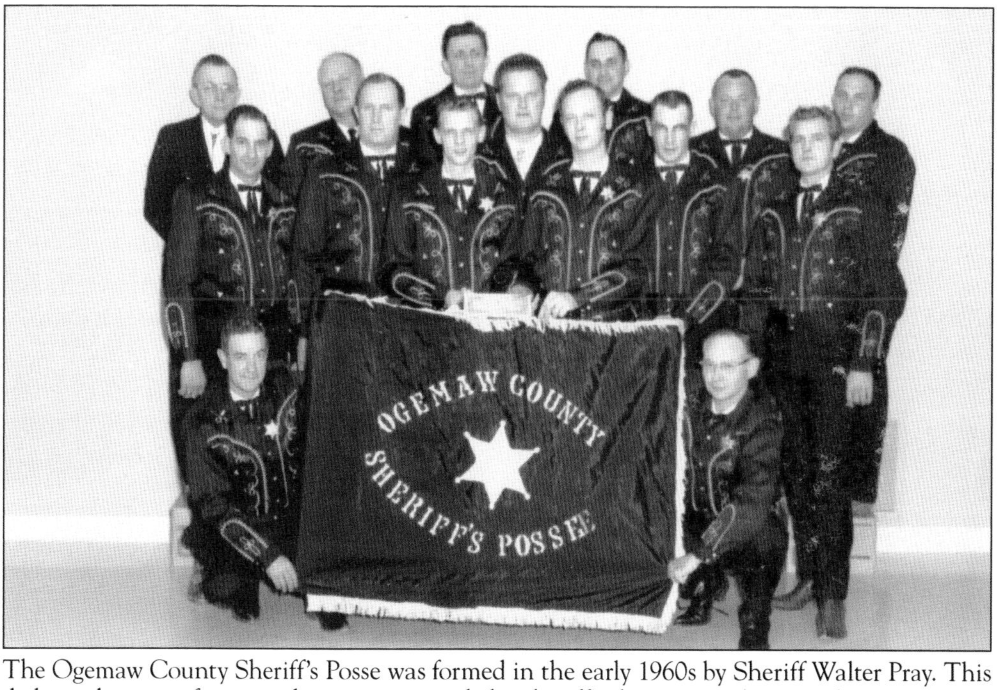

The Ogemaw County Sheriff's Posse was formed in the early 1960s by Sheriff Walter Pray. This dedicated group of men and women assisted the sheriff's department by providing security at the county fair, the tractor show, festivals, and various functions at the schools. The Ogemaw County Sheriff's Posse continues as a supportive extension of the department.

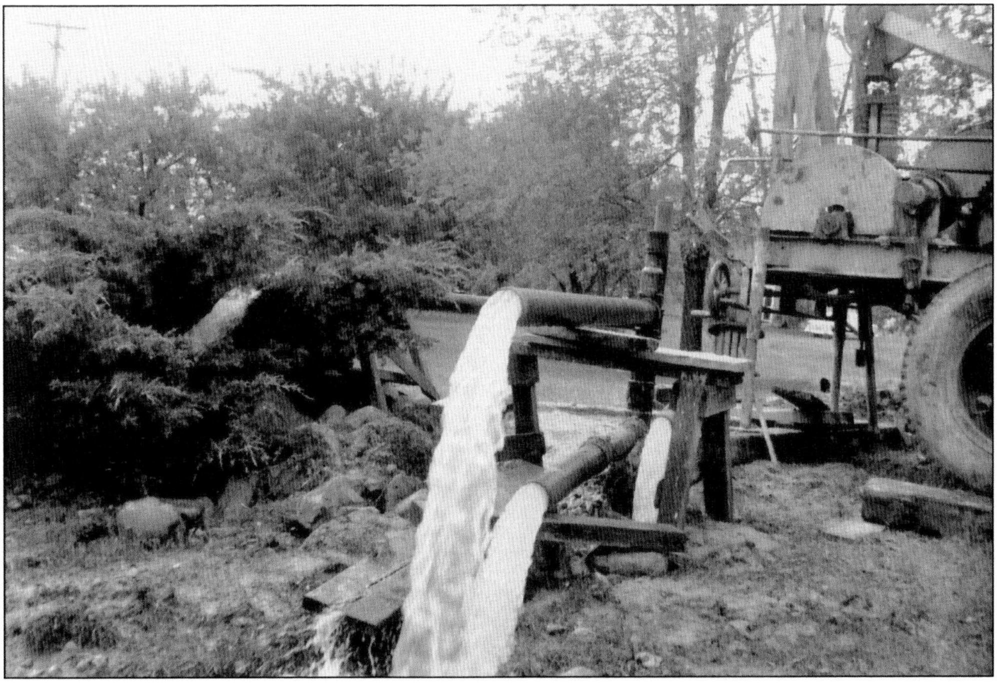

Located in many areas of Ogemaw County are flowing or artesian wells. The most popular ones are the Big Flow at Ogemaw Springs and the Metcalf Flow in Rose City. According to newspaper advertisements from as early as 1889, Ogemaw County had many artesian wells and boasted their clear, cold, clean water.

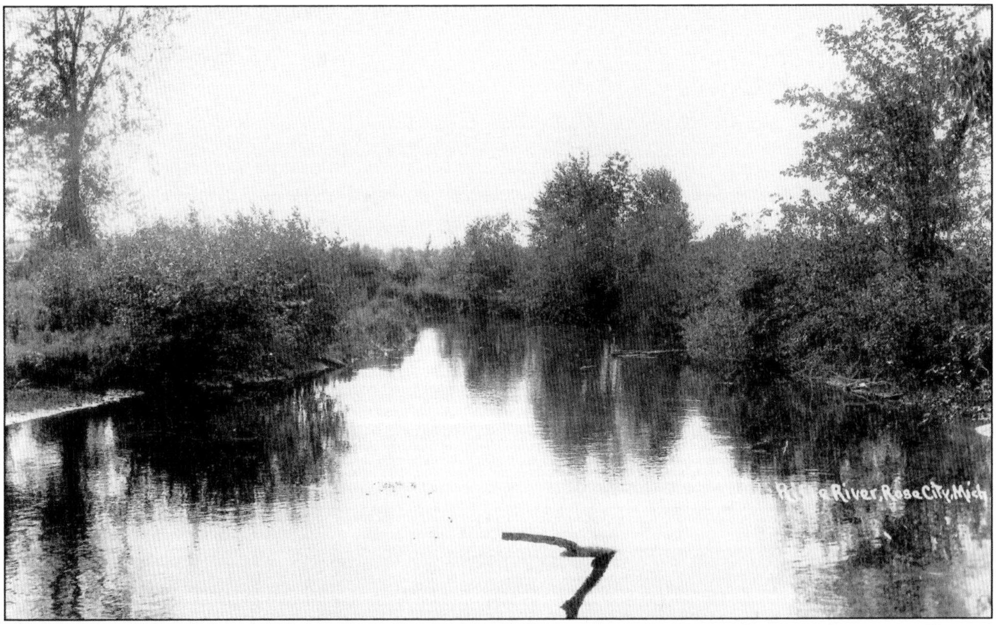

The Rifle River continues to have a huge impact on Ogemaw County. The river begins in Devoe Lake near Lupton and meanders its way south through the county. In the past, logs were floated down the river to Saginaw Bay. Today the Rifle River is a magnificent tourist attraction that provides fishing, canoeing, camping, wildlife watching, kayaking, or just river sitting.

Two

Lane Heights and Lupton

Lane Heights was a beautiful little town located about 20 miles from West Branch in the eastern part of Rose Township near the headwaters of the Rifle River. The first train came through on the lower ground south of Lane Heights in 1893. Because of the location of the railroad, the town moved about a mile to the south. At this time, the settlement became known as Lupton.

The first settlers came from Ohio in 1879. Rev. Emmor Lupton and his sons Isaac, Levi, and Martin bought about 300 acres of land and established a mill on the corner of Doll and Oyster Roads. The mill had the capacity of 20,000 feet of lumber and 25,000 shingles in a single day. This lumber was transported three miles to the Maltby switch of the Loon Lake branch of the Detroit, Bay City and Alpena Railroad.

The town of Lupton was founded on the principals of the Friends church, which are temperance and Christianity. Many of the original families were members of the Friends Episcopal Church. The first Friends church was established in Lane Heights in 1885 and was later moved to the new town.

Leander Hole built the first store in Lupton. Joshua Rakestraw ran the first post office. Jim Hamilton built the first hotel and blacksmith shop. The Dresel House was next to the hotel and housed the Lupton Land Syndicate offices. At one time, Lupton had sawmills, livery stables, a meat market, a millinery shop, a shoemaker's shop, restaurants, lumber and real estate offices, barbershops, a buggy painter, a justice of the peace, a physician, a deputy sheriff, a notary, and a bank.

From the 1930s until 1980, the town of Lupton was famous for the Graceland Ballroom, alleged to be a hangout for the notorious Purple Gang from Detroit. Lupton is now known for the beautiful Rifle River Recreation Area, which was purchased from the Harry Jewett family. The Lupton area is regarded as a neighborly and friendly place to live, work, and play.

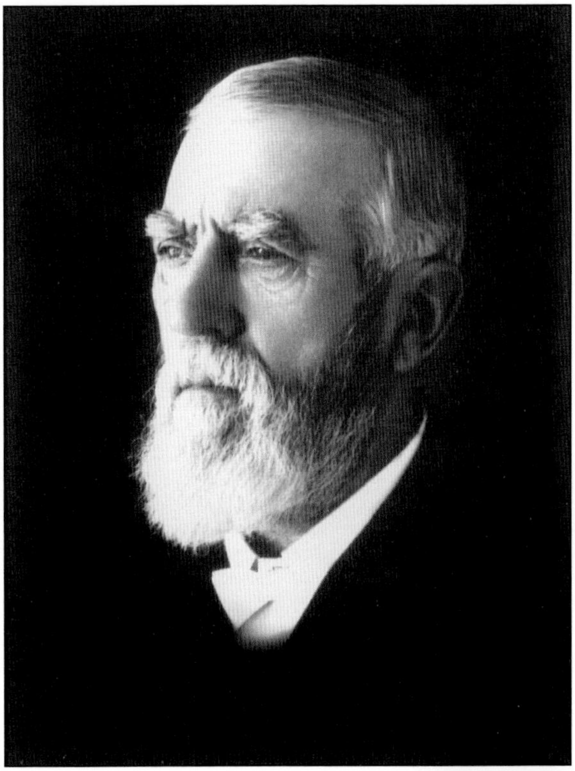

Emmor Lupton, with his wife Rebecca and five of their six children, came to this area in 1879 from Goshen, Ohio. Emmor and sons Isaac, Martin, and Levi bought over 300 acres of prime land and built a sawmill and shingle mill on Oyster and Doll Roads. The first meetings of the Friends worship were held in his home. Levi Lupton was a minister and traveled evangelist.

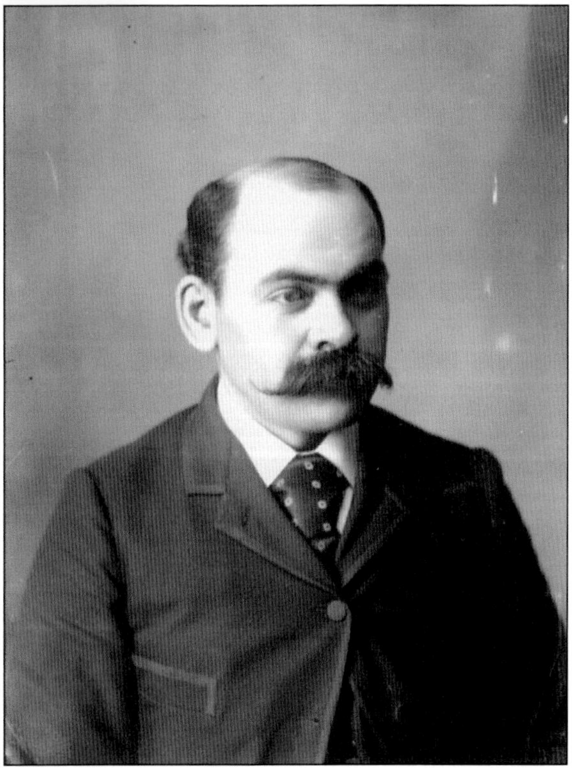

George Stanley of Selkirk, along with Isaac and Levi Lupton and Leander Hole, formed the firm of Lupton Brothers Corporation in 1892. This firm joined George H. Reissman to develop the Lupton Land Syndicate, which eventually formed the settlement of Lupton. Every deed, contract, and lease of property contained a provision forbidding the owner from the purpose of making, storing, selling, or giving away any intoxicating beverage.

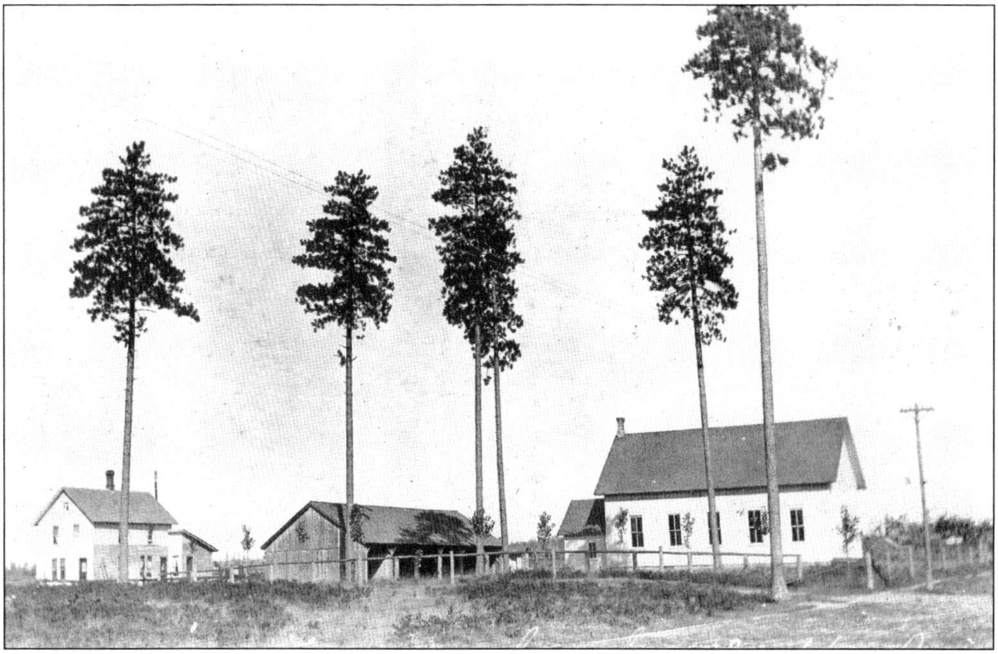

The first church services in Lane Heights were held in the home of Emmor and Rebecca Lupton. Being of strong faith and members of the Friends worship, they welcomed the First Day services, Sabbath school, and prayer meetings. In 1881, the services were moved nearby to the new school. In 1889, a new meeting hall was built. This building was moved from Lane Heights to the new town of Lupton in 1902. A parsonage was erected and used until 1954, when a new one was built. In the photograph above, notice the tall straight white pines, a reminder of how northern Michigan woods once looked. A new Friends church was built and dedicated in 1969. (Courtesy of Donald and Sharon Alderton.)

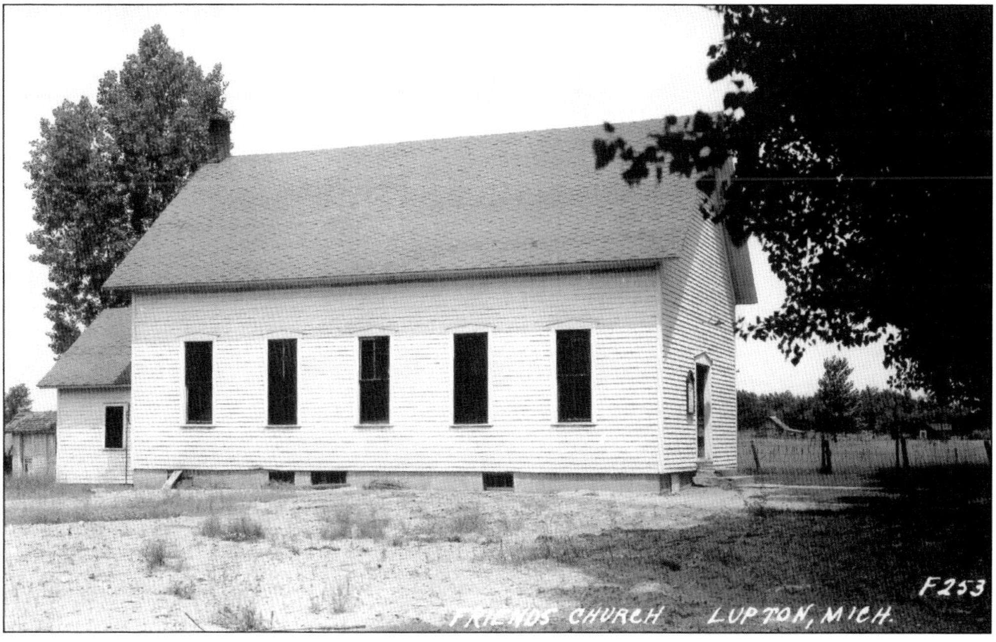

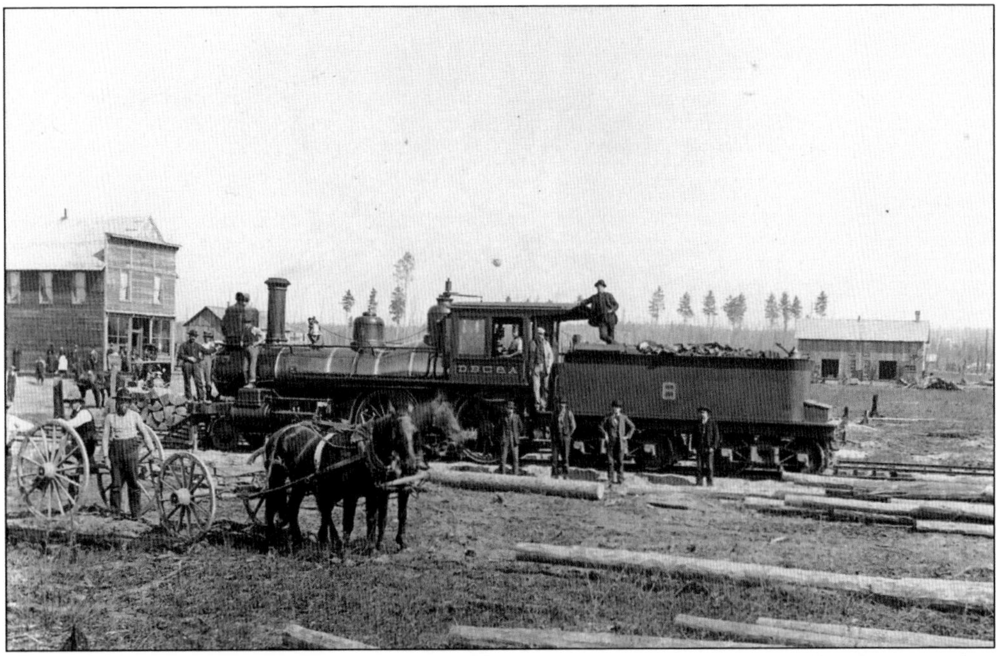

Levi and Isaac Lupton worked hard to get the Detroit, Bay City and Alpena Railroad to extend its line toward Lane Heights. Their efforts were successful, and on November 1, 1892, construction began at the edge of the new town named Lupton. The first regular train passed through town on January 1, 1893. This gave the town of Lupton its start.

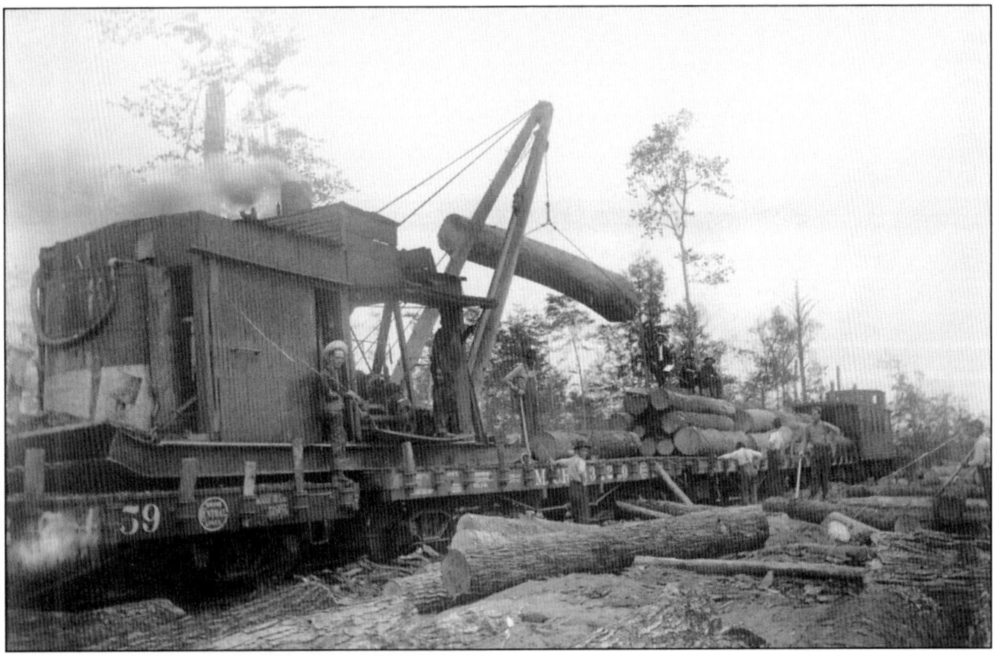

Timber resources around Lupton were extraordinarily extensive. With the Detroit, Bay City and Alpena Railroad extending into the deep forests of hardwood timber, the job of the lumber companies became easier. The rail lines moved workers, provisions, and products to the markets in the cities simpler, faster, and more efficiently.

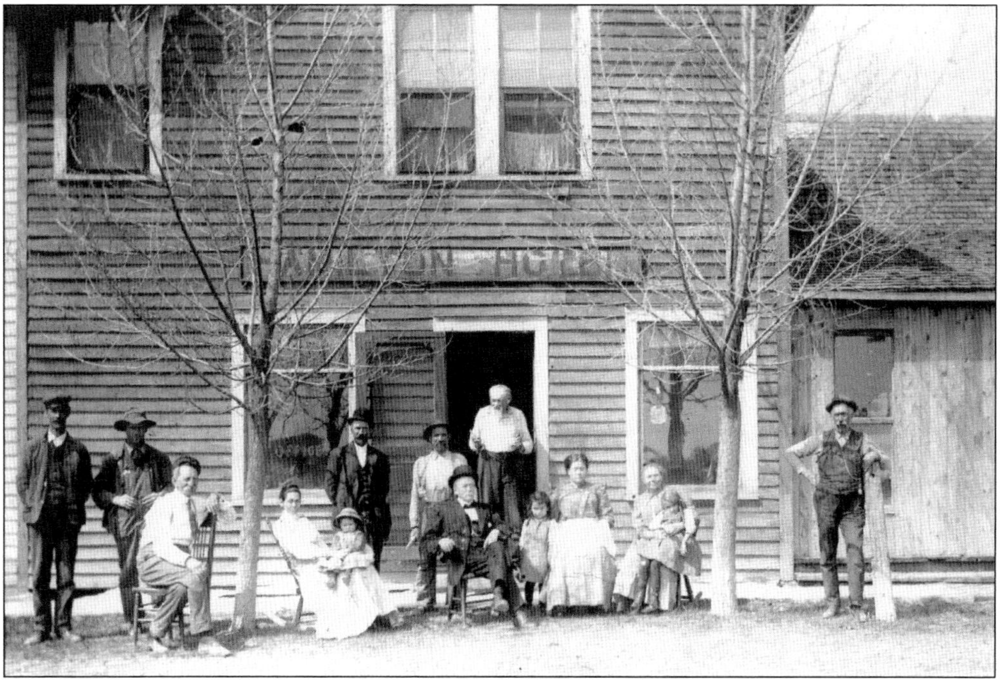

James Hamilton built the first hotel in Lupton in 1893. The Hamilton Hotel had ample accommodations for 35 guests. It provided steam heat, baths, and sanitary features and advertised the best table in this region, making it popular with commercial men and tourists.

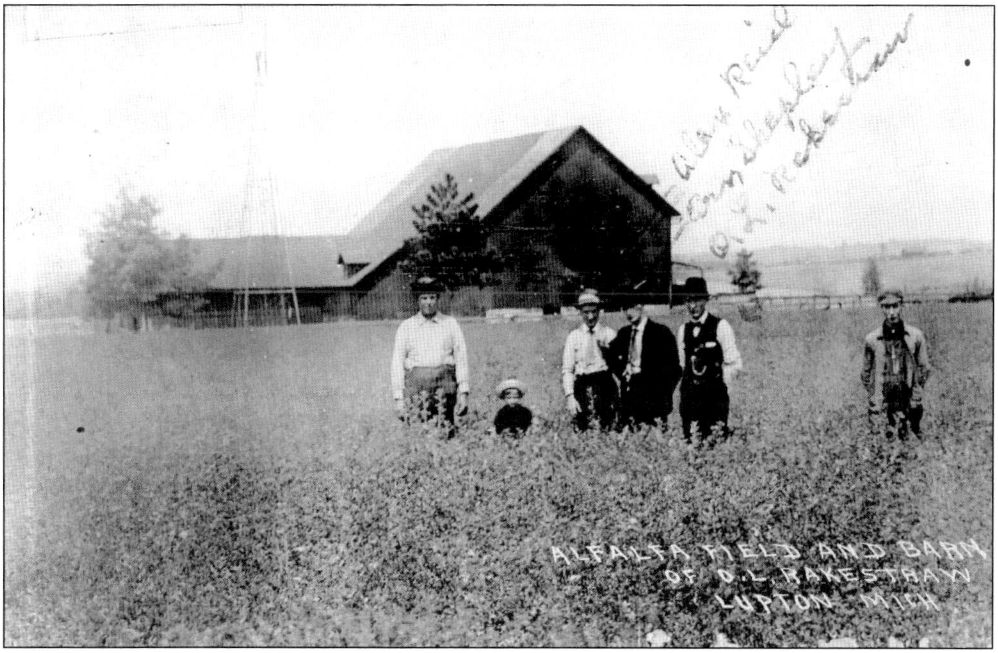

This field of alfalfa was grown on the O. L. Rakestraw farm in Rose Township. The three gentlemen in the center are identified as Alex Reid, Ern Shepley, and O. L. Rakestraw. Farming was a profitable business and hay was sold to the lumber companies and mills to feed the horses and oxen. (Courtesy of John and Vivian Mellon.)

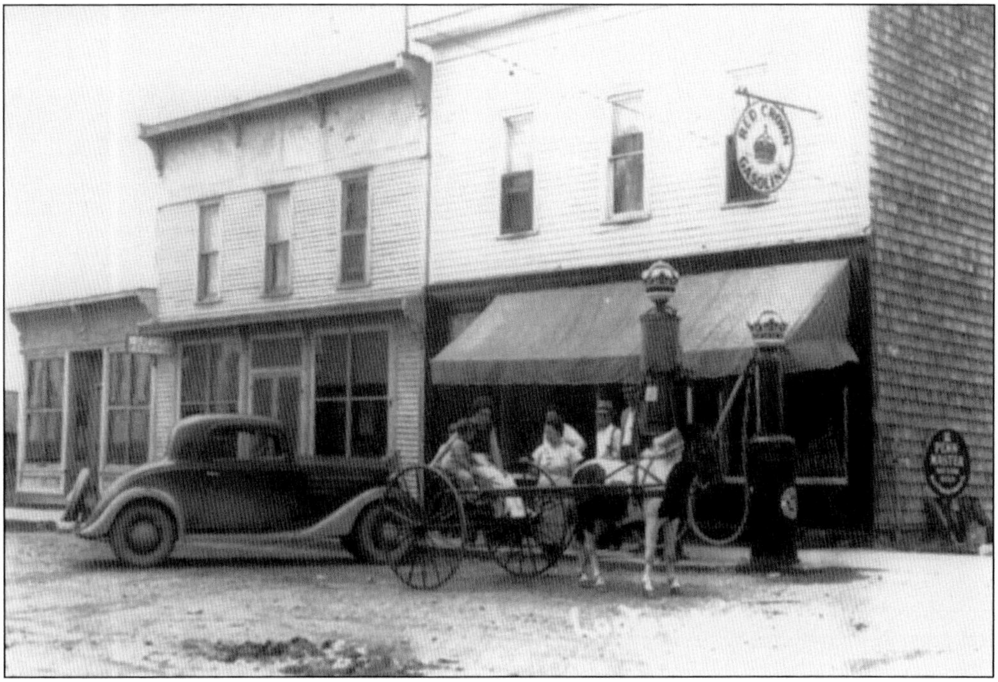

Alex Reid came to Lupton in 1900. While staying at the Hamilton Hotel, he decided to remain and work in the lumber camps. In 1903, he was contracted to build the schoolhouse. He operated the Reid Grocery Store for many years until his son, R. G. Reid, took over. (Courtesy of John and Vivian Mellon.)

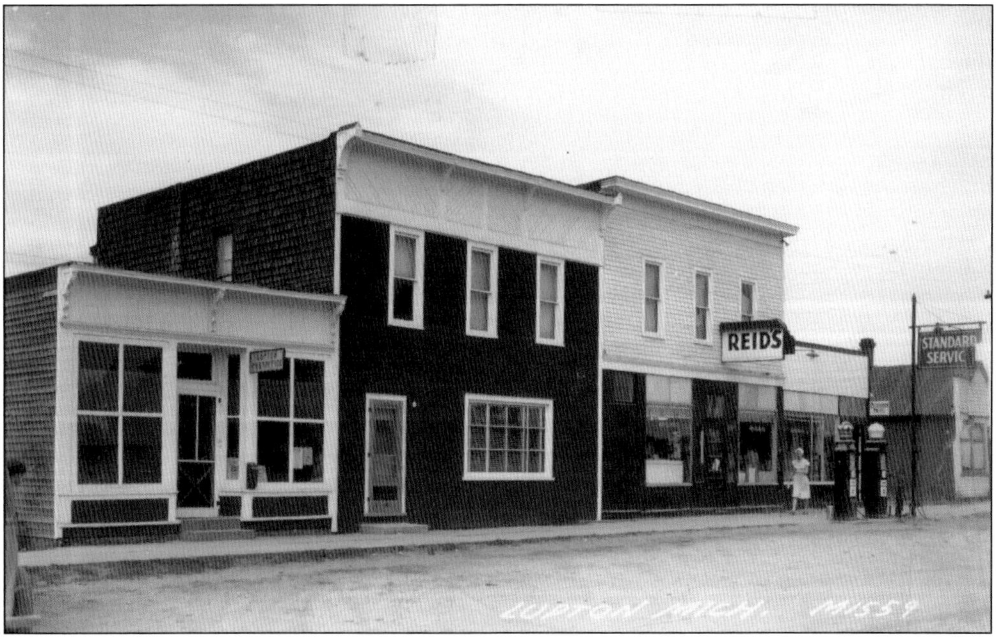

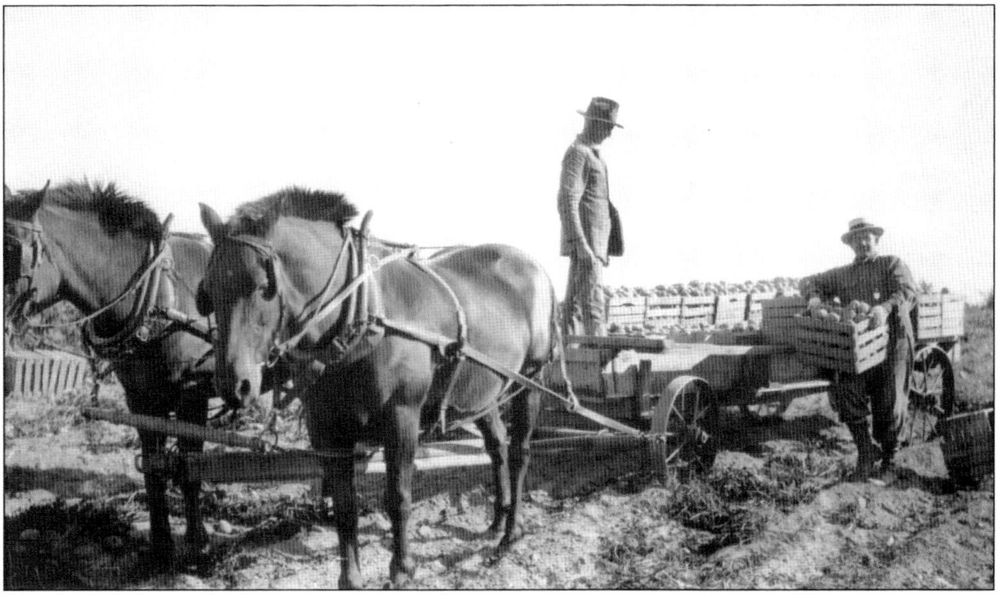

A. L. Dunlap and Guy Aurby load crates of potatoes onto the wagon pulled by workhorses Fanny and Nelly. The lumber camps were the principal markets for these potatoes grown in the rich, fine soil near Lupton. At $1 a bushel, a small clearing among the stumps could swell the pioneer farmer's pockets. (Courtesy of John and Vivian Mellon.)

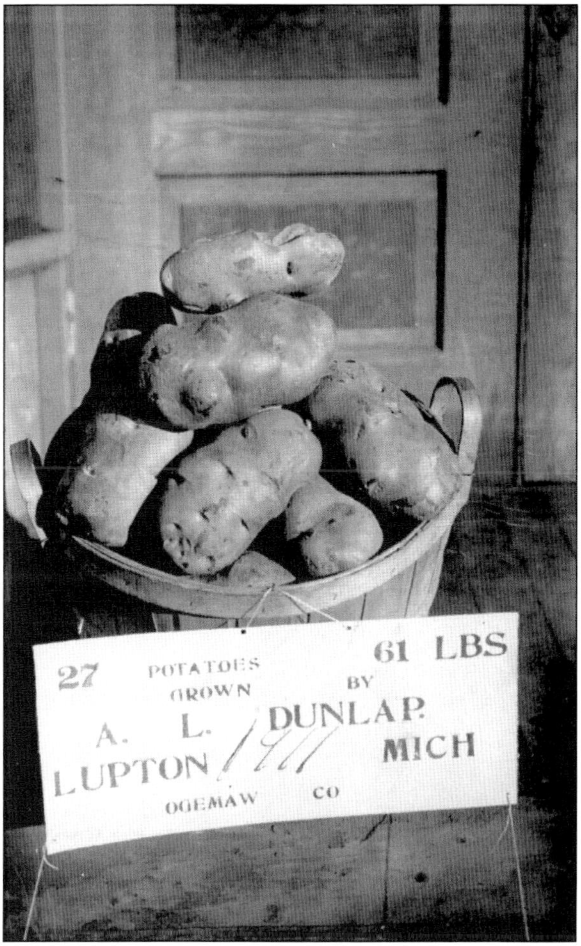

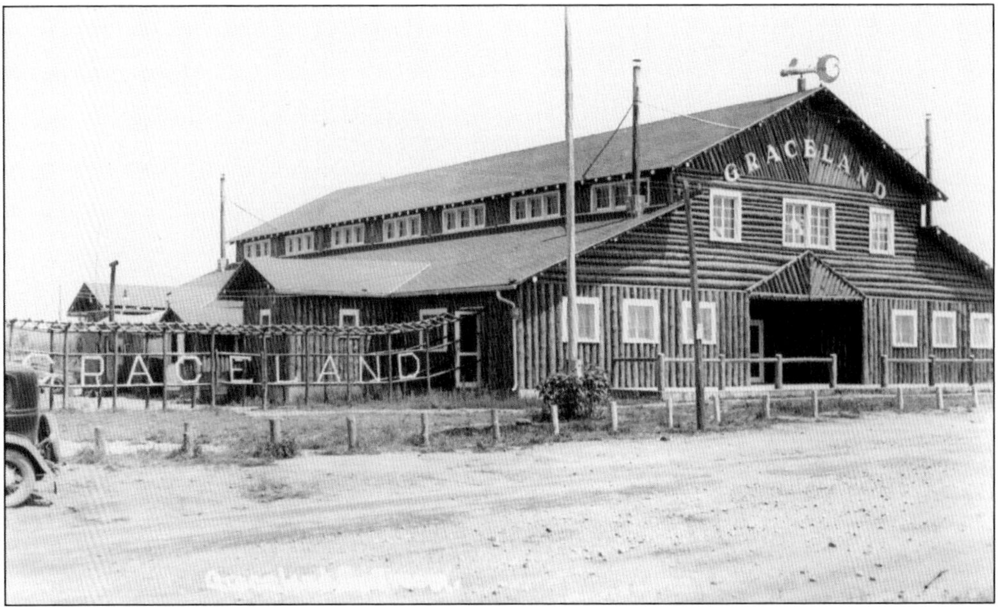

The Graceland Ballroom was built in the early 1930s during the Prohibition era. Supposedly, it was built for the Purple Gang out of Detroit. The Purple Gang members were rumrunners and ruthless gangsters. The Graceland was used as a hideaway and was owned by "One Armed Mike" Gefland and his wife Grace. Many unproven stories tell of escape tunnels and other underworld activities. In its heyday, the ballroom boasted of tourist cabins, airfield, and entertainment. Later, after Prohibition was repealed, the Graceland became a well-known local hangout featuring bands, dancing, parties, and roller-skating. (Courtesy of Donald and Sharon Alderton and Glendora Fitzgerald.)

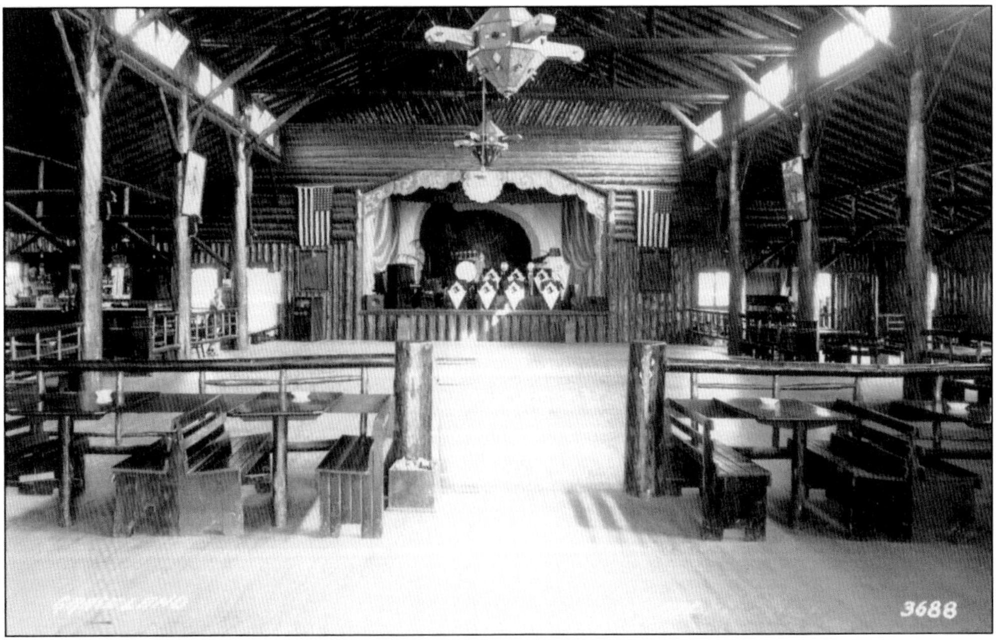

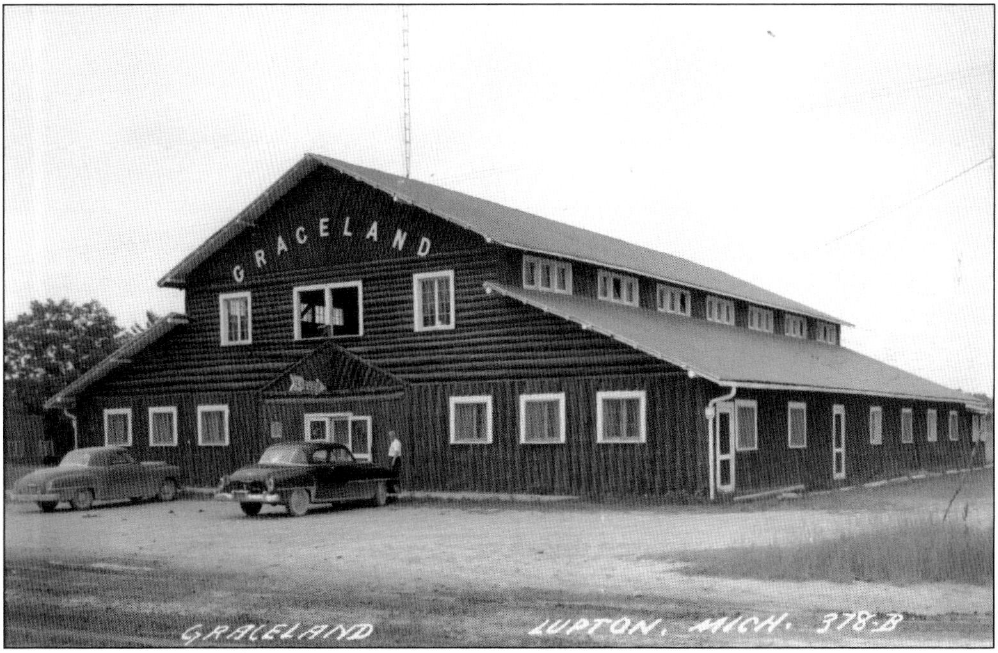

The Graceland Ballroom was a rustic log building measuring 95 feet wide by 120 feet long. It featured a large 2,400-square-foot hardwood dance floor, a beautiful stage area, a bar, and seating for about 600 patrons. A balcony, that eventually became unsafe, supported only a mannequin with a machine gun that stood guard over the dance floor. Materials for the building came from the surrounding area. The large 40-foot crossbeams were cut and stripped by hand. In the early morning of December 20, 1981, the beautiful Graceland met its demise. The building was rocked by several explosions and fire. Within an hour, the Graceland was reduced to nothing but ashes. No official cause was ever released. The Graceland was never rebuilt and remains a legend in local folklore.

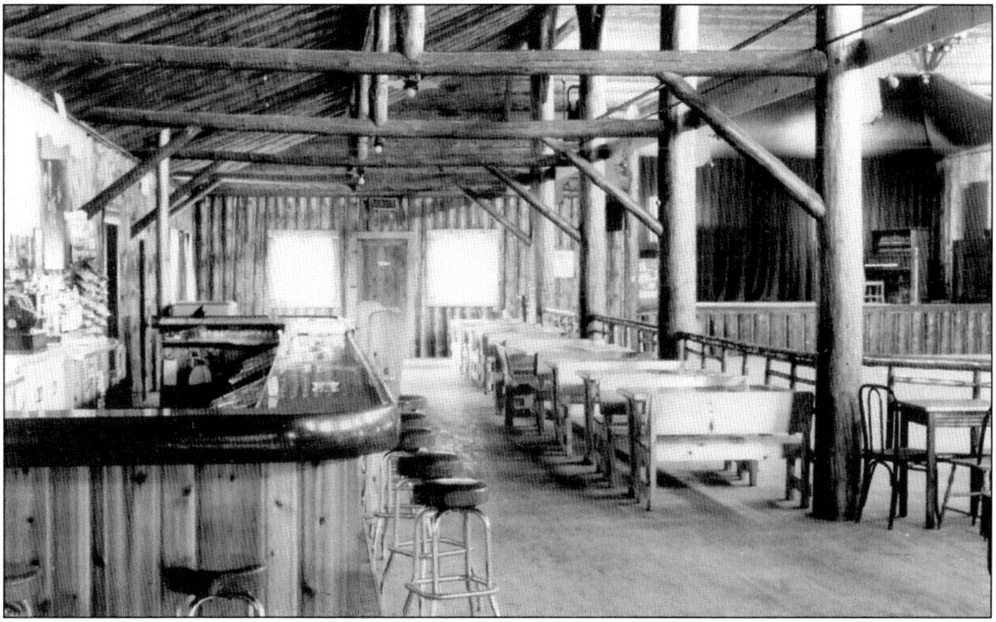

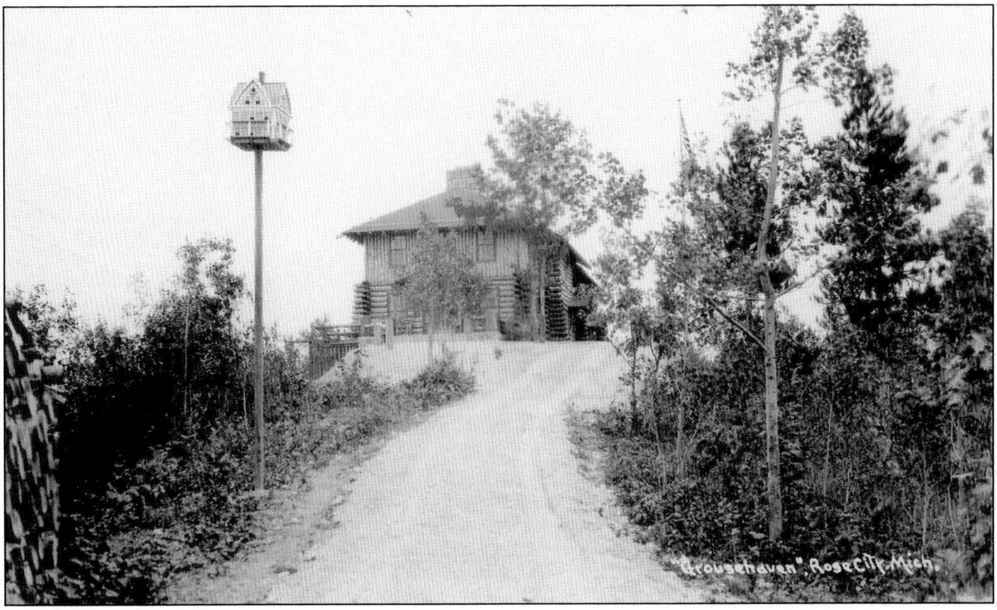

Grousehaven Shooting Preserve and Game Farm was the brainchild of Harry M. Jewett, a Detroit businessman. The 7,000 acres of former farmland was located near Lupton. In an interview with local citizen Vern Nye, he told that Jewett asked him to find a spot where he could bring his dogs and their trainers to hunt. Jewett fell in love with the area and started to buy up land. It was Jewett's intention to protect and restore the ideal situation for hunting ruffed grouse, partridge, and pheasant and to make this area a world-class preserve. Additionally, he stocked the streams and lakes with farm-raised trout. A beautiful two-story lodge with a view of four lakes was built along with other buildings. The lodge was unique as it had private baths, a beautiful stone fireplace, and electric lighting. (Courtesy of Marilyn Pachota.)

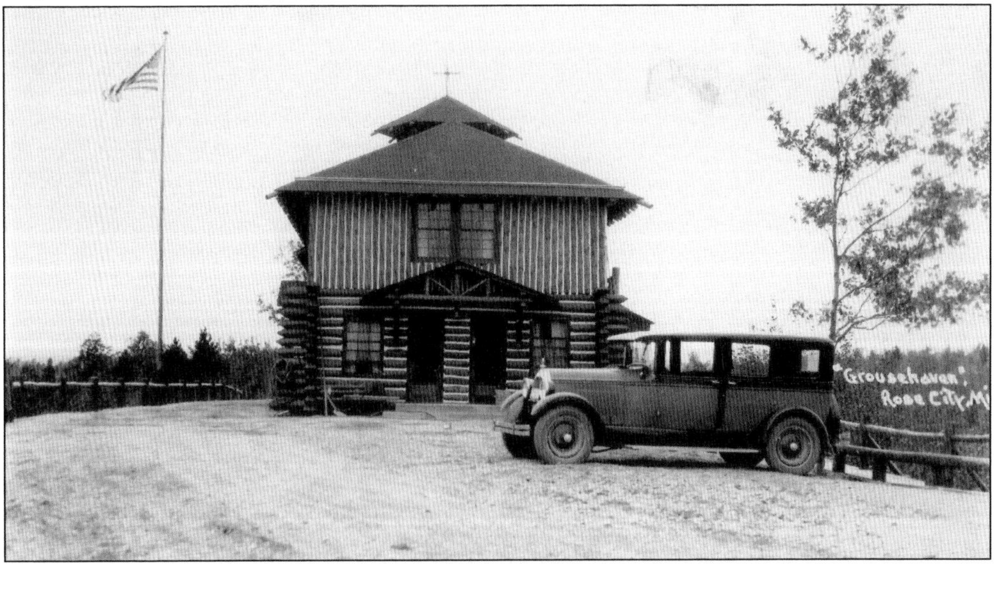

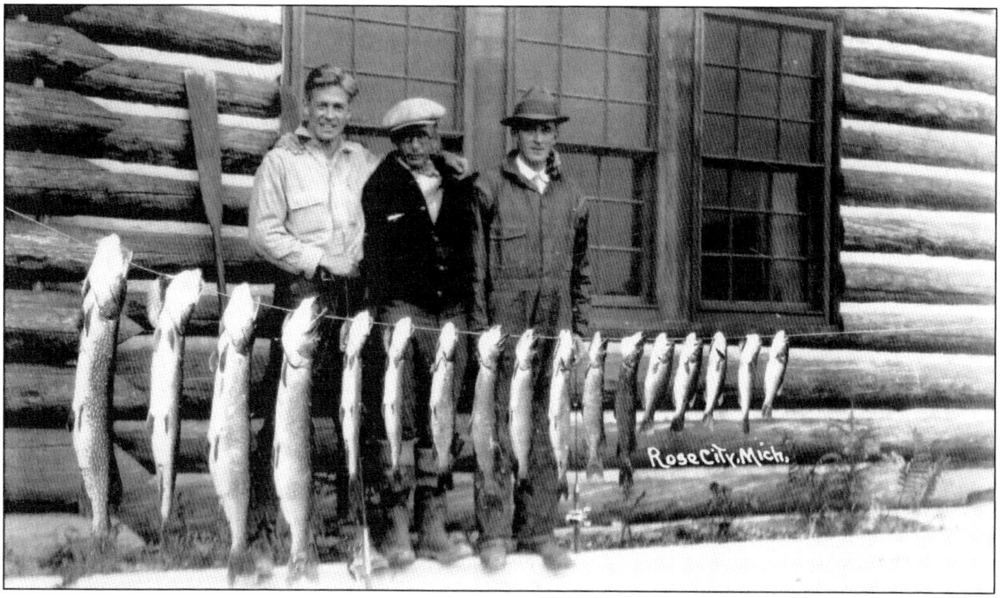

Local resident Lew Wolfe was hired to blow up stumps at $1 each. With Jewett's untimely death in 1933 at the age of 62, the dream came to a halt. In 1945, Mrs. Jewett sold 4,318 acres to the Michigan Department of Conservation, Fisheries Division, for $75,000. Pictured above with a nice stringer of fish are, from left to right, Ned Jewett, Byron Baird, and Clyde Karcher. The photograph below is one of the farm buildings on the property.

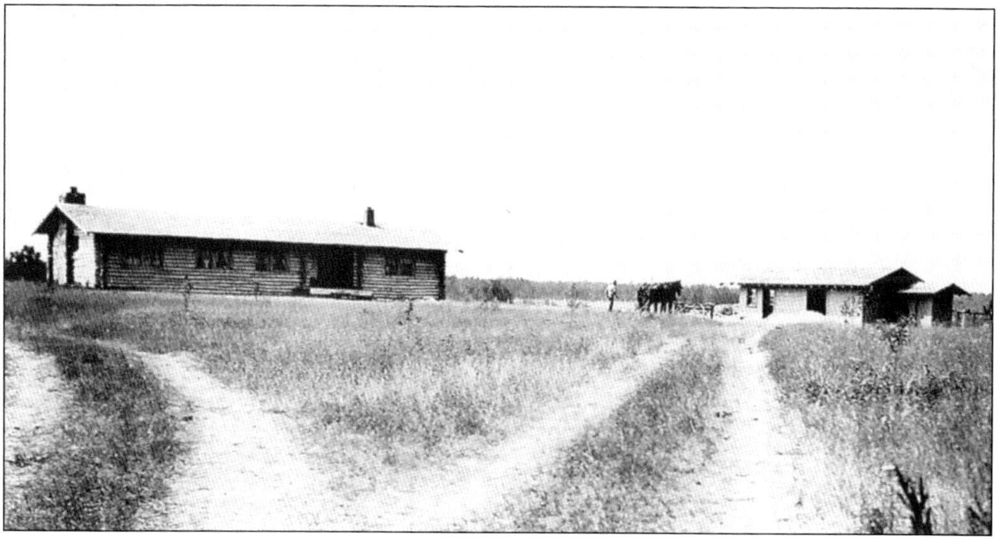

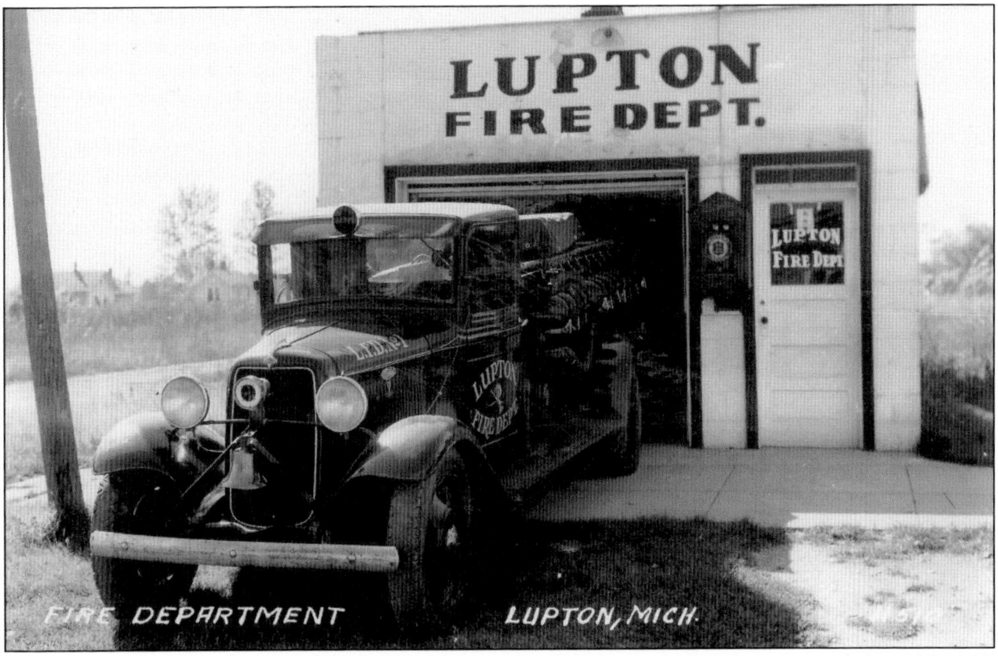

The newly formed Lupton Fire Department, spearheaded by R. G. Reid, converted this 1934 V-8 Ford farm truck into a fire truck. It was equipped with a 500-gallon water tank and 500 feet of hose. Much of the equipment was donated by the City of Saginaw Fire Department. Standing on this fire truck, from left to right, are Lawrence Matthews, Sandy Parker, R. G. Reid (first fire chief), Jimmy Parker, Cecil Weston, Lew Wolfe, Lou Brindley, and Devere Rakestraw. (Courtesy of John and Vivian Mellon.)

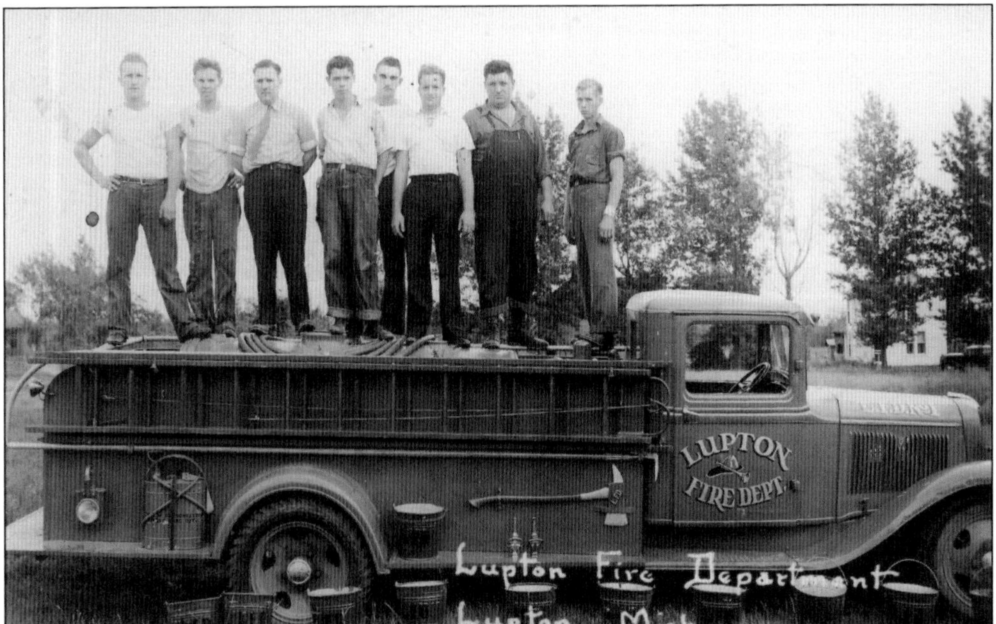

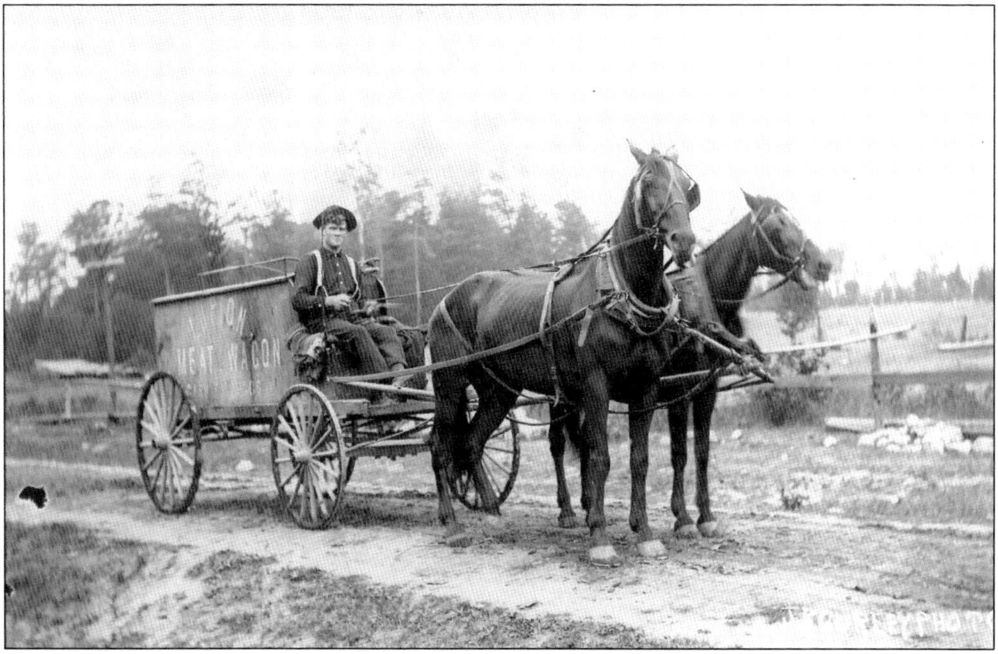

The Lupton Meat Wagon was used to sell and deliver groceries to rural homes in the Lupton Area. (Courtesy of John and Vivian Mellon.)

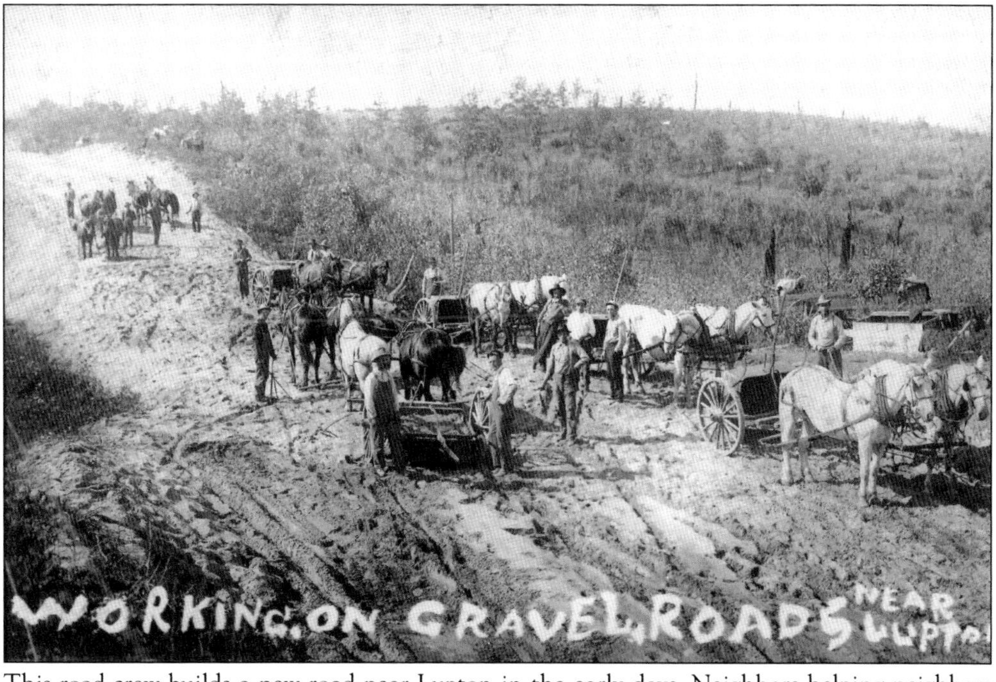

This road crew builds a new road near Lupton in the early days. Neighbors helping neighbors was the name of the game. Early roads were often nothing more than trails through the woods. Many of the roads near Lupton led through swamps and low areas and many yards of fill had to be brought in to make them passable.

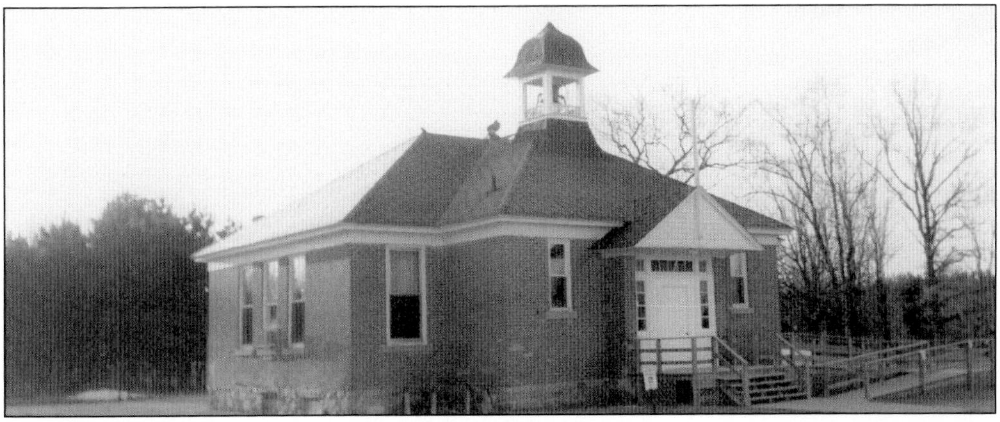

The Lupton School was an impressive brick building. The school consisted of two large rooms separated by two giant doors. Students in kindergarten through 10th grade attended this school. After the 10th grade, an official graduation ceremony was performed. For a 12th-grade diploma, students traveled to Rose City.

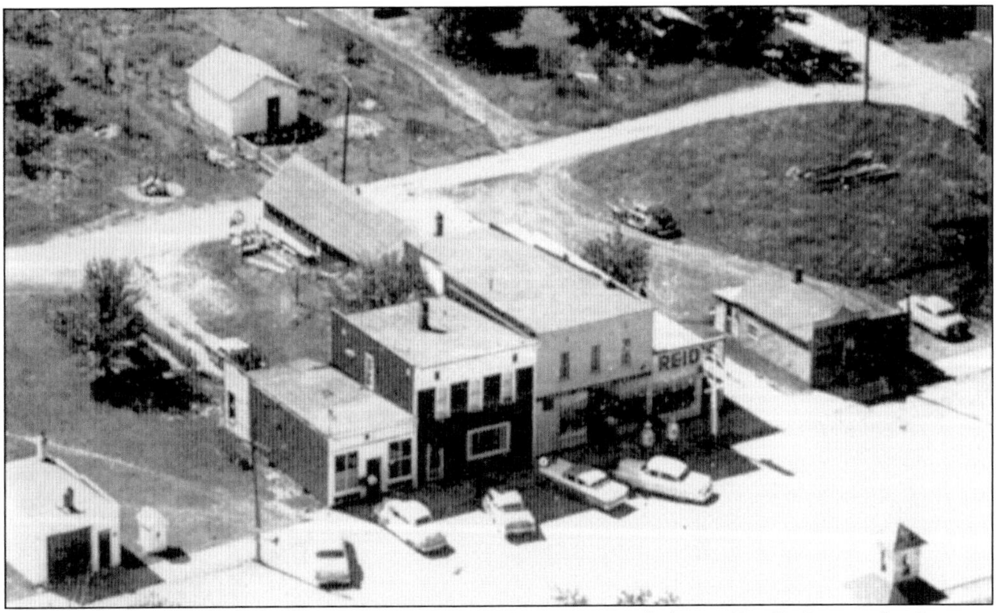

This view of downtown Lupton was taken in the 1950s and shows Reid's Store, the Lupton Garage, the post office, and other buildings in town.

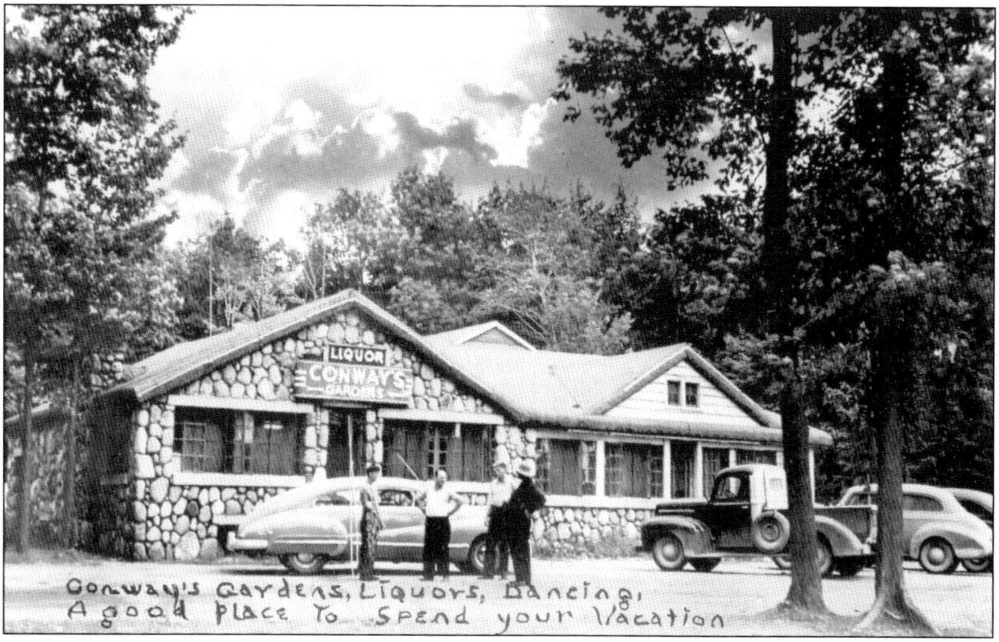

Shady Shores Park began on August 14, 1928, with the formation of the George and Rifle Lake Resort Company in an area known for its hunting, fishing, and boating. Ninety acres were bought from James O'Connor on August 3, 1926, by Ceil Conway of Vassar and Andrew Foster of Detroit. Ceil Conway's brother Paul was a builder and he and his family were living across the lake at Dyer's Landing. Paul was hired to clear the land and build roads. The properties were sectioned into lots and were sold from the back of a Republic truck. Paul built an estimated 60 homes and a store in the park. In 1926, he built the first wooden and stone arch to welcome visitors to the park. (Below, courtesy of Sharon and Don Alderton.)

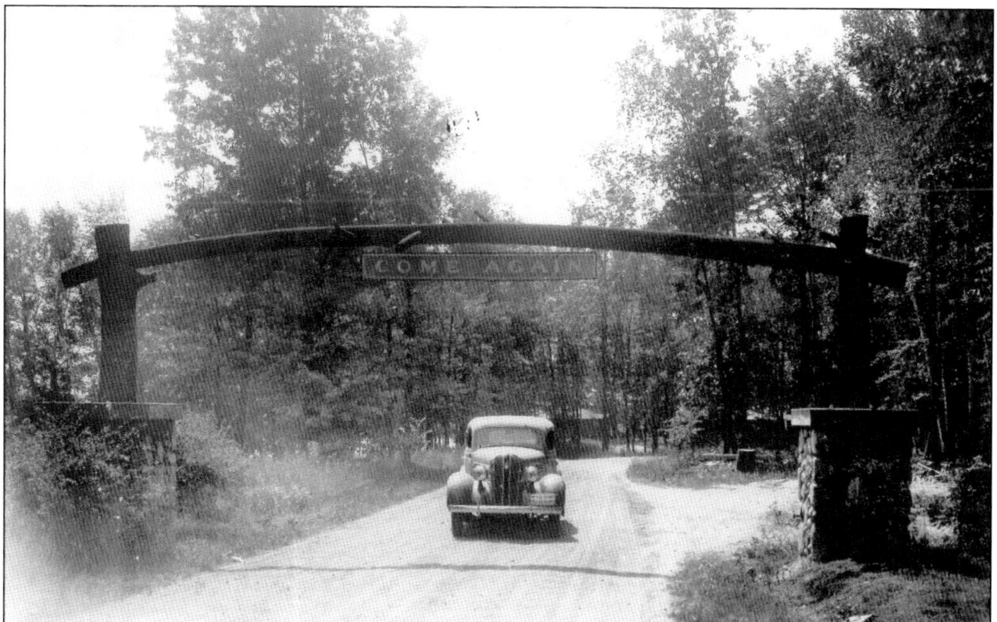

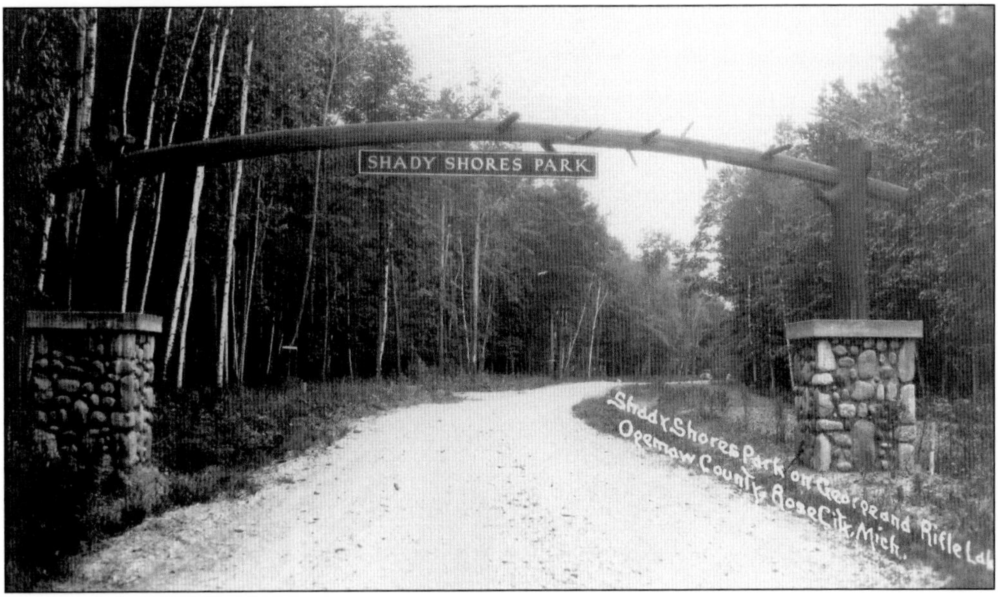

A community building was built in the late 1920s and is still being used as a gathering place for those who vacation or own homes in Shady Shores. The beautiful wooden arch was replaced with a cement one on Fourth of July weekend in 1949. In 2003, a cement truck accidentally took down that arch. The community rallied and a new arch was dedicated on July 1, 2006. In the summer of 2008, Orison Conway, son of the original builder of the arch, along with his three sons, Melvin, Randy, and Douglass, helped lay the new stonework, which covers the base of the arch. Shady Shores remains a great place to visit and spend the summer months fishing and boating. (Courtesy of the Conway family.)

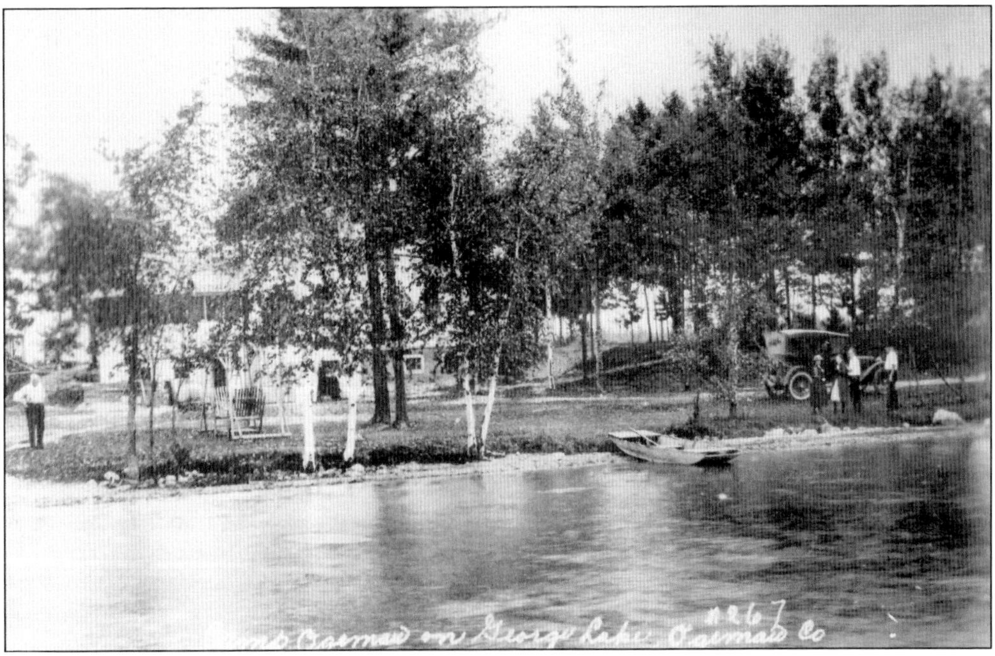

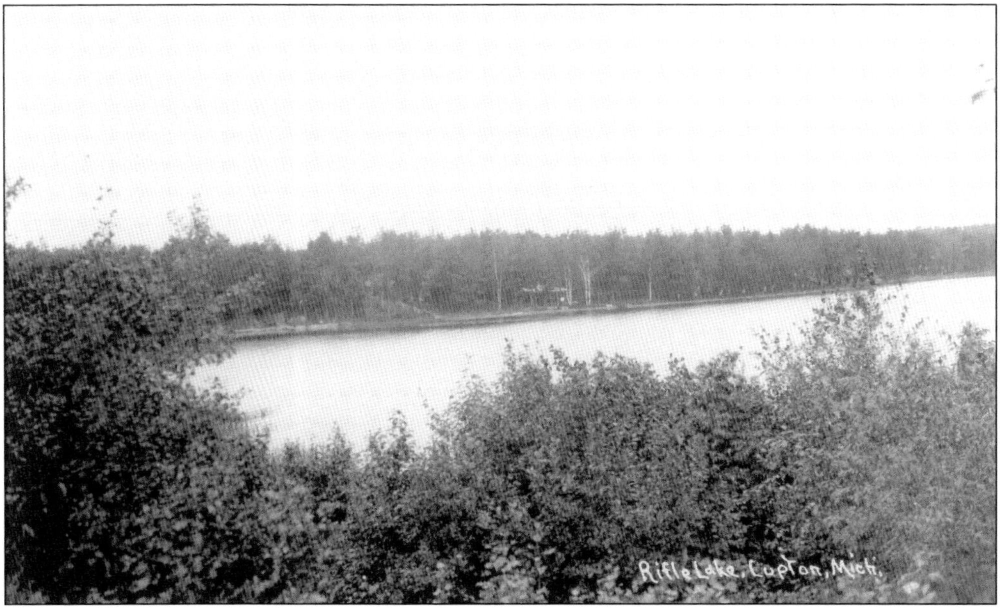

Rifle Lake is one of the lakes that encompasses Shady Shores Park. George Lake is the second lake. Both lakes are known for their excellent fishing and swimming areas.

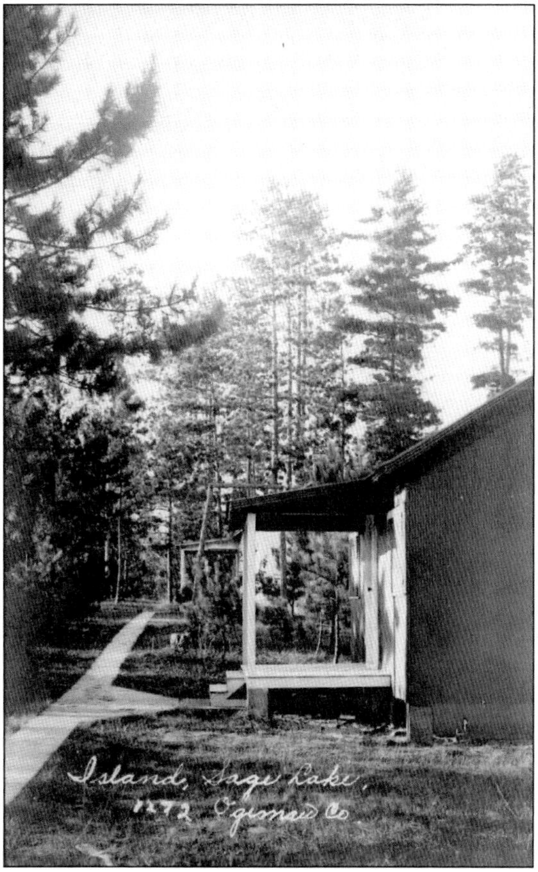

First Island of Sage Lake is not furnished with electrical power. Charles Martin Kenyon (1842–1915) once owned this island plus a small section on the northeast side of the lake, which he sold prior to buying the 2,000 acres where he built the Kenyon's Landing Resort.

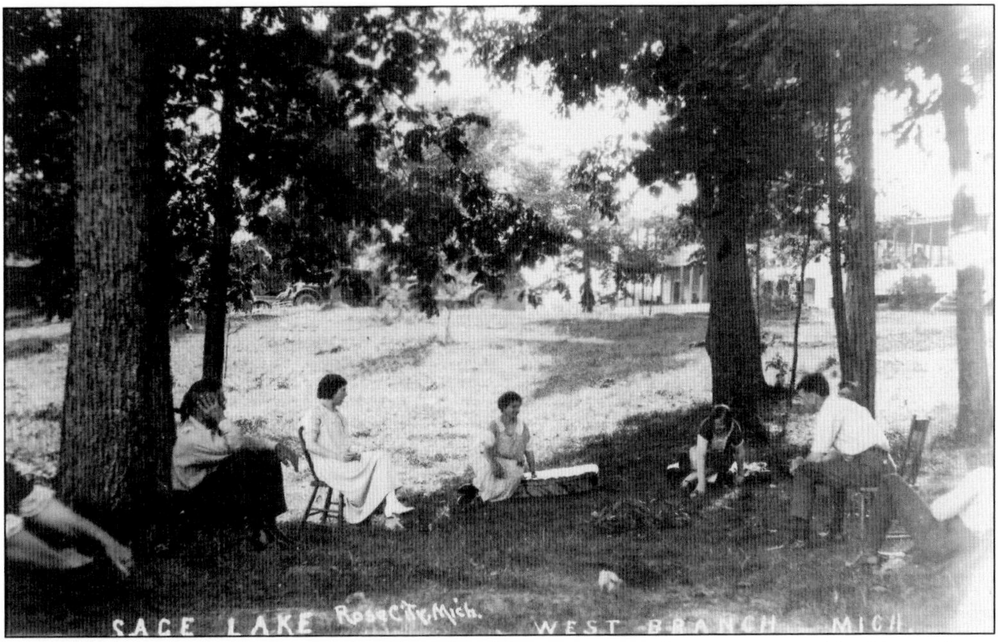

Sage Lake got its name from the Sage Land and Improvement Company owned by Henry Sage, John McGraw, and W. C. Grant. It is the largest lake in Ogemaw County, being a mile across at the widest point and three miles long. There are three islands in the lake. The smallest is called First Island. Second Island has many cottages and Third Island is owned by one family. The headwaters of the AuGres River begin at Sage Lake. During the lumber era, logs were held in the lake, then later floated down the river to Lake Huron, where they were loaded onto barges and taken to the sawmills.

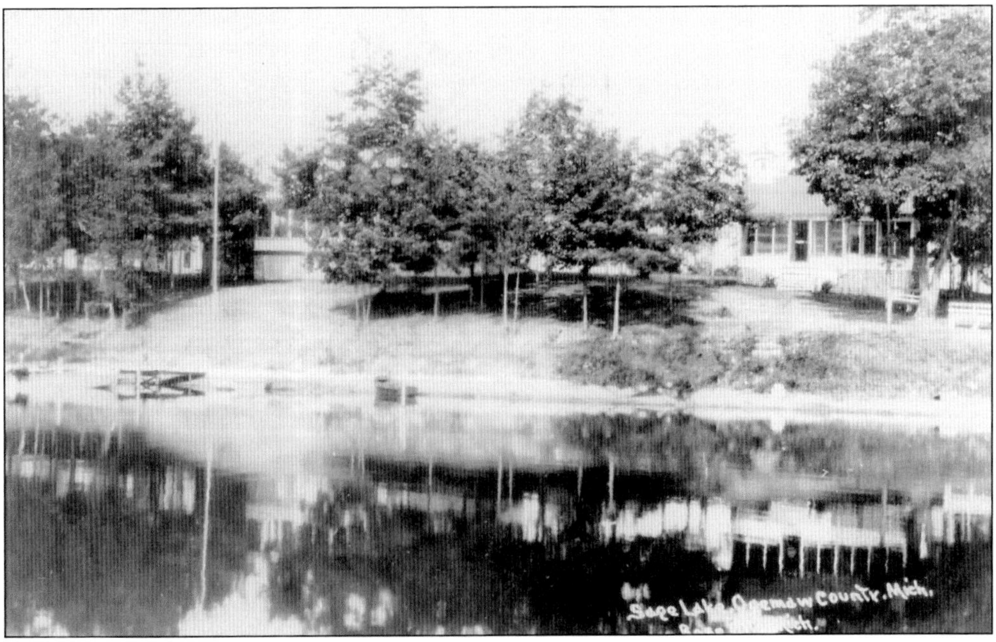

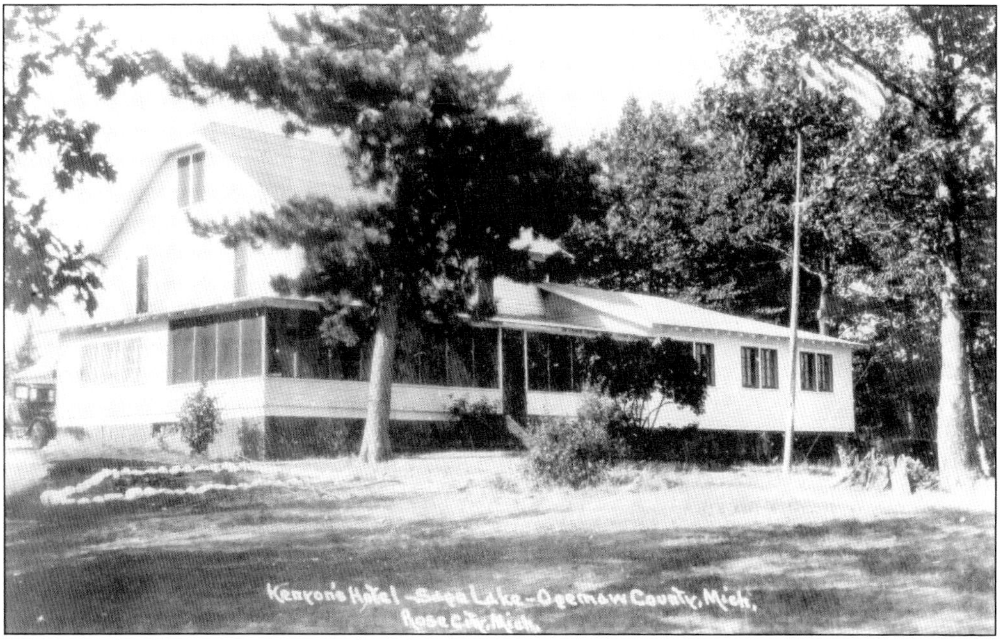

In 1903, Charles Martin Kenyon bought 2,000 acres on the west and south sides of Sage Lake extending to State Road. He built the original Kenyon's Landing, consisting of a home and six cabins. After his death in 1914, the business was run by several family members. Kenyon's was a thriving business into the 1940s and 1950s, when several new buildings were erected to accommodate more guests. The hotel had a long porch overlooking the lake, a lounge area, fine dining restaurant run by French chef Pierre, fishing boats, and a riding stable. Recently the resort has been owned by several others, rather than members of the Kenyon family.

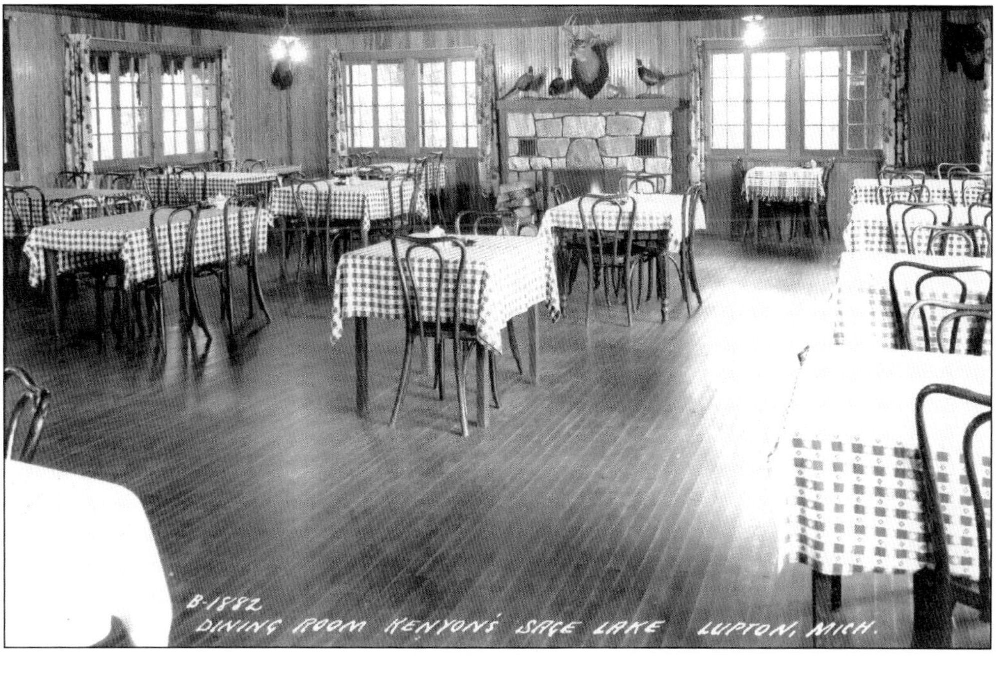

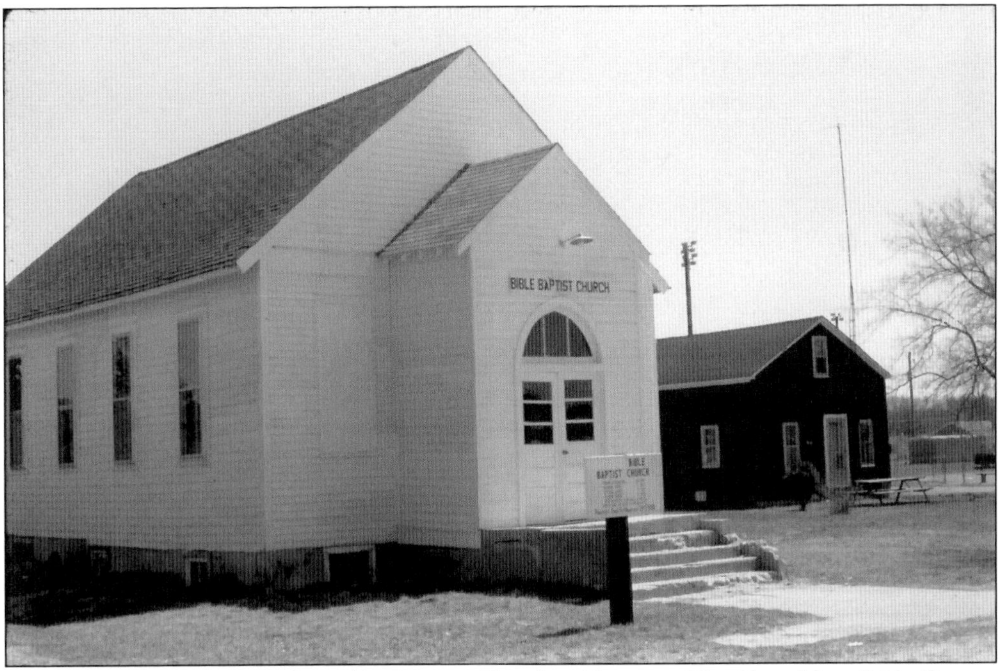

The photograph above is the Bible Baptist Church of Lupton. The Friendship Bible Baptist Church was organized at its current location in 1976. Its name was changed to avoid confusion with the Friends church already located in Lupton.

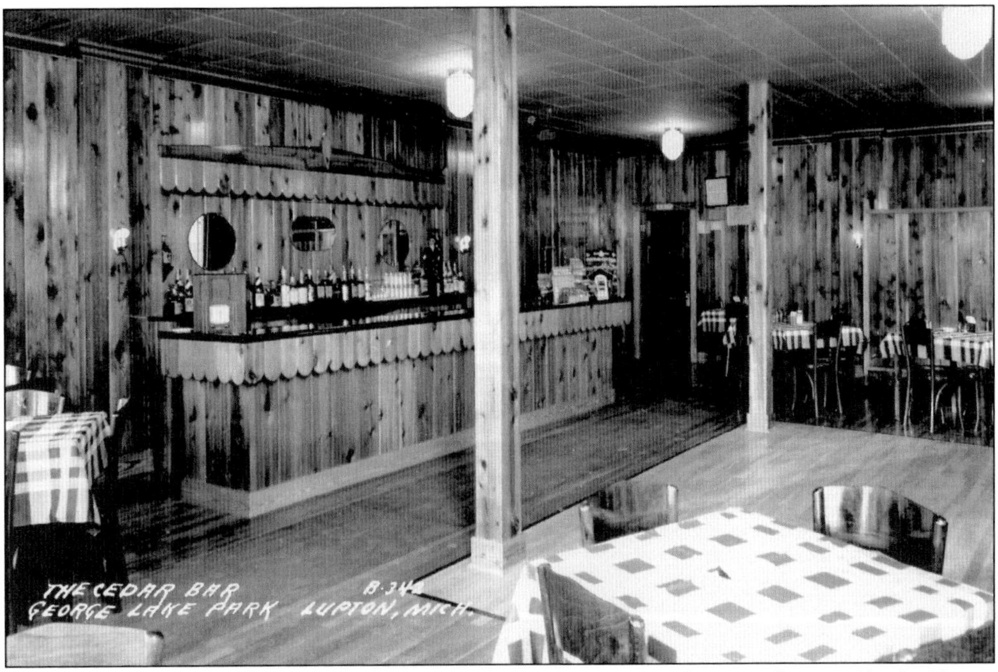

The Cedar Bar is located on the corner of Shady Shores and Wiltse Roads near Shady Shores Park and is as popular today as it was in the past for good food and excellent entertainment. It was established in 1932.

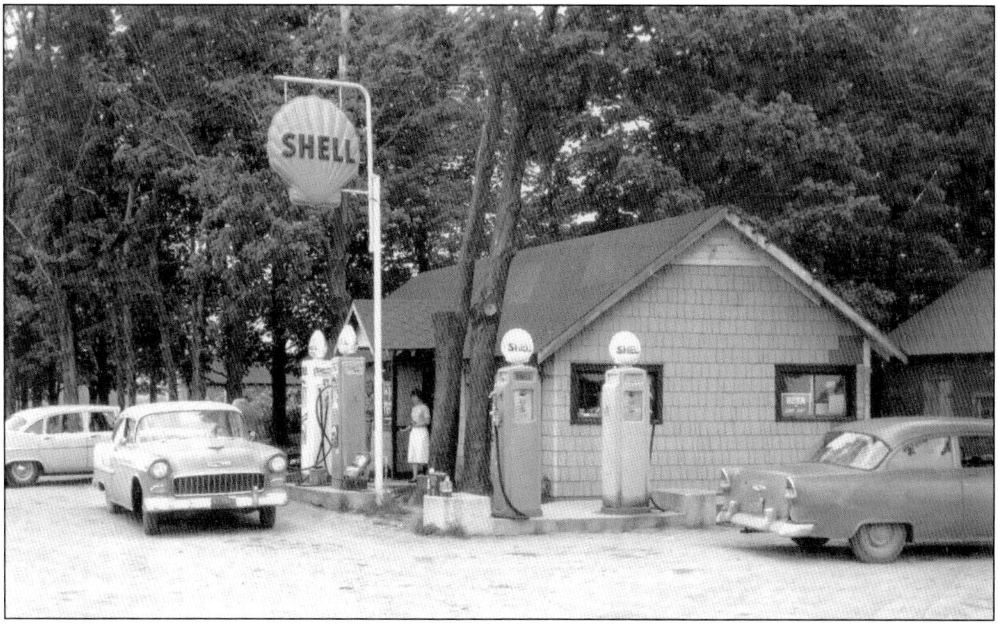

Lovewell's Corner Store opened in 1905 on the northwest corner of Wiltse and Sage Lake Roads. Frank Lovewell came from Monroe County in 1895 and operated a sawmill with his father, Robert, and a Mr. Hobart before opening the store. The store has seen many changes, ranging from a blacksmith to car repair, grocery, and boatbuilding businesses. The store is owned now by the fourth generation of the Lovewell family. (Courtesy of Connie Stasiak.)

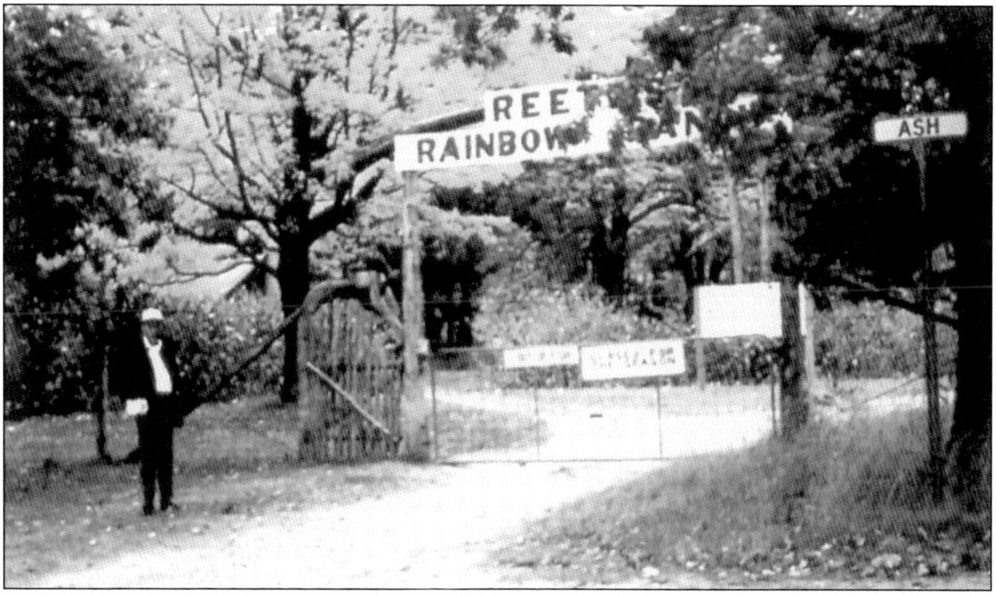

Al Reetz bought this property in 1950 and filled the ponds with runoff from the school's flowing well. He started with three ponds and ended up with seven, which he used for raising trout. In the 1960s, he opened the Reetz's Rainbow Ranch to fishing. For $3 a pound, grandfathers emptied their wallets making their grandchildren happy catching trout. The facility has since closed to the public, the family now uses it as a gathering place for making memories and remembering. (Courtesy of John Reetz.)

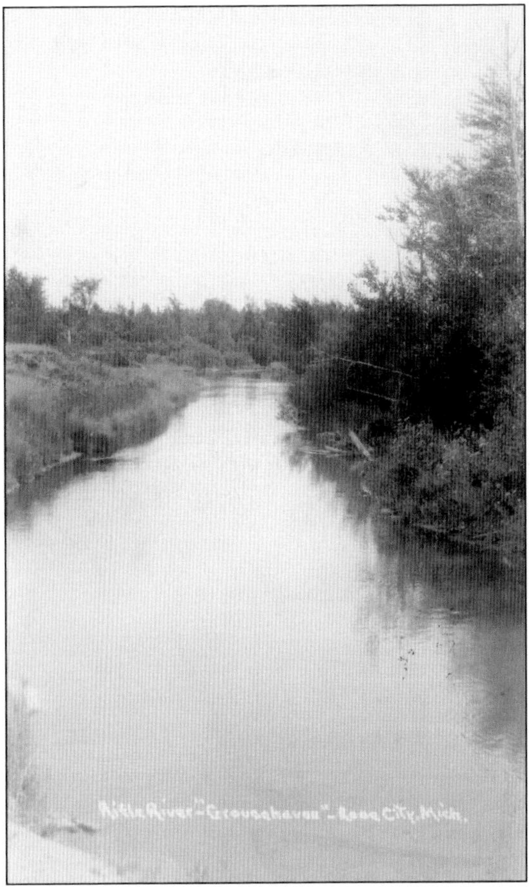

In 1965, through the efforts of four local men—namely Bernard Card, Clarence Cooley, R. G. Reid, and Lyle Wallace—Grousehaven became the Rifle River Recreation Area under the administration of the Michigan State Parks and Recreation Division. The purchase was made possible through the sale of fishing and hunting licenses. This huge area of wilderness was once the private retreat of Detroit entrepreneur Harry M. Jewett. This action allowed the area to become accessible to all campers, fishermen, hunters, and outdoor enthusiasts as a state park. Today it boasts campgrounds for 100 people, 7 lakes, 13 miles of trails, and 7 miles of trout streams. An observation tower with a magnificent view replaced the once beautiful log lodge when it was condemned.

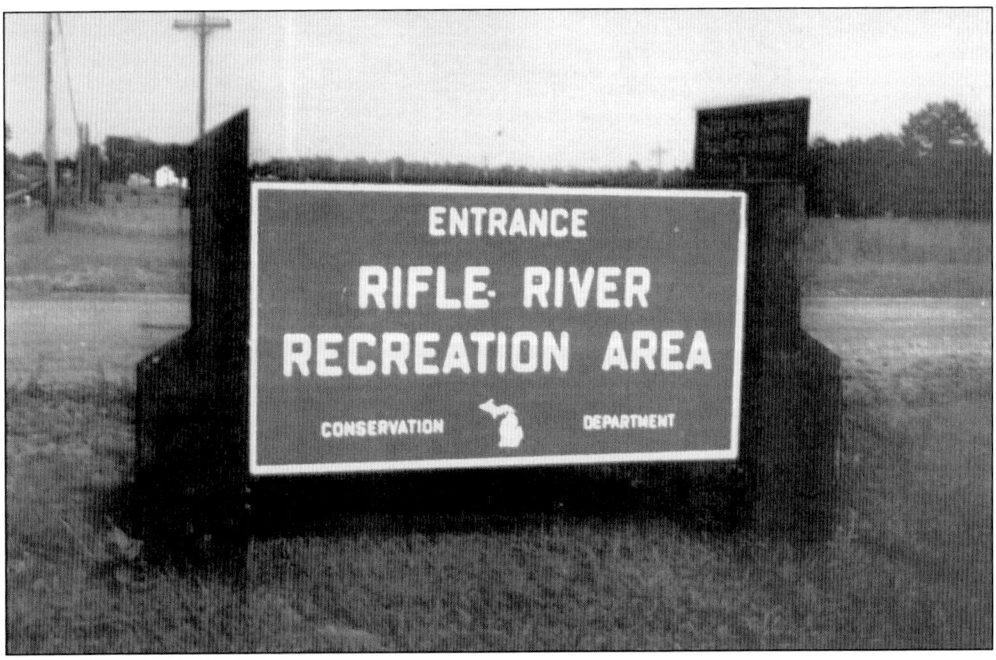

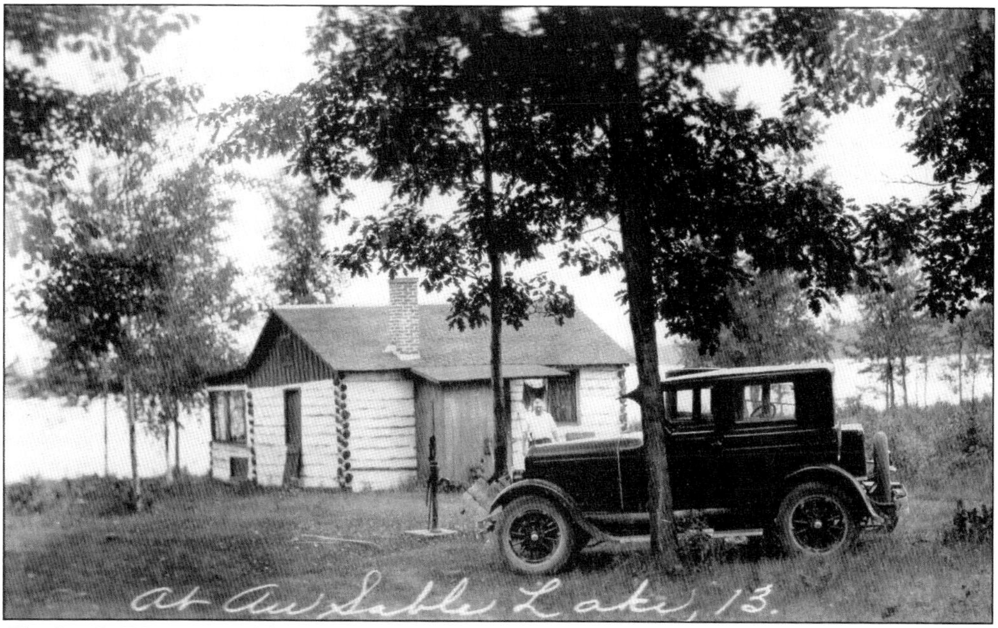

Charles C. Winnery and his wife Virginia from Toledo, Ohio, came on the train to Long Lake in Iosco County on their way to Alpena. While in Long Lake, they traveled west and found peaceful AuSable Lake. They bought property in 1912 and moved there permanently. Charles and Virginia bought the land, cattle, and started a resort with seven cabins and a large barn. The Winnery Resort entertained guests with excursions to the AuSable River and fishing trips. In 1952, the resort was renamed Duggan's Resort when Virginia, their daughter, married John Duggan. The Duggan family still owns the property today.

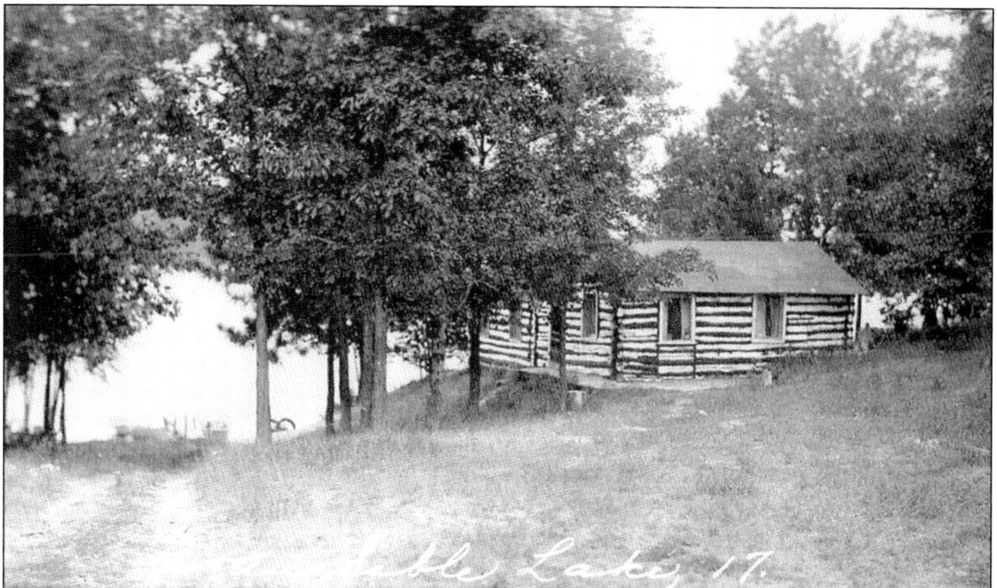

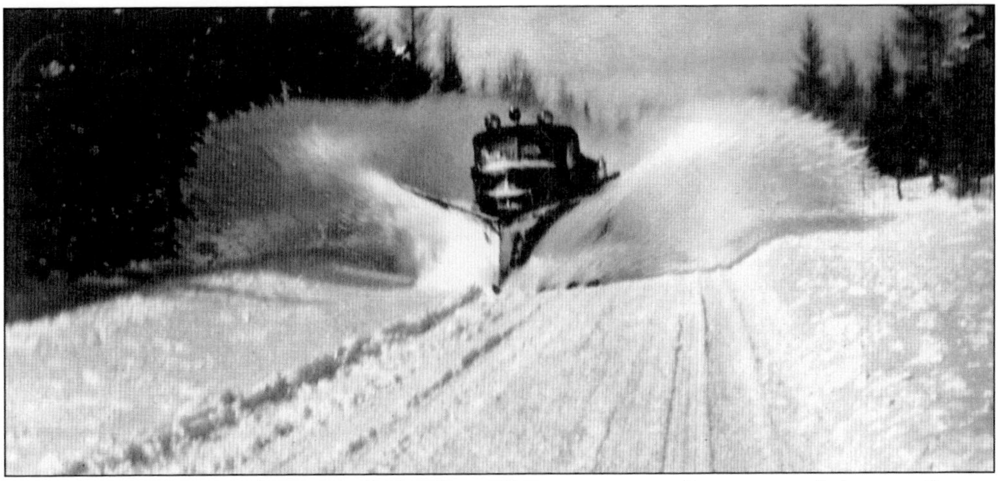

Winters in northern Michigan can be harsh, and Lupton is generally in a snow-belt area of heavy winter snows. The winter of 1976 was extremely harsh. Snow accumulated by the foot and travel became a challenge.

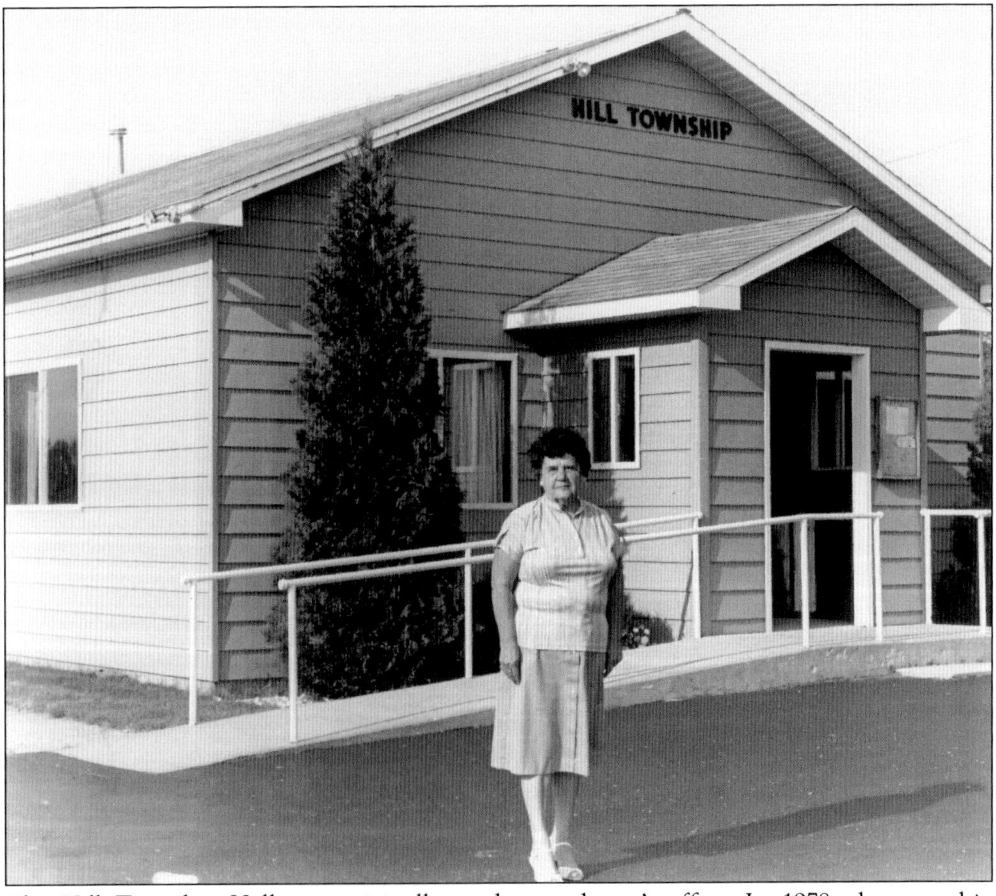

The Hill Township Hall was originally used as a doctor's office. In 1978, the township acquired the building and added a large hall as a place to hold meetings, play cards, or to have social gatherings.

Three

The Prescott and Skidway Area

Richland Township of Ogemaw County was formed in 1879. No one knows why the township was named Richland, but possibly the rich land that produced some of the most supreme timber in the state of Michigan provided an easy-to-remember label.

Prescott was the major center of trading for Richland Township. Several historical documents state that the lumbering community of Camp Six became known as Prescott, a popular stop on the rail line between Shearer and Mills. Prescott was named for Charles H. Prescott, a daring businessman with strong religious convictions. Born in Maine in 1828, Rev. Charles H. Prescott ventured to Michigan from Pennsylvania in 1878 to harvest the bountiful crop of virgin white pine that stood on 8,500 acres he acquired in a bankruptcy sale. His lumbering ventures led to investments in the railroad business, then later to cattle ranching. The Charles H. Prescott family dominated the Richland Township area of Ogemaw County during the lumbering, railroading, and early farming eras.

The community of Prescott was incorporated as a village in June 1947. Before that time, the small town was managed by the Richland Township Board. In 1957, voters from Prescott and Whittemore approved to consolidate the small local schools to form Whittemore-Prescott Area Schools. In 2000, the population of Prescott was 286.

Mills Township of Ogemaw County was created in 1884. The township was named after Barney Mills, an ambitious pioneer lumberman and businessman that moved to the area from St. Clair County. Most of the harvested Mills Township's timber was stored in Skidway Lake, where later the logs were skidded from the lake to area sawmills and local buyers. Barney Mills built the first general store in Camp Six.

Currently, Skidway Lake is an unincorporated community in Mills Township. The lake resort area supports many thriving businesses, a modern volunteer fire department, and a law enforcement unit. The Rifle River meanders through the center of Mills Township and provides fishing, canoeing, and kayaking entertainment. Residents of the area have either a Prescott or Alger address.

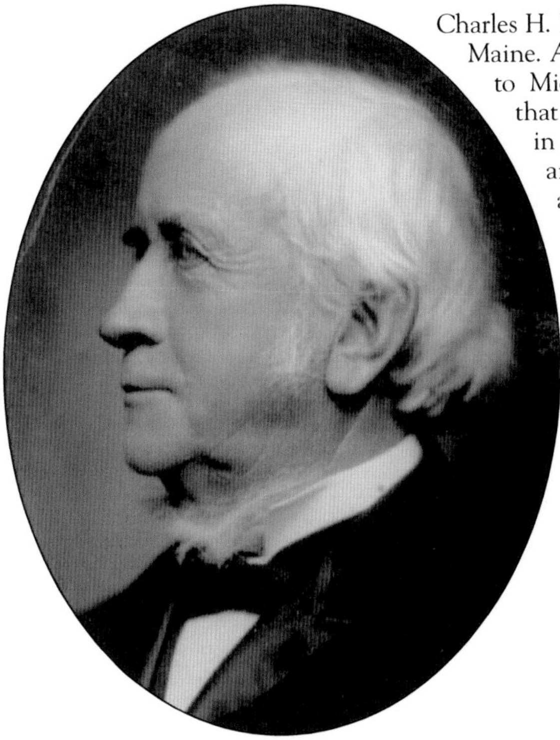

Charles H. Prescott (1828–1913) was born in Sidney, Maine. As an ordained Baptist minister, he came to Michigan from Pennsylvania in 1878. At that time, he purchased 8,500 acres of land in Richland Township of Ogemaw County and Burleigh Township of Iosco County at a bankruptcy sale. After 20 years of harvesting timber, he promoted the entire agricultural arena of the state by farming and grazing that same land.

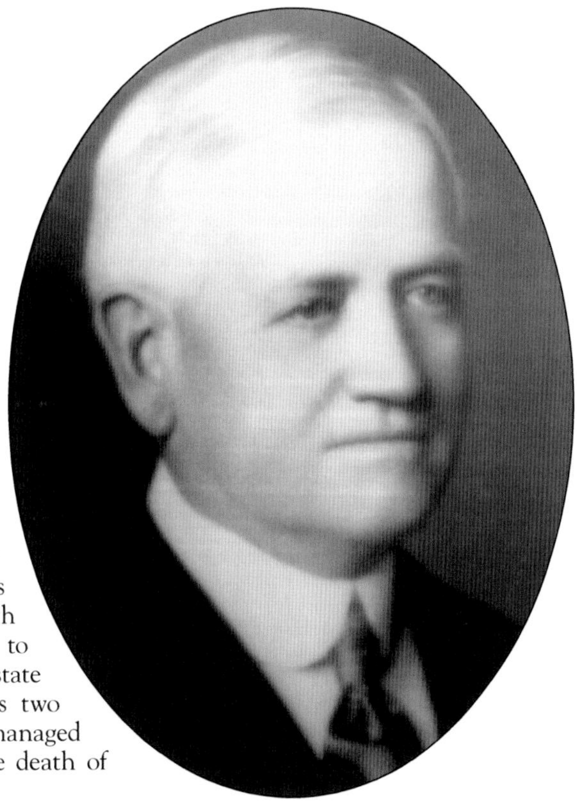

George A. Prescott Sr. (1862–1927), born in Pennsylvania, was the son of Charles H. and Sarah Prescott. He was a Michigan state senator for the 28th District from 1895 to 1898. From 1905 to 1908, he was Michigan secretary of state under Gov. Fred Warner. He and his two sons, Charles T. and George A. Jr., managed the extensive Prescott Ranch after the death of Charles H. Prescott in 1913.

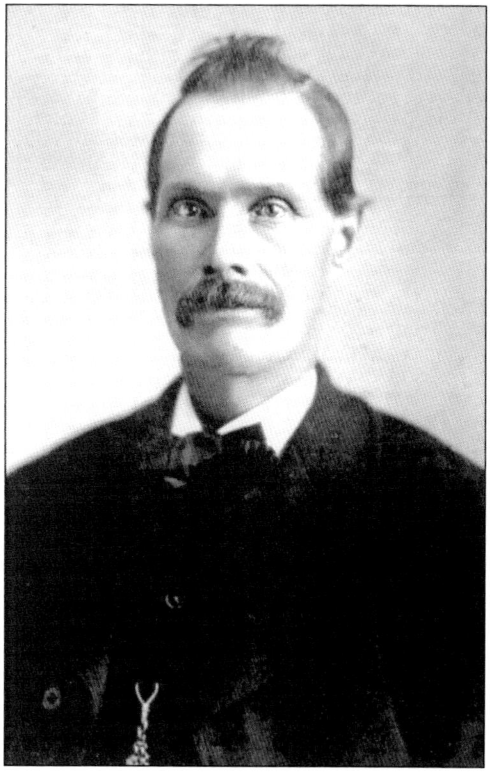

Barney Mills (1828–1905) was an ambitious pioneer lumberman and businessman of the area. He came here from Marysville, St. Clair County, where he and his brother Nelson were progressive lumbermen and sawmill owners. Barney owned several hundred acres of land north and west of Camp Six and provided much of the lumber for area buildings. Barney built the first general store in Camp Six. (Courtesy of Dave Mills.)

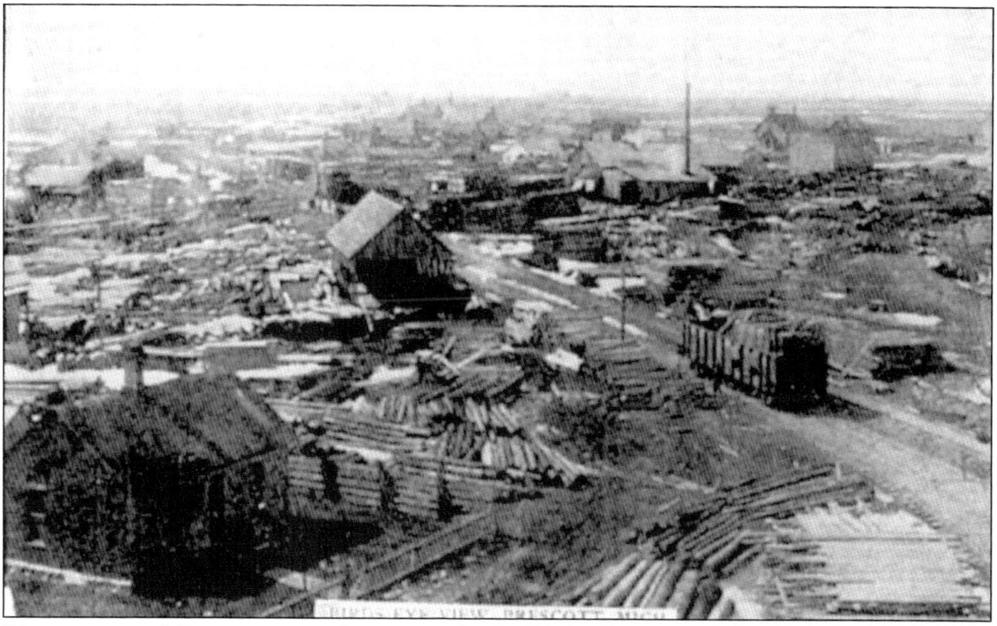

This picture of Prescott was taken around 1896 from the top of the first elevator looking southwest. The rail line shown in the photograph is that of the Detroit and Mackinac Railway. John Wilson's sawmill is seen in the center. During the lumbering era, Prescott was known as Camp Six. As early as 1886, Camp Six was called Prescott. The first elevator was built here in the mid-1890s.

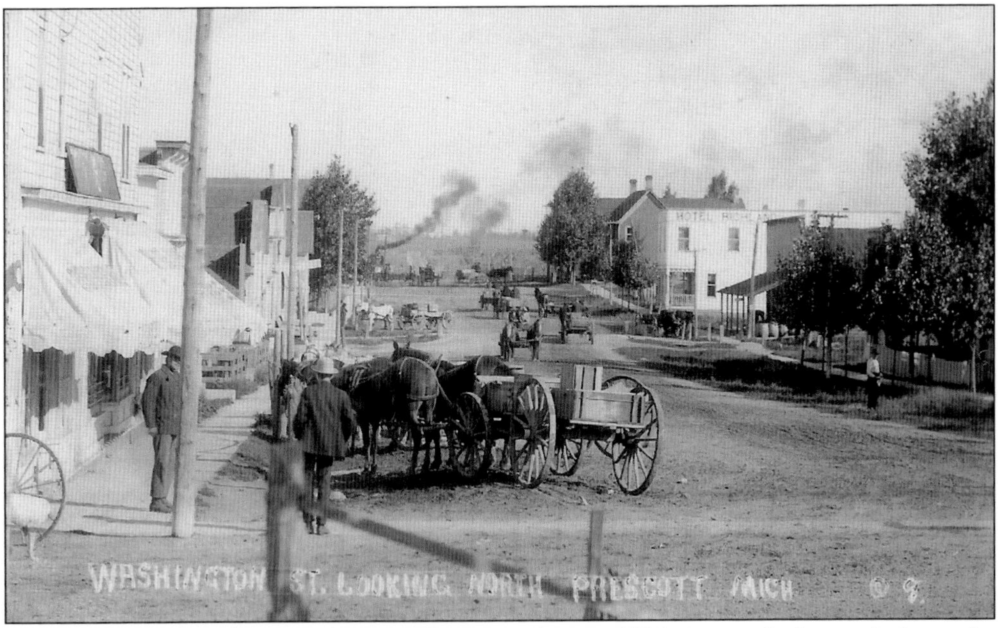

This is a view of Washington Street in Prescott taken in 1908. As one looks north down the street, the large white building on the right is the Richland Hotel. Smoke is flowing from the train engine as it approaches the depot. During the 1890s, Charles H. Prescott established narrow-gauge rail lines to all six of the lumber camps he owned in the area. (Courtesy of Ron McCarthy.)

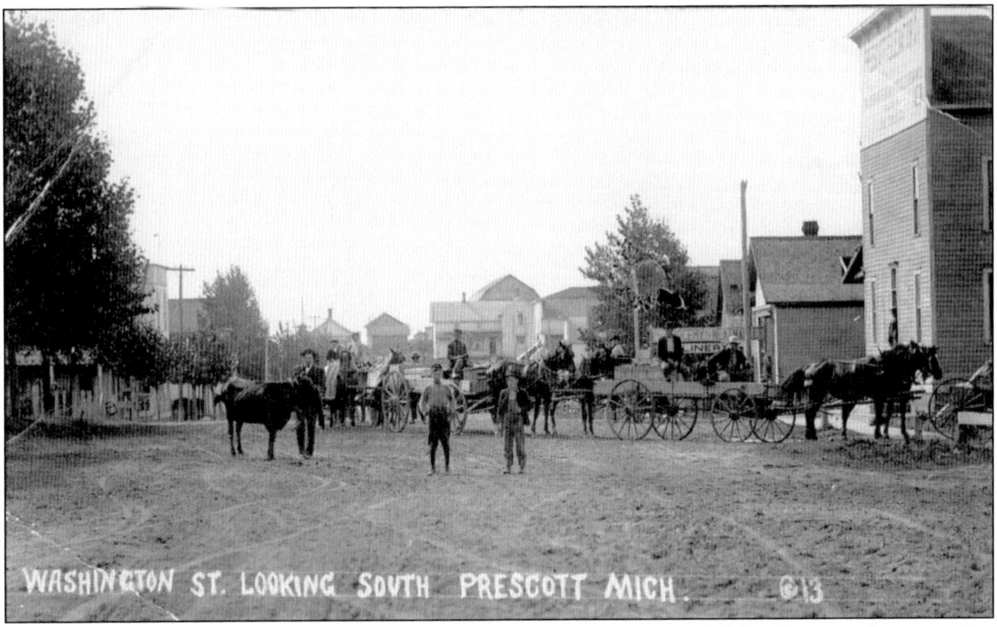

This is the same Washington Street as in the above photograph, probably taken on the same day in 1908. However, in this photograph the viewer is looking south down the street. At the dawn of the 20th century, lumbering was the major industry, but as land was cleared, crop farming and livestock raising became more prevalent. Before the invention of the automobile, the Prescott farms employed approximately 100 men.

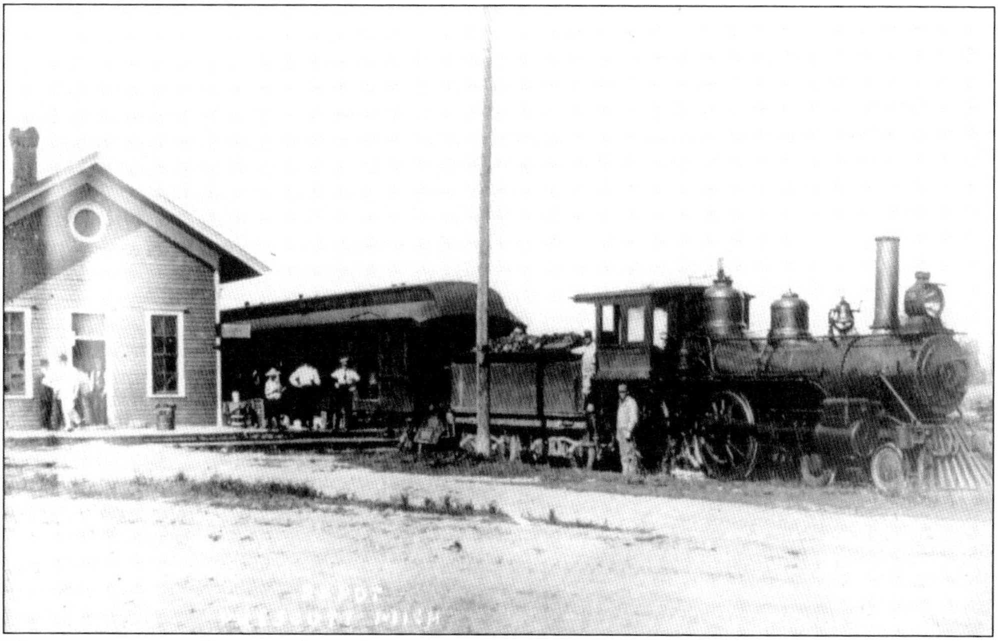

The train was significant to the early development of Prescott. Not only was the train important for carrying harvested timber to the Tawas area for milling, but it also provided transportation services for the people, the mail, and the supplies and staples required for a thriving community. This is a photograph of the first Prescott depot, which burned in 1907.

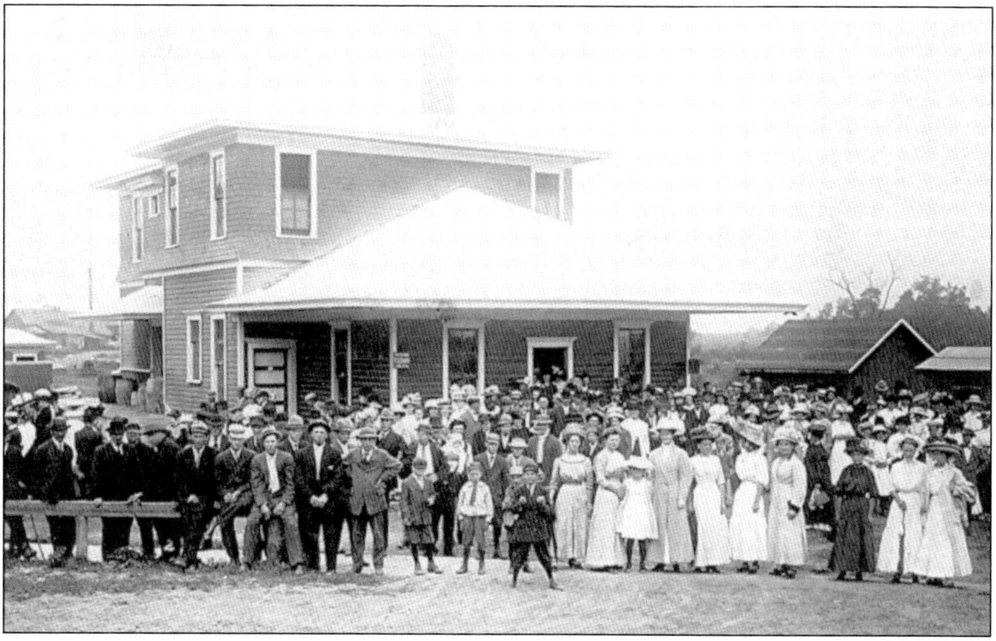

The second depot in Prescott was built between 1908 and 1910. This photograph from 1913 shows a large crowd eagerly awaiting the arrival of the train for the annual excursion. Each year the train would make a one-day trip to a special place, such as Tawas Bay or Wenona Beach near Bay City. The excursions were discontinued in 1917.

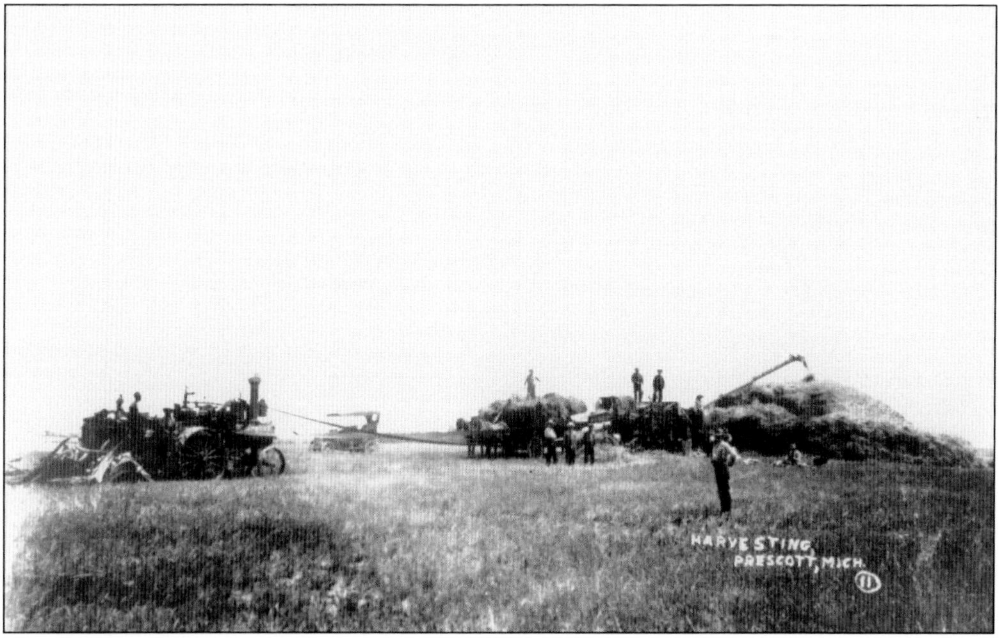

A hearty threshing crew harvests a bountiful crop of wheat just south of the town of Prescott around 1915. This particular threshing machine was owned by Bruce Solomon, Mr. Nichols, and Mr. Shepard. Threshing crews moved throughout the area while completing the harvest at hand. (Courtesy of Neil Erickson.)

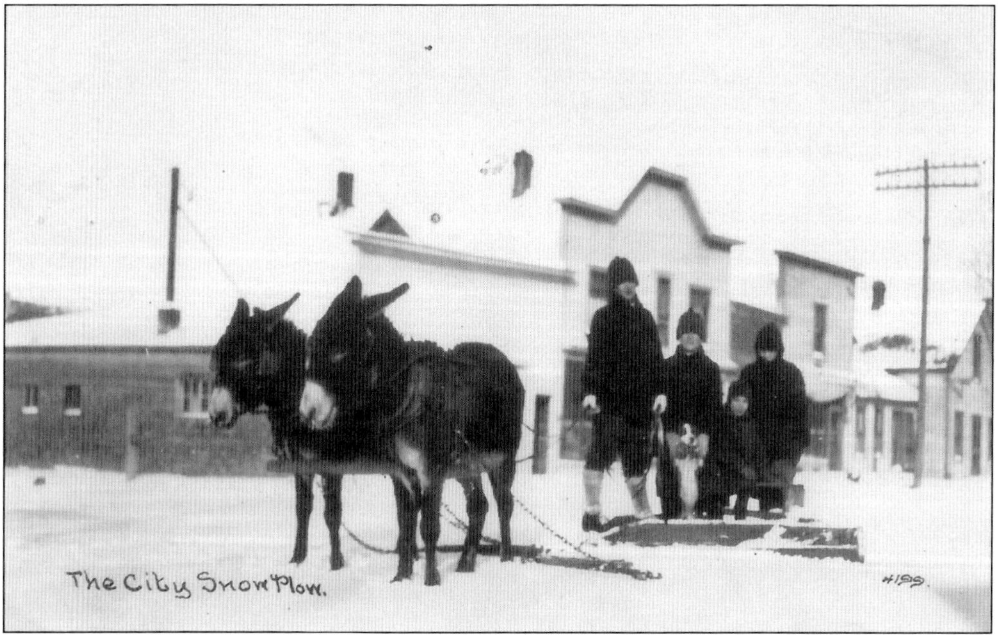

George (left) and Melvin Stoutenburg, along with Jay Zeran (seated) and another unidentified helper, plow the streets of Prescott with a sturdy pair of donkeys.

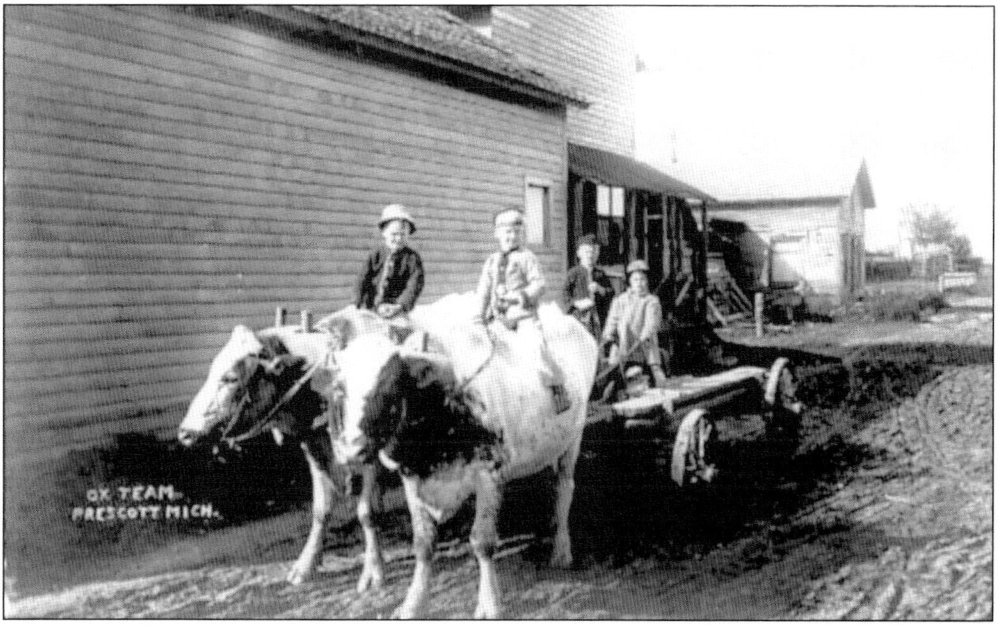

Cattle of any breed or gender that are used for draft purposes are called oxen. Before significant use of the automobile, oxen were a major mode of transportation for folks that resided in the Prescott area. Several photographs of oxen in Prescott have survived the tests of time. Supposedly, George Goings was the last man around Prescott to drive a team to town.

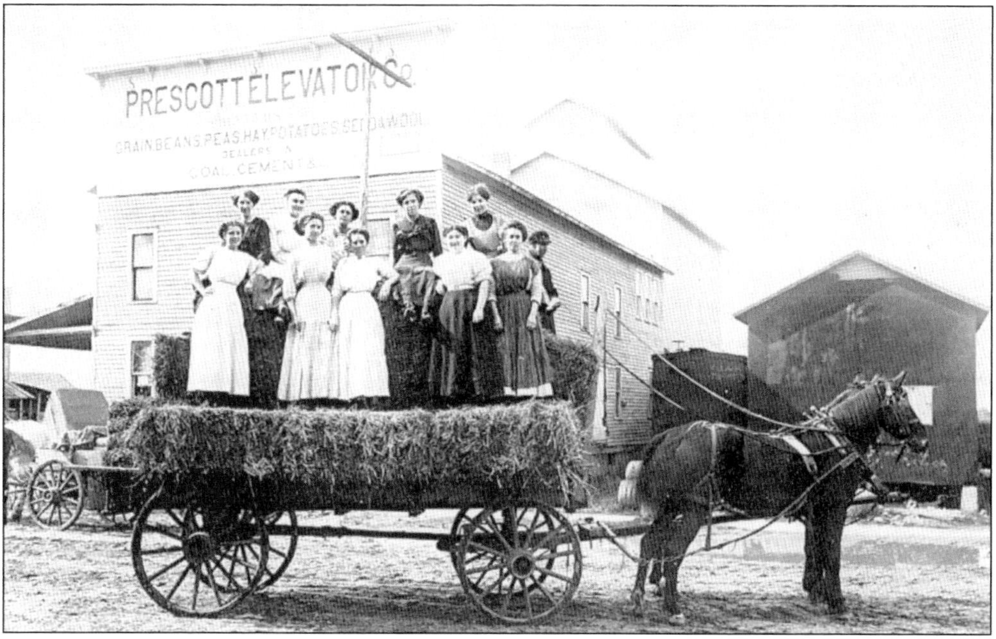

The first elevator in Prescott was built by Fred Server and marketed goods produced by local farmers. This structure burned down and was rebuilt by Finn Carr. After Carr's death in 1912, the Saginaw Milling Company bought the business. This building also burned and was rebuilt by a farmer's cooperative around 1920. The elevator always included a bean-cleaning business. Perhaps the women in this photograph are those that cleaned beans.

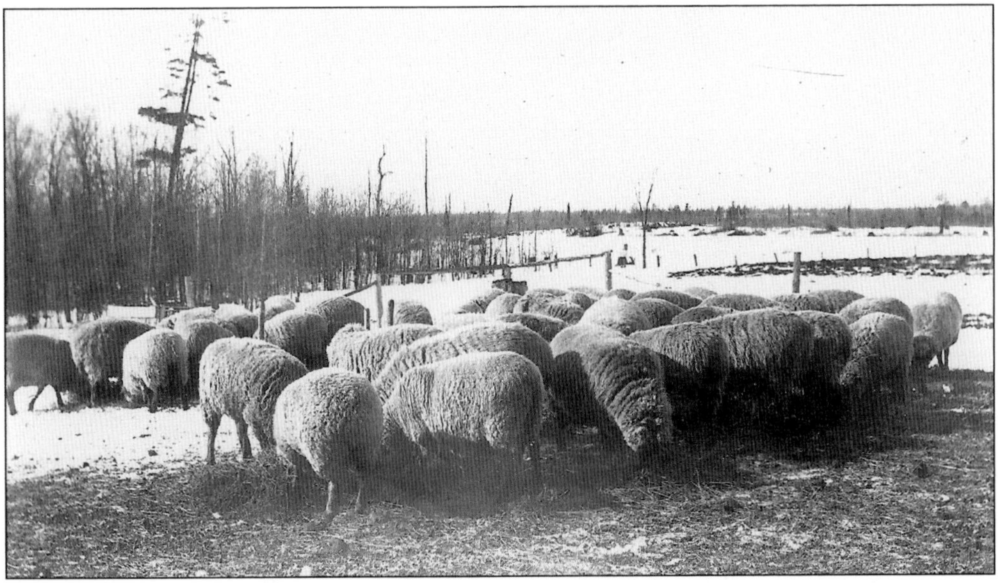

George Gage and Guy Mitchell were partners with Charles H. Prescott in a sheep-raising business in the Prescott area. Sheep were delivered on railcars, unloaded in Prescott, then driven to grazing lands north of town. Both the Prescott Ranch and the Logan Ranch raised large flocks of sheep. At one time, over 9,000 sheep in the area enabled a wool marketing business and a wool carding mill in Prescott.

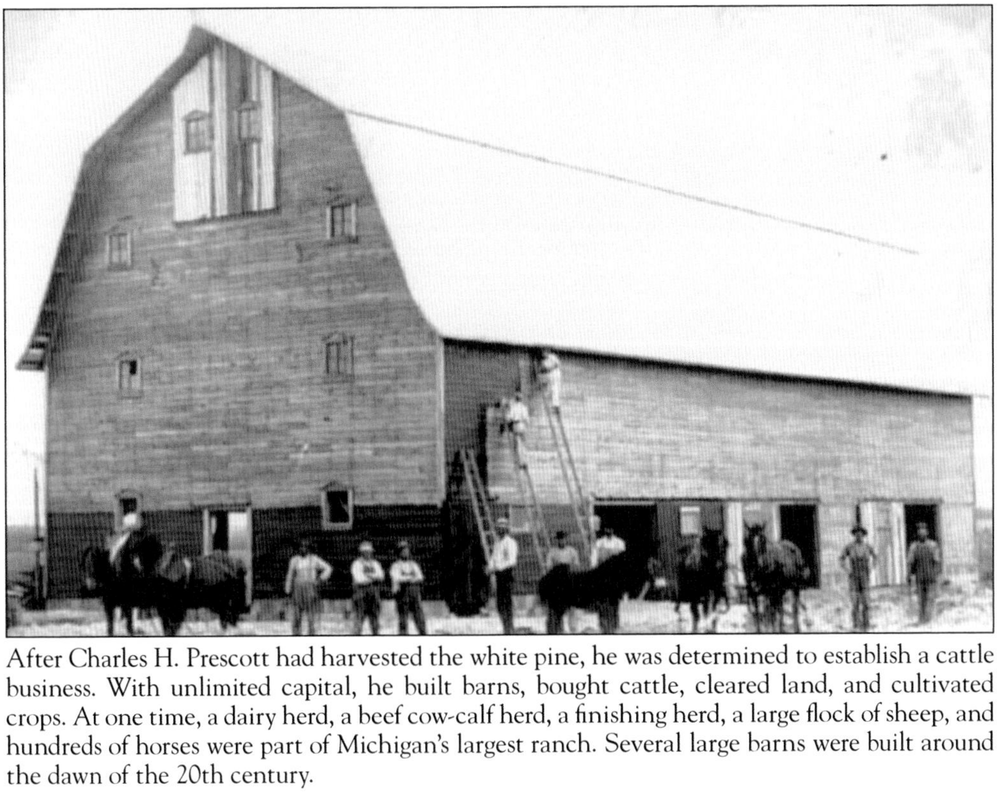

After Charles H. Prescott had harvested the white pine, he was determined to establish a cattle business. With unlimited capital, he built barns, bought cattle, cleared land, and cultivated crops. At one time, a dairy herd, a beef cow-calf herd, a finishing herd, a large flock of sheep, and hundreds of horses were part of Michigan's largest ranch. Several large barns were built around the dawn of the 20th century.

Sen. Charles T. Prescott, grandson of Charles H. Prescott, drives cattle owned by the Prescott Ranch to another pasture in this 1953 photograph. About 1910, C. T. began buying cattle for the ranch and bought the entire spread in 1931. C. T. was born in October 1884 in Tawas City. He served as state senator from 1947 to 1961, when he died in office.

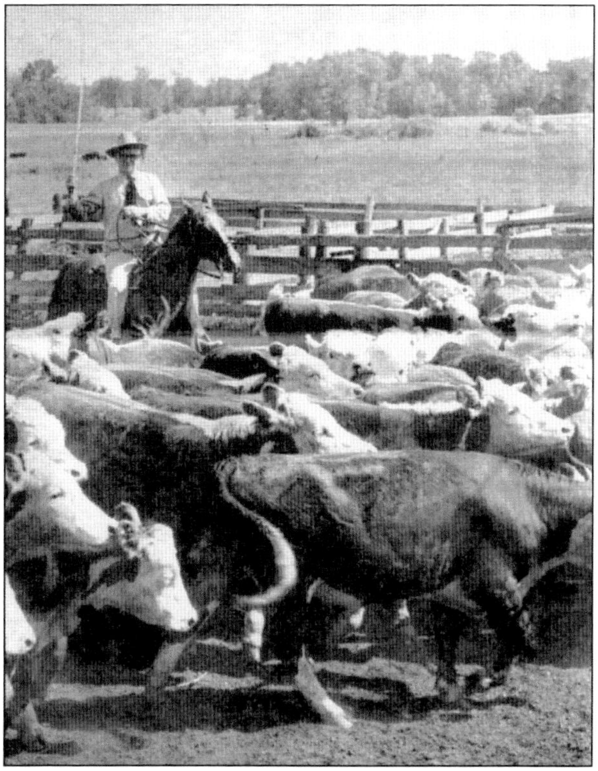

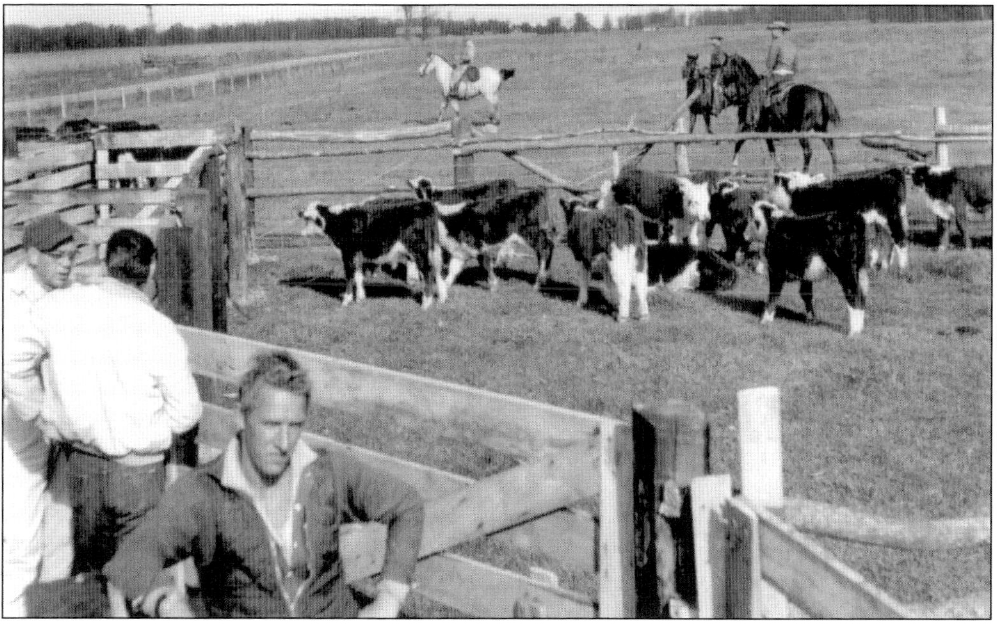

C. T. sold the Prescott Ranch to Warren Huff in 1958. At that time, this large agricultural enterprise was known as the Rowala Ranch. Huff hired Wayne Survant as ranch manager, who bred Angus bulls to Hereford heifers, thereby producing whiteface crossbred beef cattle. Huff owned the ranch until 1968, when it spanned nearly 5,000 acres and was home to 2,000 cattle. (Courtesy of Wayne Survant.)

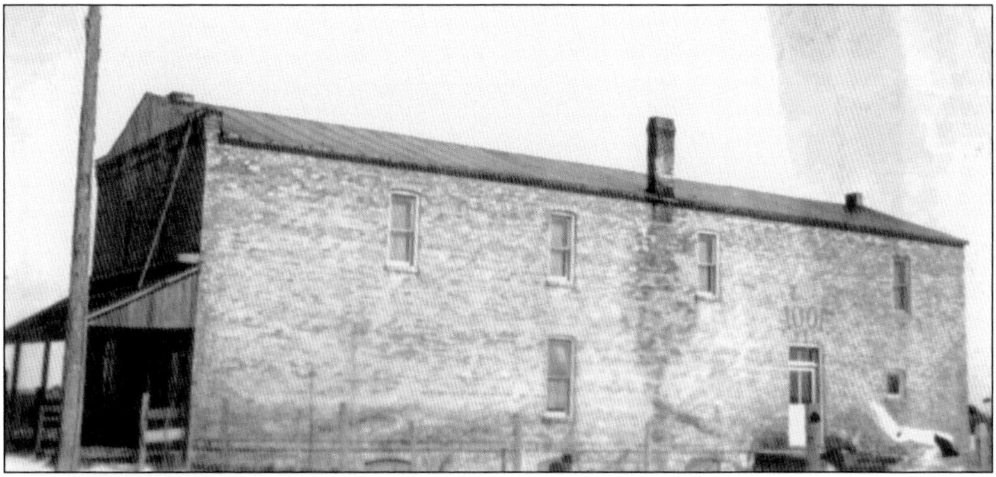

This building housed one of the first general stores at Camp Six. The two-story brick building was erected by Barney Mills on Sherman Street before 1900. The bricks for this structure were made by the Malcolm McLean Kiln in Shearer, a lumber town located southwest of Camp Six. After Mills closed his store, the building was bought by the International Order of Odd Fellows (IOOF) lodge. Later it became the Haskin's Recreation Hall.

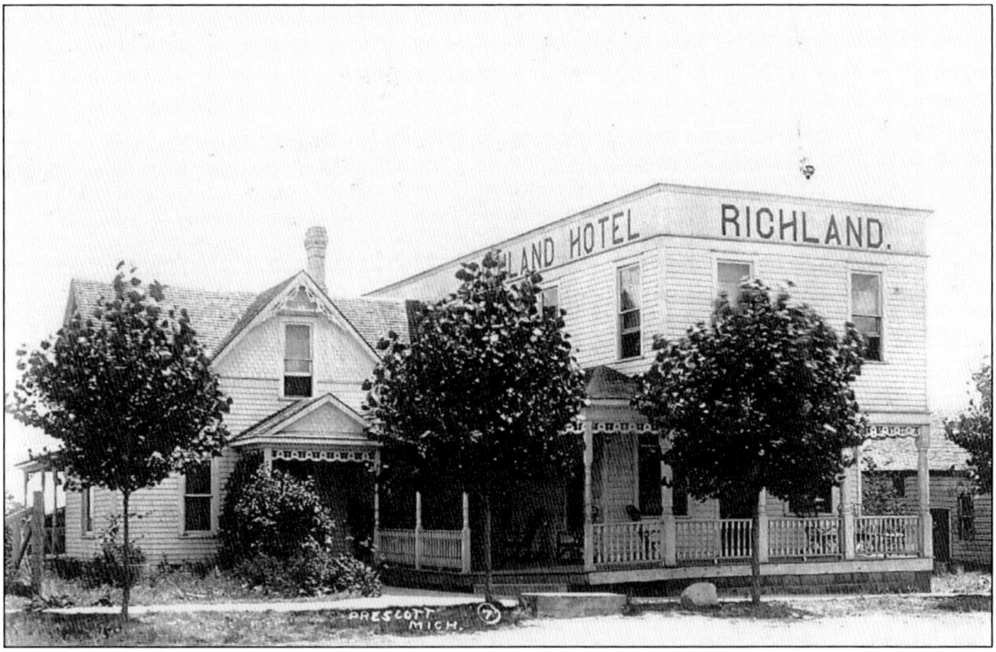

The town of Prescott has had six hotels. For several years, two hotels operated at the same time. Finn Carr built the Richland Hotel in 1908. After his death in 1912, the hotel was bought by Fred Rice. After changing hands many times, the building was used as an apartment house. A pool hall was established in the downstairs lobby.

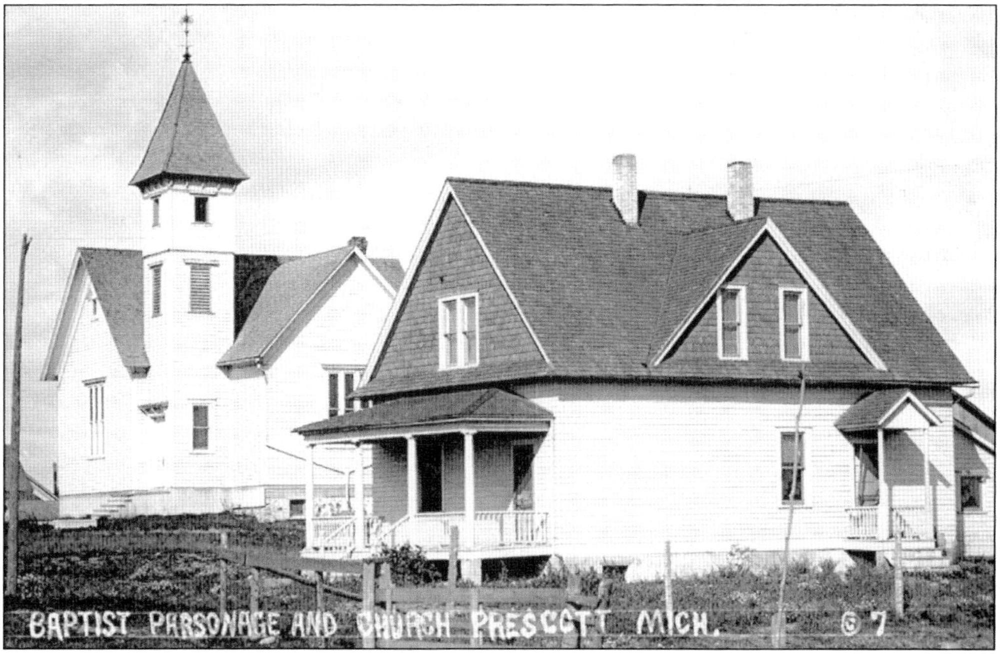

Charles H. Prescott organized and furnished lumber to build the Judson Baptist Church. Construction of the church began in 1892. Most of the work and materials to build the church and parsonage were donated. Rev. A. Waterbury was the first pastor. The name Judson was chosen to honor Adoniram Judson, a pioneer missionary to India. The original church was demolished in 2007 to make way for a more modern facility.

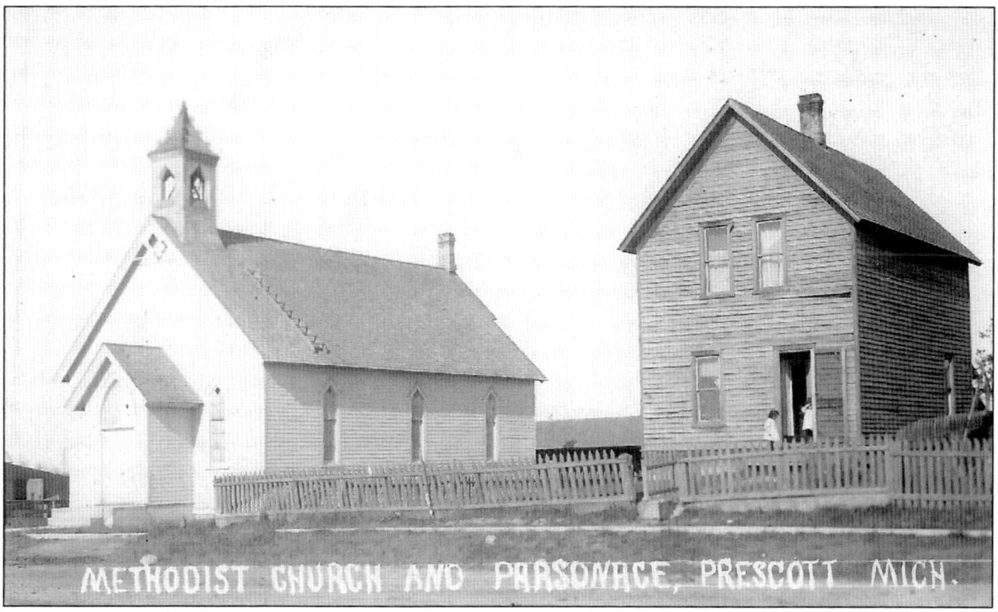

The first pastor of the Prescott Methodist Church, Rev. George Smith, arrived in the community before the church was built in 1896. The church and parsonage were built with donated materials and labor under the diligent leadership of Reverend Smith. The Methodist congregation discontinued church services in Prescott in 2005. (Courtesy of Ron McCarthy.)

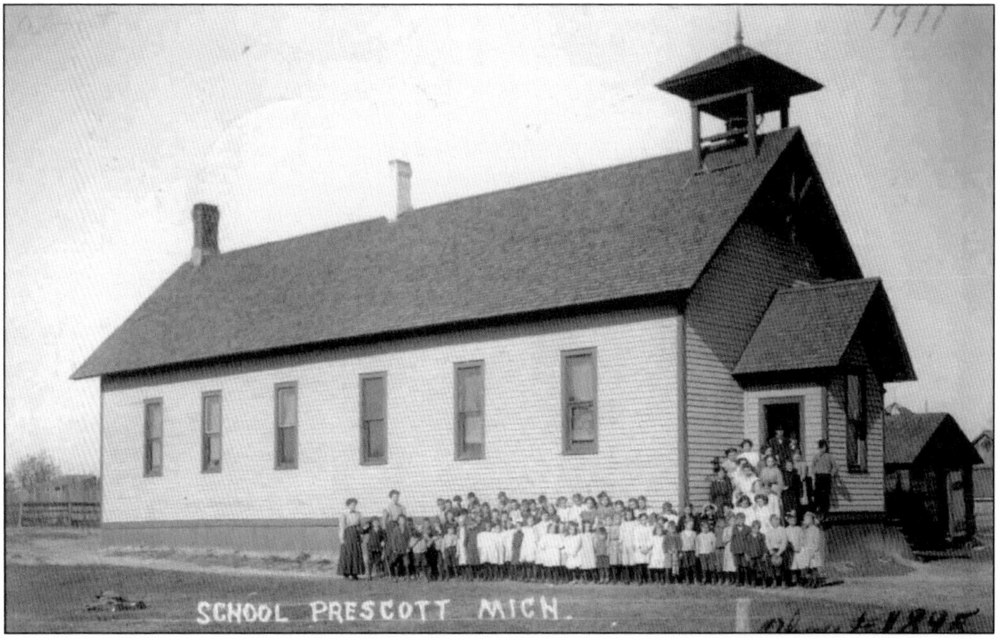

The first two-room schoolhouse was built on Sherman Street in Prescott in 1895, which is the date of this photograph. Grades 2 through 5 gathered in the west room for classes, and grades 6 through 10 met in the east room. Kindergarten and first grades met across the street in the IOOF building. When a new school opened in 1915, this building was sold and moved.

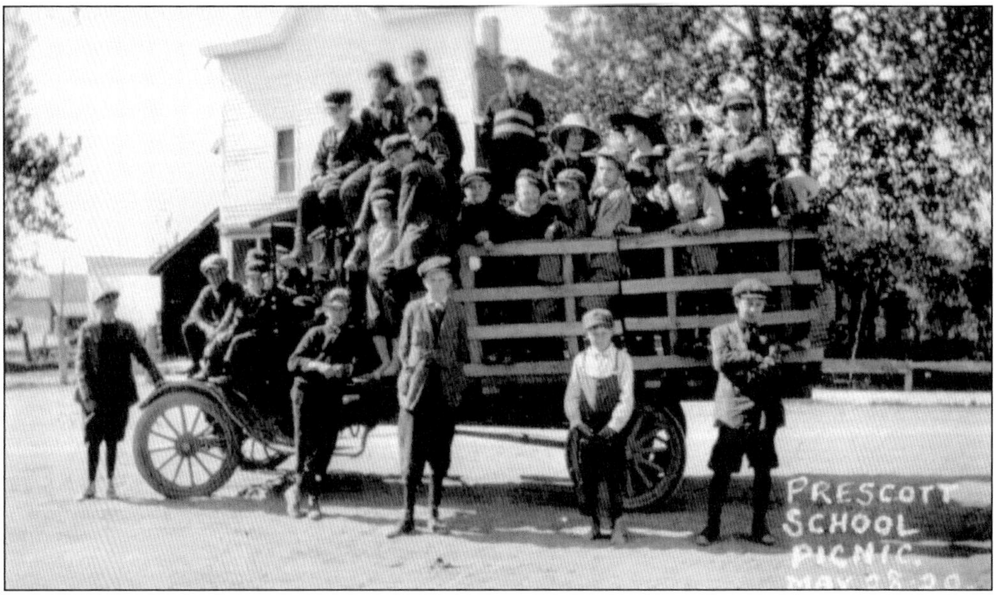

This photograph was taken in Prescott on May 28, 1920, for a school picnic. Included are Leroy Stoutenberg, Buff Eymer, Shirley Voorhees, Martin Siegrist, Roy Stalker, Walt Hoover, Art Thorne, Russell Currie, Edmond Rockefeller, Harold Melrose, Maynard McKnight, Burton Osborne, Harold Eymer, Devere Dockhan, Barney Cliff, Wilma Mott, Harold Siegrist, Lawrence Ecker, Harold Carl Raby, and Glen Voorhees. The teachers were Jessie McWethy and Mary Baxter.

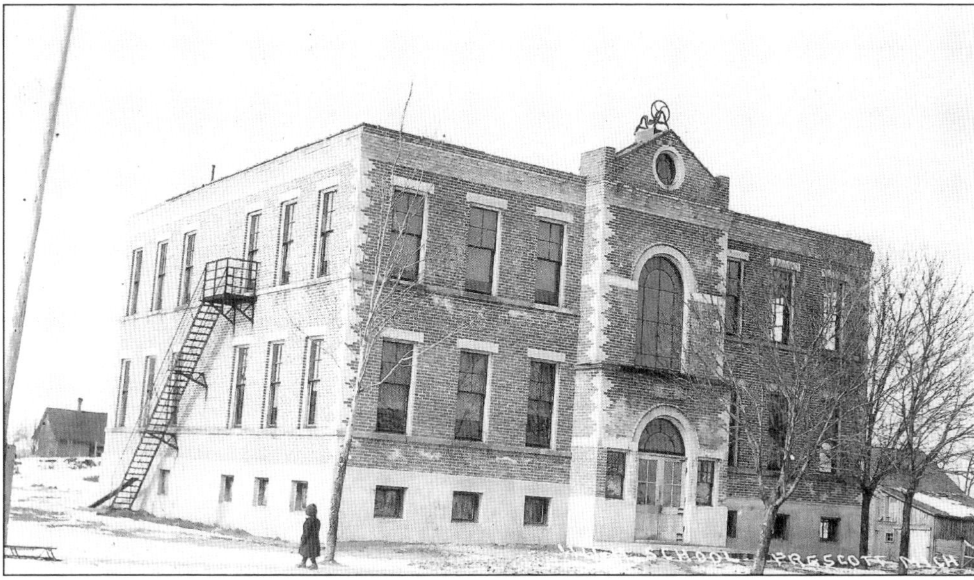

This two-story brick building opened for classes in the fall of 1915. In 1920, this school, located on Sherman Street, became a complete high school, offering classes for grades kindergarten through 12. A gymnasium was added to the building in 1936. On June 5, 1941, this school building burned to the ground. At the time of the fire, 350 students attended classes here. (Courtesy of Neil Erickson.)

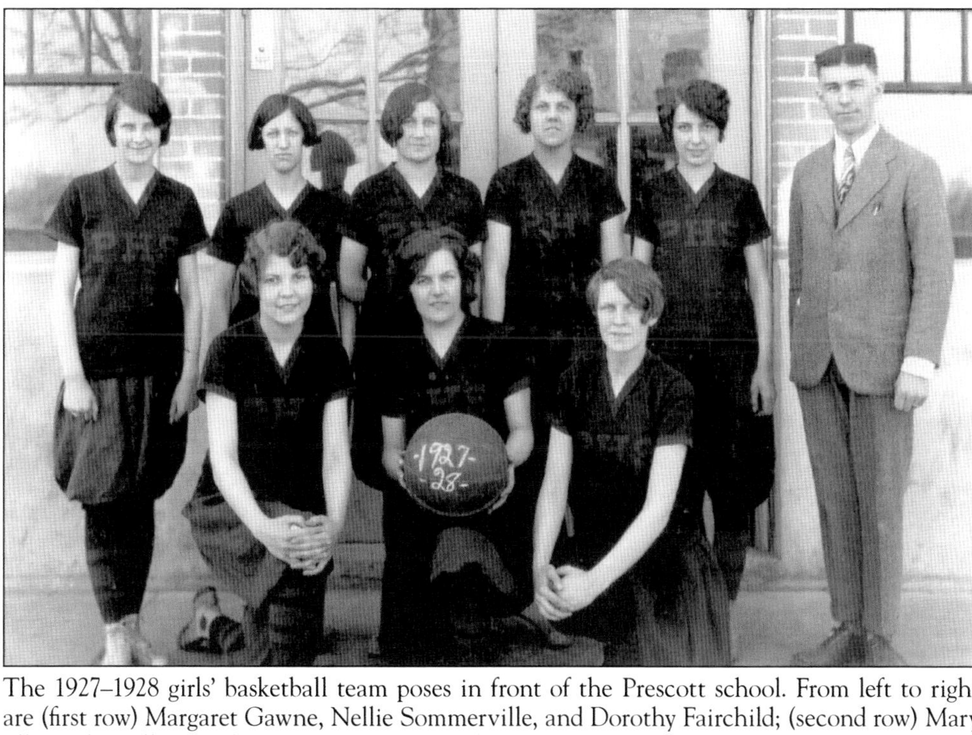

The 1927–1928 girls' basketball team poses in front of the Prescott school. From left to right are (first row) Margaret Gawne, Nellie Sommerville, and Dorothy Fairchild; (second row) Mary Ellsworth, Nellie Combs, Winona Gibson, Wilma Mott, and Esther Sommerville. The coach is Francis Pettit. The Prescott High School mascot was a pirate, sporting orange and black as the school colors. (Courtesy of Neil Erickson.)

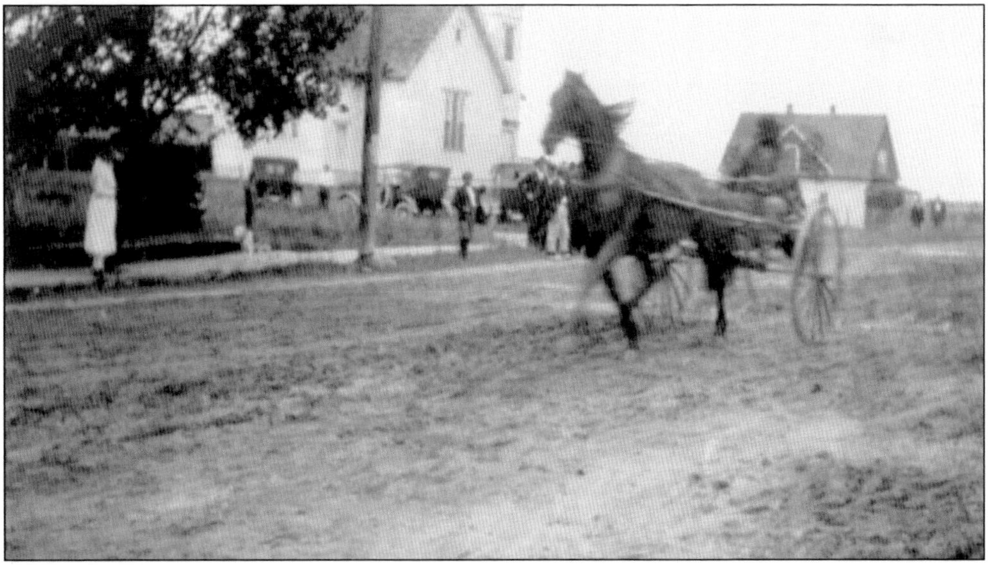

William Stoutenberg drives Ogemaw Belle, a famous local racehorse, in front of the Judson Baptist Church and Parsonage on Harrison Street in this early photograph. Prescott was home to three different racetracks over the years. The latest track, complete with grandstand and lights, was developed by Ralph Thompson on 40 acres east of town during the 1930s. Snowmobiles raced on the track in the winter.

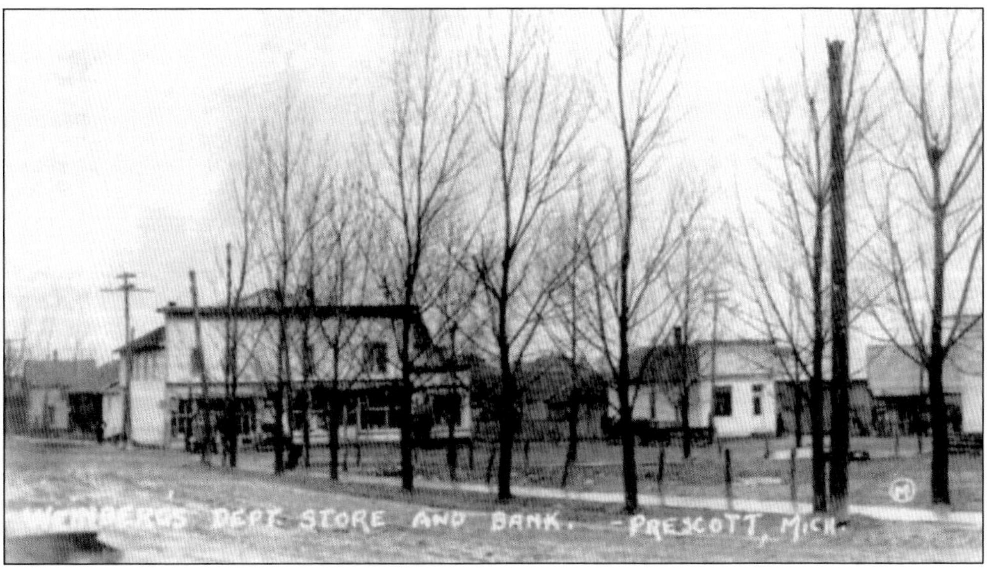

E. J. (Jake) Weinberg came to Prescott around 1890 and sold goods door to door. Eventually he established a department store business in Prescott, which is the building on the left in this photograph. This building burned in 1962. The small building to the right is the bank, which was opened by James McKay in 1903. This building is the current barbershop in town, once owned by Jim and Monica Harper.

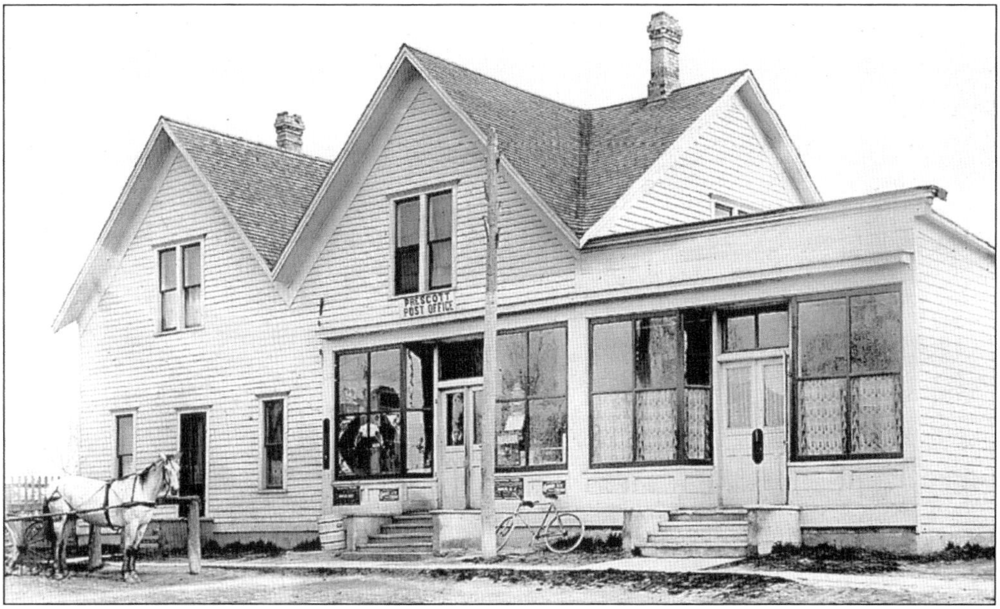

The first post office in Prescott was located in this building, which was built by Henry Zeran in 1898. The first post mistress for Prescott was Julia A. Davidson, who served from October 27, 1882, until January 25, 1883. Over the years, this 16-room building housed the post office, hotel, ice-cream parlor, drugstore, and tavern. The building was razed in June 1969. (Courtesy of Ron McCarthy.)

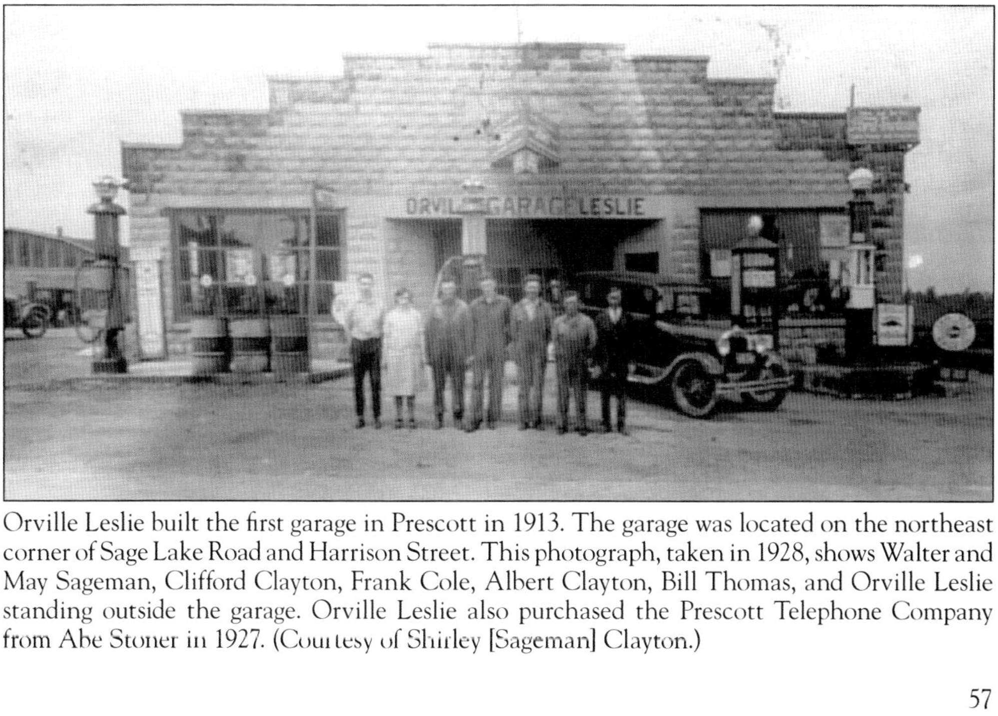

Orville Leslie built the first garage in Prescott in 1913. The garage was located on the northeast corner of Sage Lake Road and Harrison Street. This photograph, taken in 1928, shows Walter and May Sageman, Clifford Clayton, Frank Cole, Albert Clayton, Bill Thomas, and Orville Leslie standing outside the garage. Orville Leslie also purchased the Prescott Telephone Company from Abe Stoner in 1927. (Courtesy of Shirley [Sageman] Clayton.)

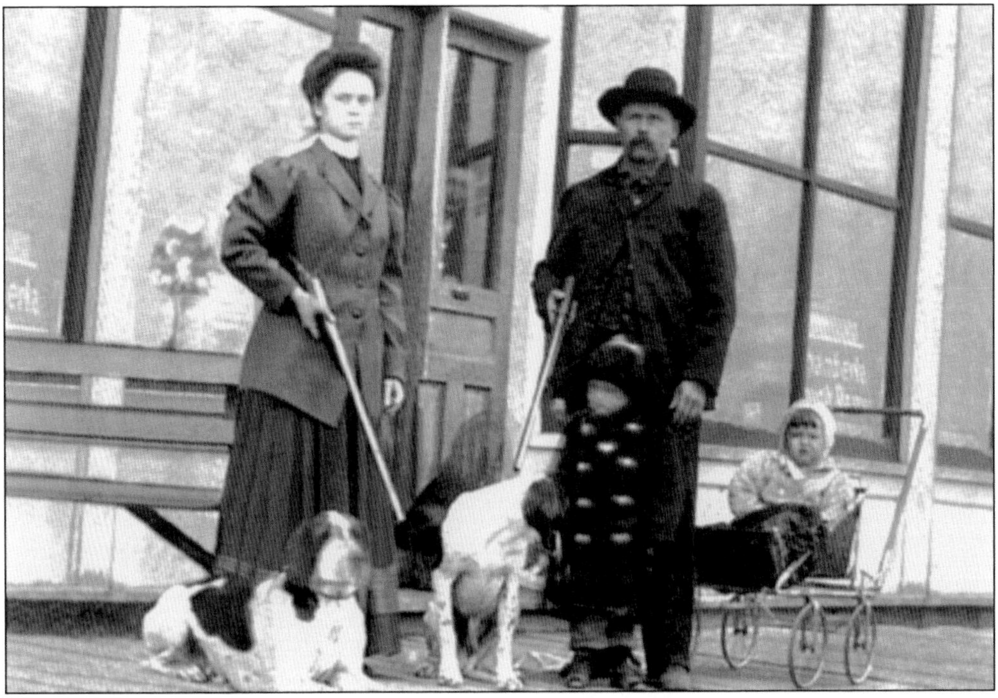

Mable (Zeran) Eymer poses with her father, Henry Zeran, and her sons Harold (standing) and George (in the buggy) outside Zeran's Drug Store. Mable married Harry Eymer in 1906. Harold was born on October 20, 1906, and George was born February 19, 1908. The Zeran and Eymer families were prominent developers of early Prescott. Eymer family businesses still operate in the area in 2008.

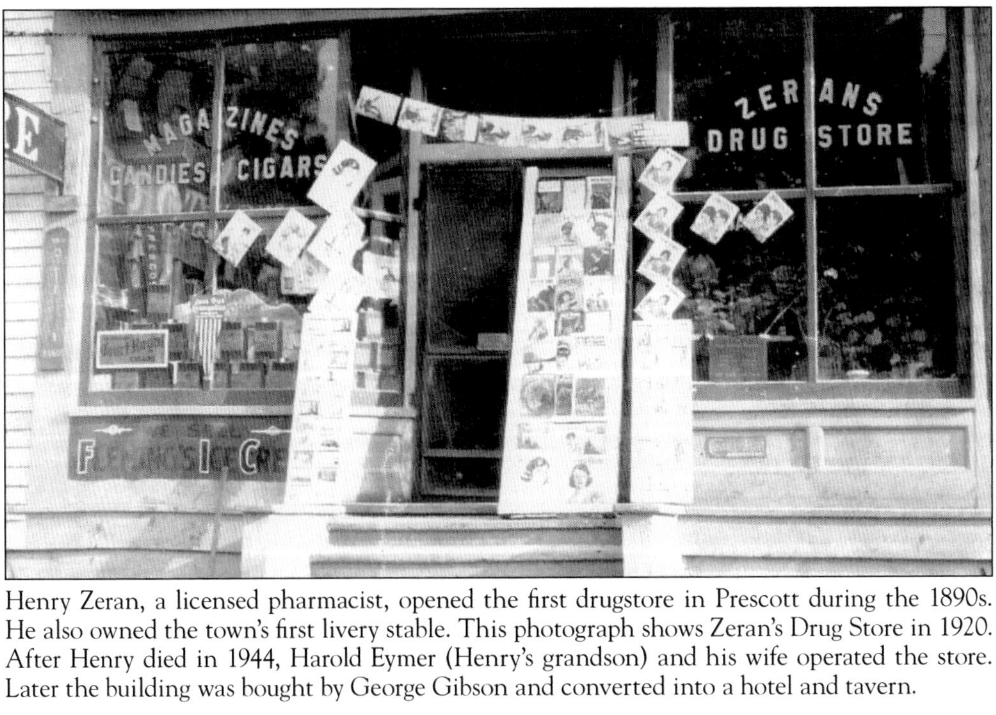

Henry Zeran, a licensed pharmacist, opened the first drugstore in Prescott during the 1890s. He also owned the town's first livery stable. This photograph shows Zeran's Drug Store in 1920. After Henry died in 1944, Harold Eymer (Henry's grandson) and his wife operated the store. Later the building was bought by George Gibson and converted into a hotel and tavern.

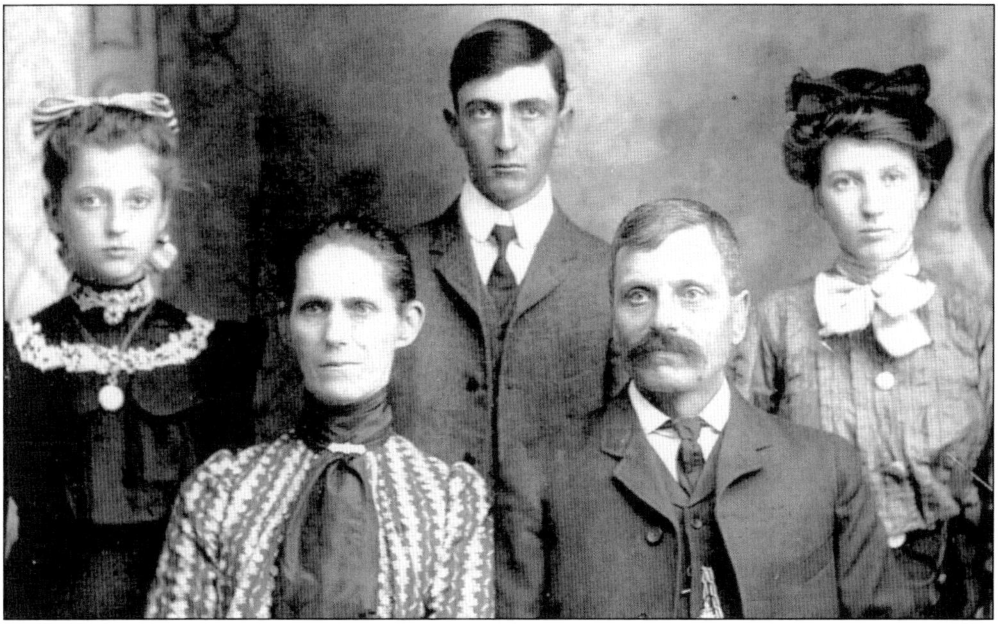

George Eymer (1852–1926) was born in Allegany County, New York. He ventured to Michigan in 1874 and operated a store in Sterling, Arenac County, in 1880. He followed the lumbering movement to Camp Six, where he became a notable entrepreneur with diverse business interests. In this photograph he is seated next to his second wife, Katharine. Three of his children, Blanche, Harry, and Grace, stand behind him.

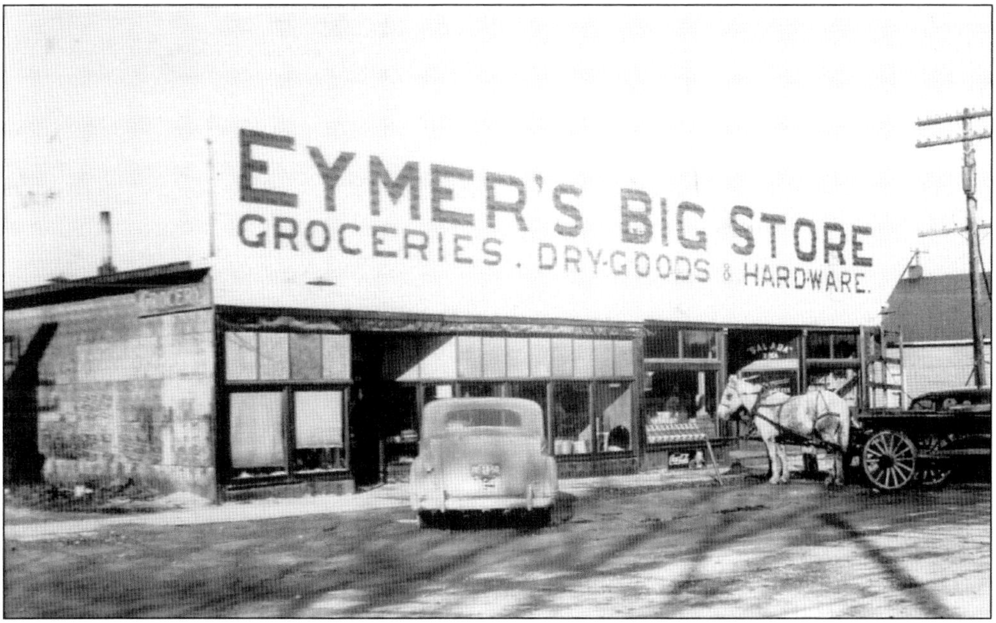

In 1906, George Eymer and son Harry opened a large general store in Prescott across the street from the Judson Baptist Church. Eymer's Big Store was a landmark in the village for several years. George Eymer also established the first implement dealership in Prescott. After George retired in 1916, Harry continued the business. Descendants of George Eymer continue local business enterprises in the Skidway Lake area today.

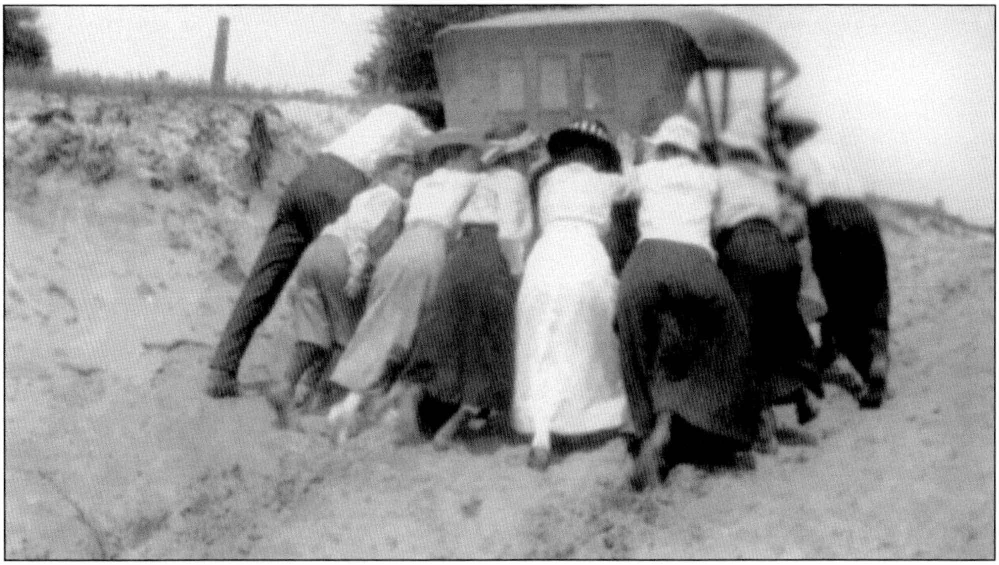

Bill and Hazel Zeran, Hank Zeran, Emma Martin, Charles and Flora Craner, and Russell and Addie Martin push their automobile through the mud on Sage Lake Road in Richland Township. Roads were often difficult to navigate while shared by horses and the early vehicles. During this era of history, property owners exchanged road improvement labor for property taxes at the local level. (Courtesy of Phyllis [Currie] Druley.)

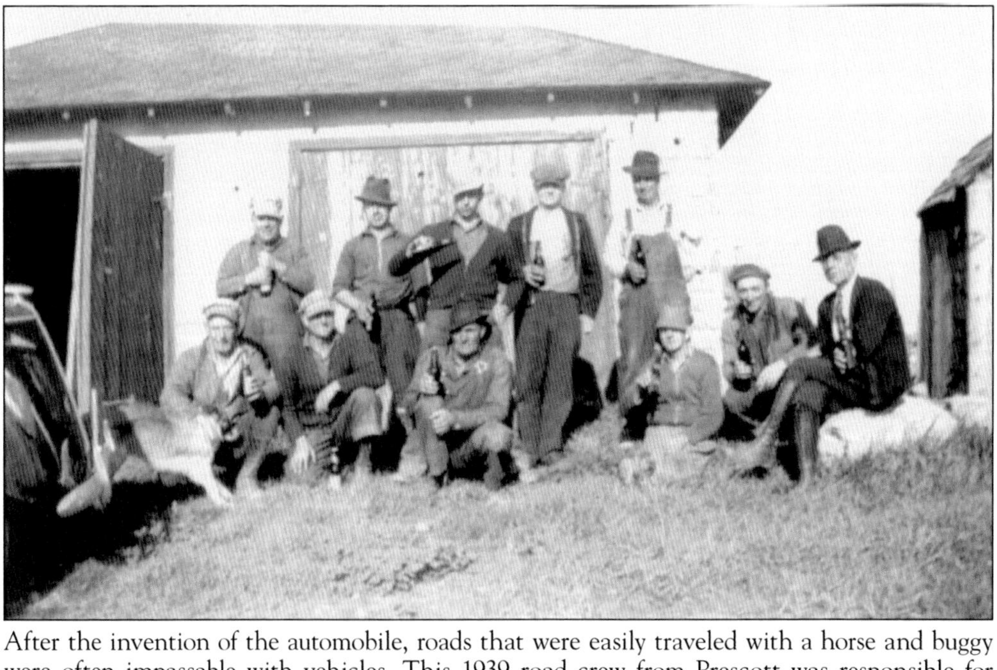

After the invention of the automobile, roads that were easily traveled with a horse and buggy were often impassable with vehicles. This 1939 road crew from Prescott was responsible for improving road conditions. Pictured from left to right are (first row) James Foote, unidentified, Neil Currie, Barney Cliff, Fred Webster, and Sie Sedore; (second row) Wilfred Lawrence, Lee Sedore, two unidentified, and George Corey.

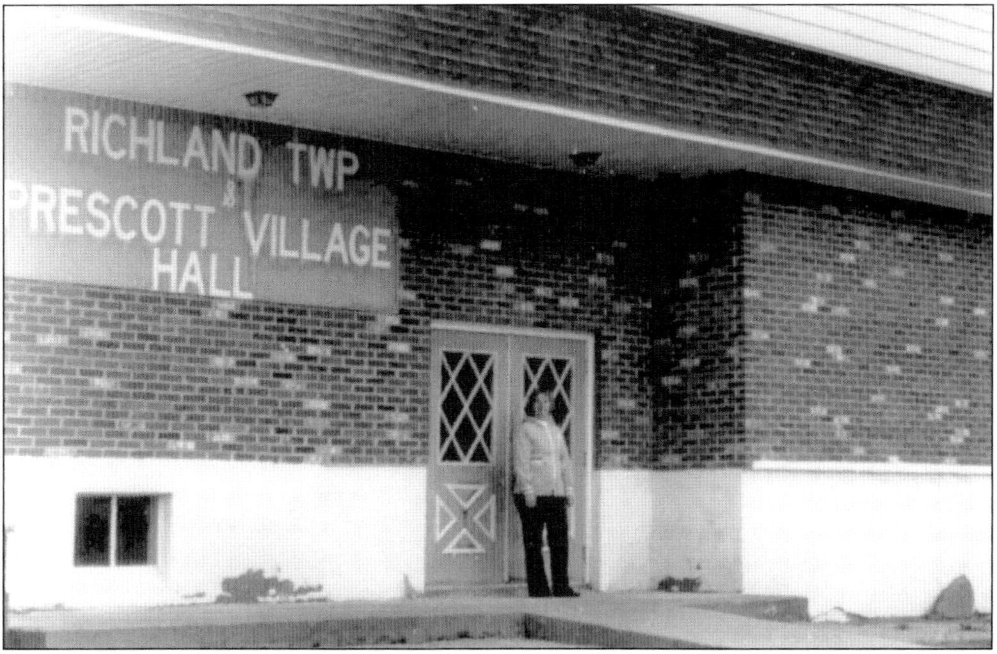

For many years, Richland Township and the Village of Prescott shared office and conference space in this building on Sherman Street. The local volunteer fire department was also housed in this building with the government entities. This building was erected during the summer of 1957 on the foundation of the Prescott High School that burned in 1941.

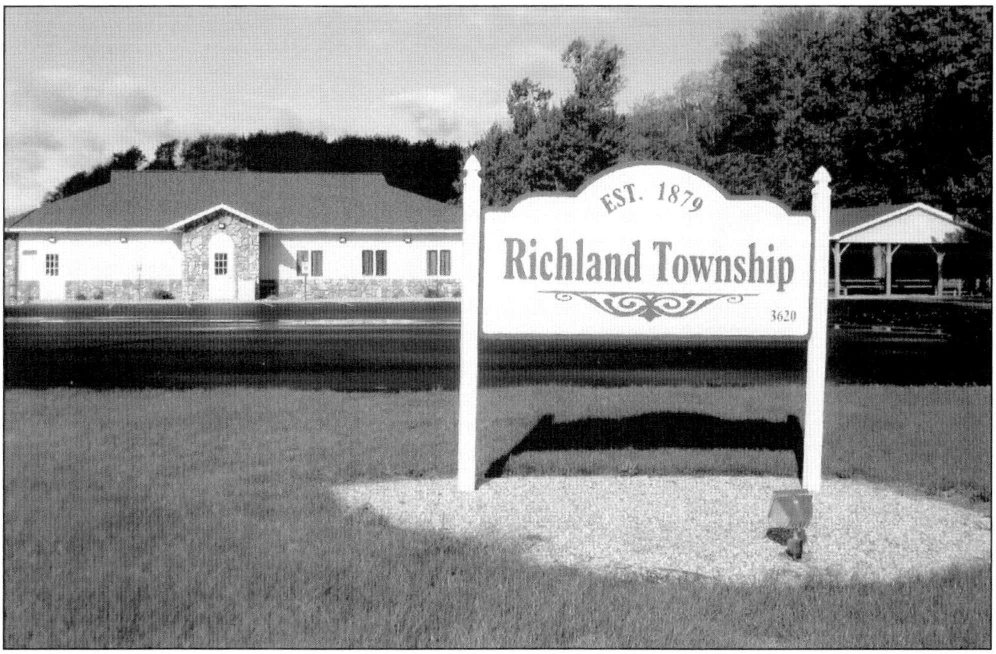

On October 11, 2003, a new Richland Township Hall was dedicated to the community. The hall was built on property located on McLean Road, around the corner from the Richland Township Cemetery on Sheffer Road, southeast of the village of Prescott. This property had been owned by the township since November 18, 1889. The pavilion was added to the site in 2004.

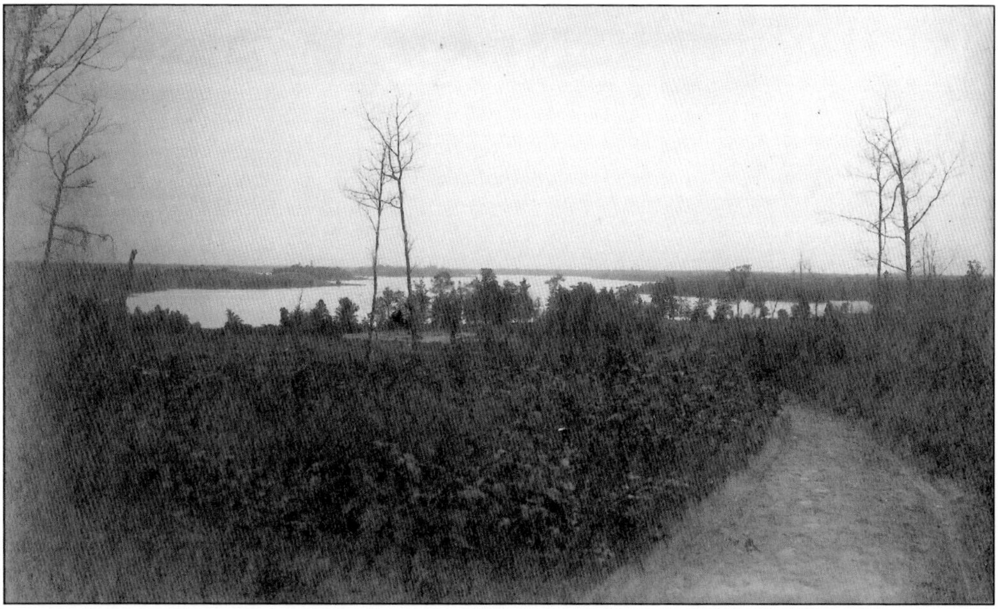

Feeding Grounds Lake was located east of Skidway Lake, in the vicinity of the current St. Stephens Catholic Church. At one time, huge log buildings were located here that housed facilities for feeding lumbering crews and the horses that pulled logs from the woods. Therefore, the label Feeding Grounds Lake was given to this lake area.

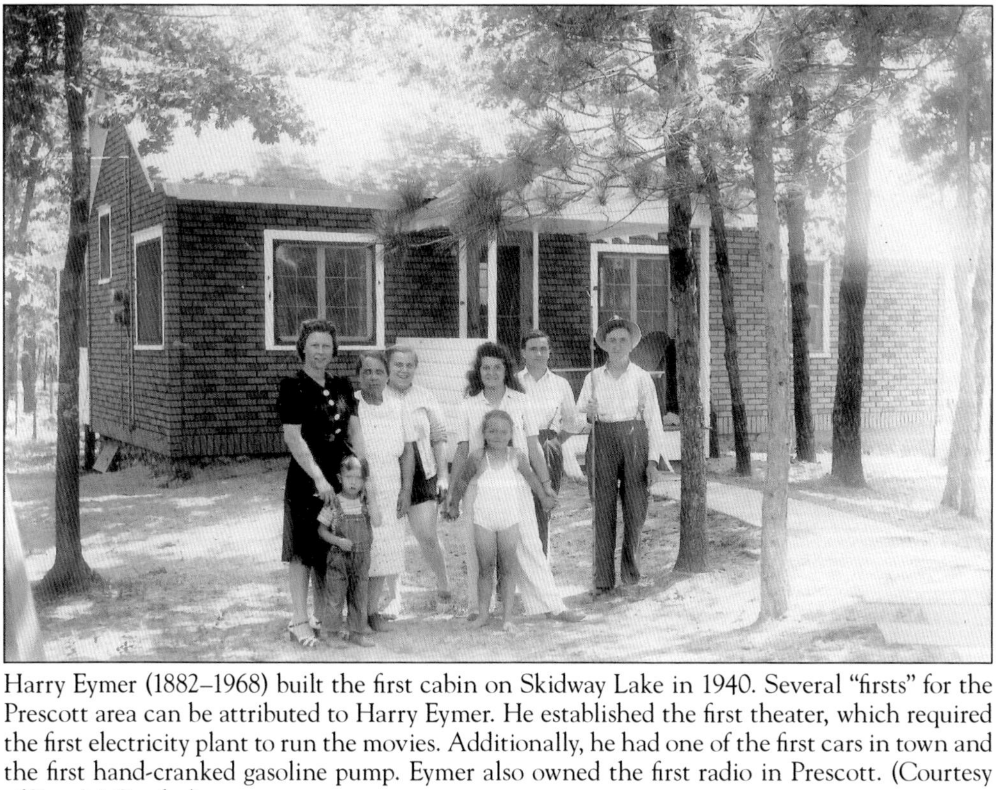

Harry Eymer (1882–1968) built the first cabin on Skidway Lake in 1940. Several "firsts" for the Prescott area can be attributed to Harry Eymer. He established the first theater, which required the first electricity plant to run the movies. Additionally, he had one of the first cars in town and the first hand-cranked gasoline pump. Eymer also owned the first radio in Prescott. (Courtesy of Ron McCarthy.)

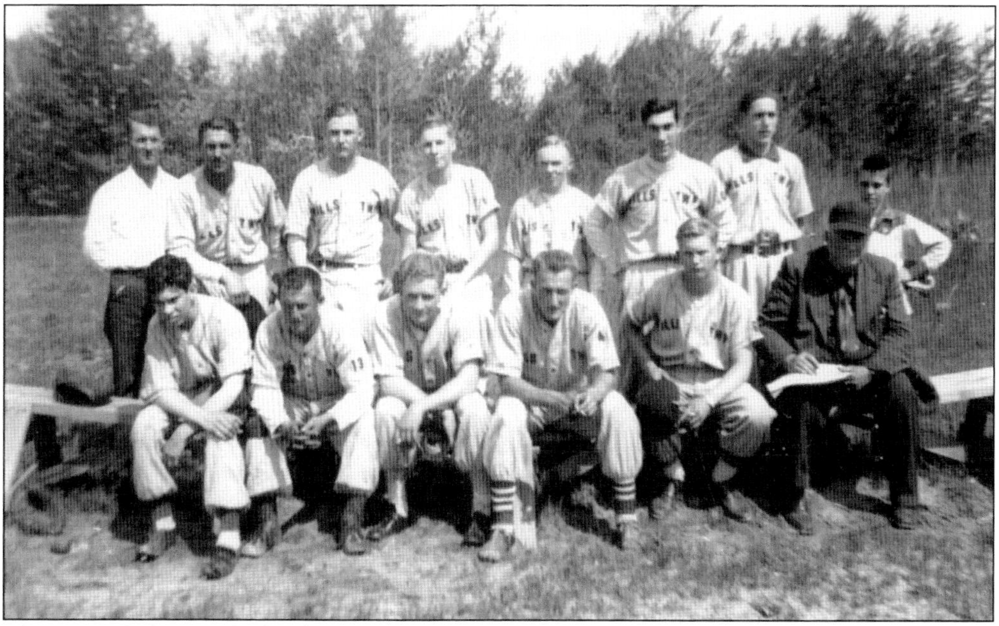

The 1950 Skidway Lake baseball team had a record of 2 wins and 11 losses. Seen here are (first row) unidentified, Paul Arndt, Grover McCord, Bill Clayton, Bill Cliff, and Elmer Cornwell; (second row) Barney Cliff, Dennis Arndt, Wayne McCord, Don McCord, Jerry Vincent, Jerry Sageman, Duane Hall, and Dale Currie. Earl Smith was the manager of the 1950 team. In 1951, Wayne McCord coached the same team to a 13-2 record.

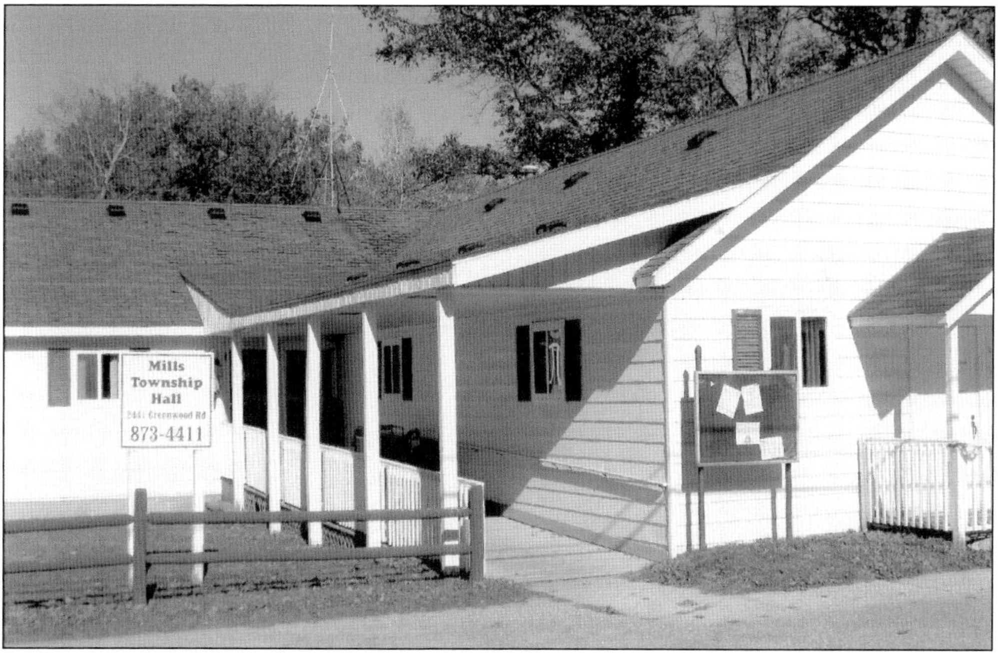

The Mills Township Hall is located east of Skidway Lake on Greenwood Road. Because the Rifle River flows through the heart of Mills Township, and several small lakes are prevalent within its boundaries, this area is a popular tourist and fishing destination. As of the 2000 census, there were 4,005 people, 1,705 households, and 1,159 families residing in the township.

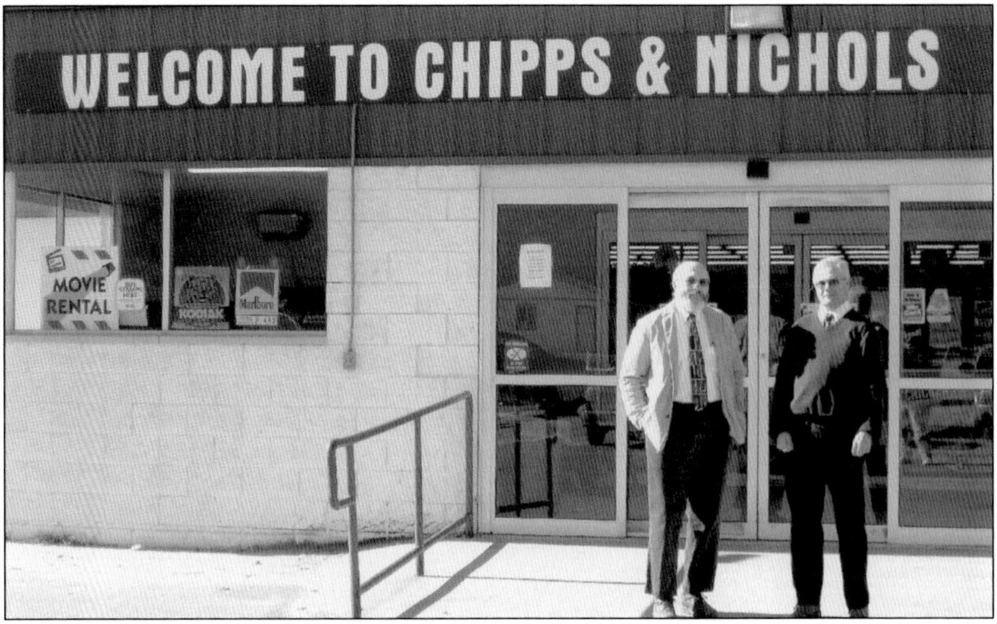

Brothers Bob (left) and Chuck Nichols, sons of Earl Nichols, pose outside the Chipps and Nichols Store located in Skidway Lake. In 1941, Charles Chipps started a grocery business with George Eymer. In 1952, Charles Chipps and his son-in-law, Earl Nichols, formed a partnership and developed the Chipps and Nichols IGA in Prescott, which moved to Skidway Lake in 1974. Today the 23,000-square-foot store employs 40 people.

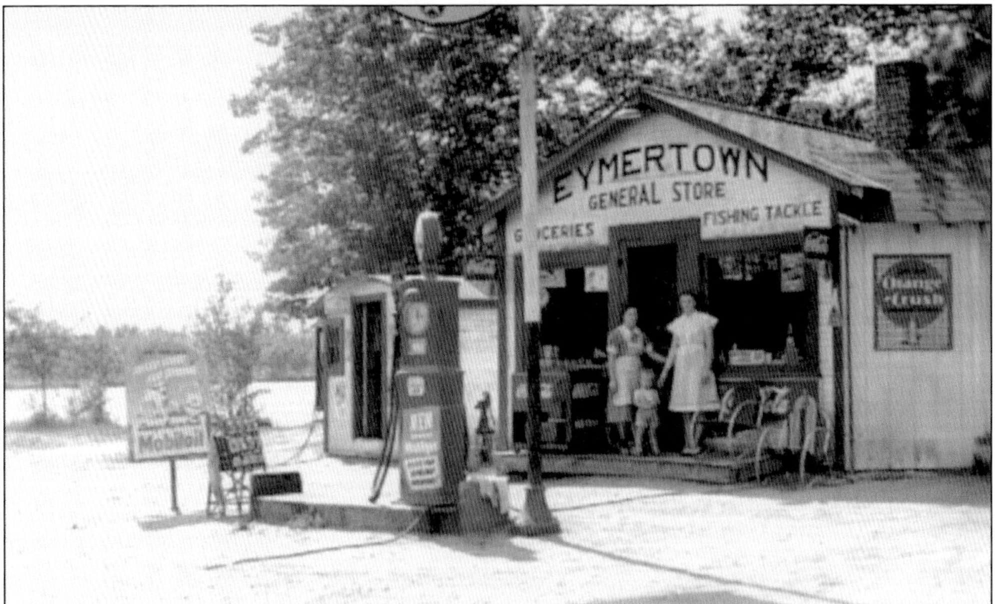

The Eymertown General Store sat east of Skidway Lake where the Roos Pharmacy once stood. Chet May (1920–1999) purchased Eymertown from Harry Eymer in 1945 and opened the store as May's Resort on December 1 of that same year. He added a restaurant to the building in 1946. May established May's Redi-Mix in 1959, which was sold in 1987 and became Swanson's Excavating. (Courtesy of Larry Eymer.)

Four

The Rose City Area

Rose City was first named Churchill and was located one-half mile west of its present location. In 1872, it boasted a population of eight, but by 1877 it consisted of a general store, post office, boardinghouse, and homes. In 1871, William "Deacon" Rose and Hiram Hodge came to Churchill from New York to homestead. Deacon Rose was followed by his sons Allan and Hiram. In 1875, the first post office was established with Allan as postmaster. The first log school was built in 1878. The town was often referred to as Rose Settlement or Rose Town, which became Rose City in 1905. Hiram and Allan Rose built a sawmill and gristmill near the settlement on Spring Brook. Soon a hotel was erected to house the builders of the new Heading Mill.

In 1892–1893, the Detroit, Bay City and Alpena Railroad built a rail line through Lupton to just east of the old settlement of Churchill. The first train pulled into town on Christmas Day, 1893. Eventually, Rose City became a boomtown. The population soared to over 700, and it seemed new people moved to the town daily. But the town had major problems, as streets were poorly maintained and improvements were slow. The town is situated in Rose Township and Cumming Township and neither wanted to take responsibility for the costly repairs. On April 14, 1905, the state legislature granted a charter and the new city of Rose City held its first election.

After a fire on April 3, 1910, the future of Rose City took a dramatic turn for the worse. Within an hour, most of the buildings on Main Street were gone. Reconstruction began at once but the town would never enjoy the growth it had at the dawn of the 20th century. Train service ended in the early 1930s, and tourism became the leading business.

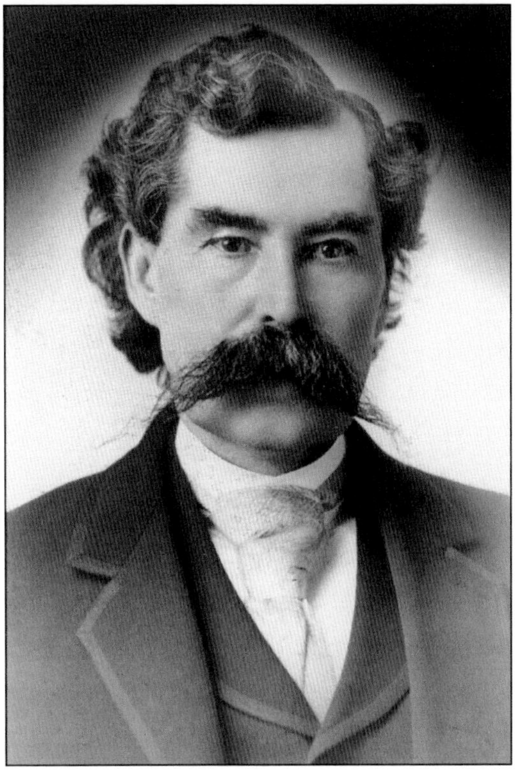

Allan S. Rose (1842–1915) was a pioneer of Churchill Settlement. In 1871, with his father and brother, he built a log structure that contained a general store, post office, meeting room, and living quarters. Rose became the first postmaster, register of deeds, probate judge, and later county treasurer.

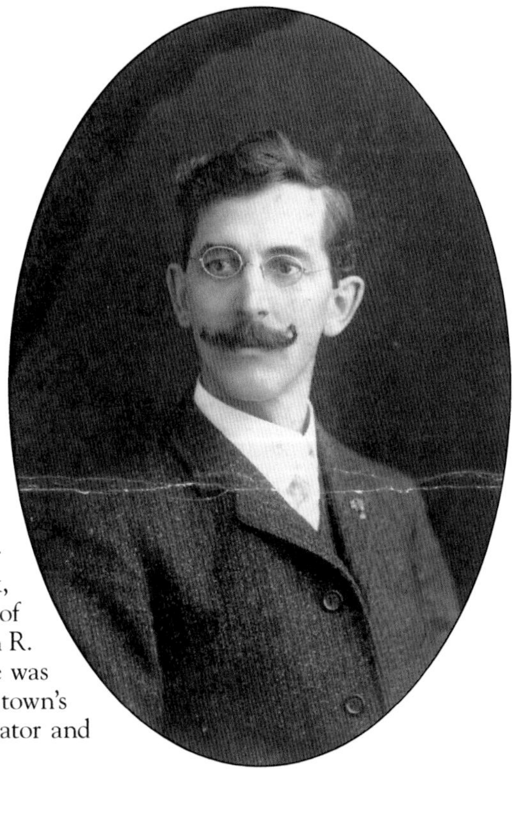

Horatio S. Karcher (1868–1939) came to Rose City in 1888 to teach school. He was a member of the board of school examiners, a store clerk, the postmaster, and the first superintendent of the Rose City schools. In 1904, he and Dr. Leon R. Ingleright established a drugstore. In 1905, he was appointed judge of probate and became the town's first mayor. In 1923, he was elected state senator and held that position until 1928.

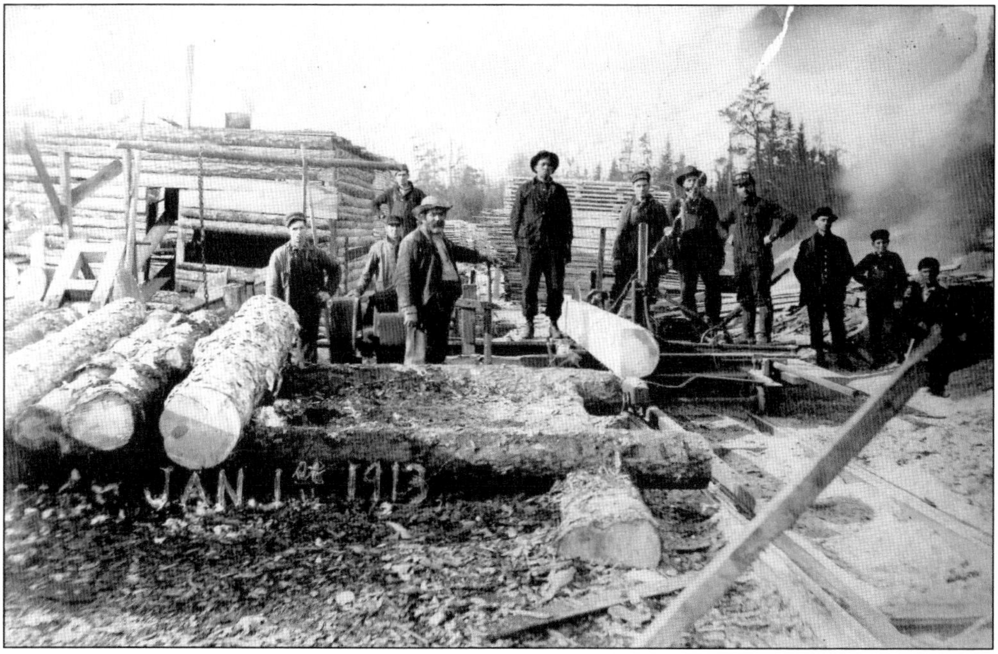

Miller's Mill, pictured above, was located about one and one-half miles east of Rose City. Willard Rose built the Heading Mill, below, just east of town on Houghton Creek, a tributary of the Rifle River. The mill had a capacity of 4,000 board feet per day. A gristmill was also constructed at this time.

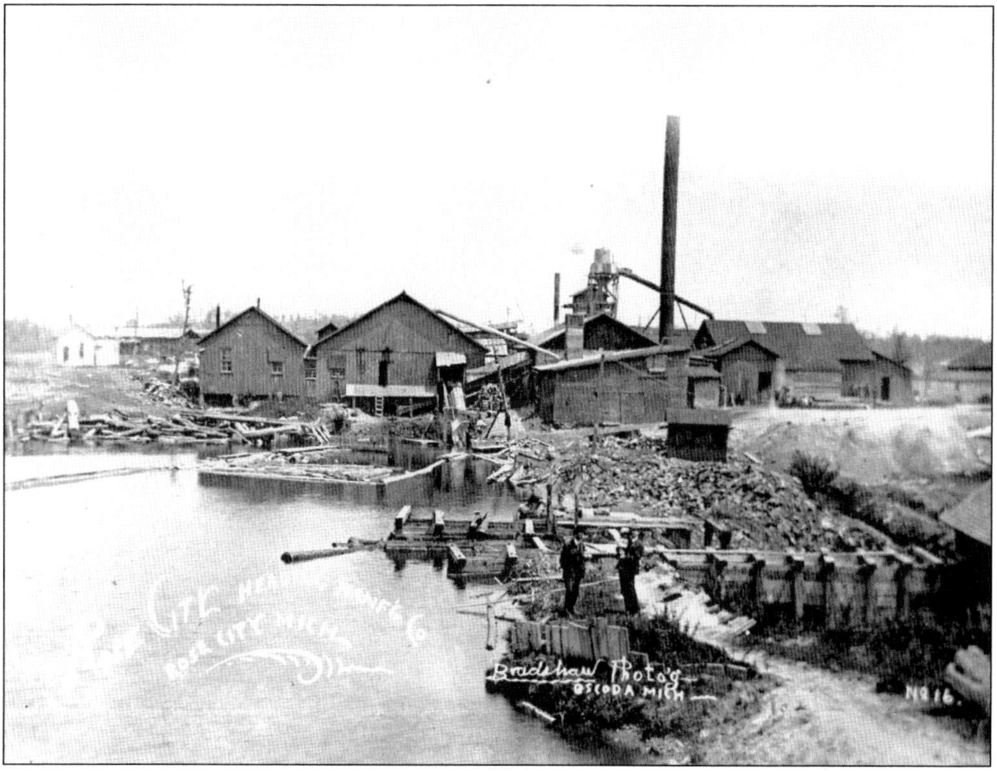

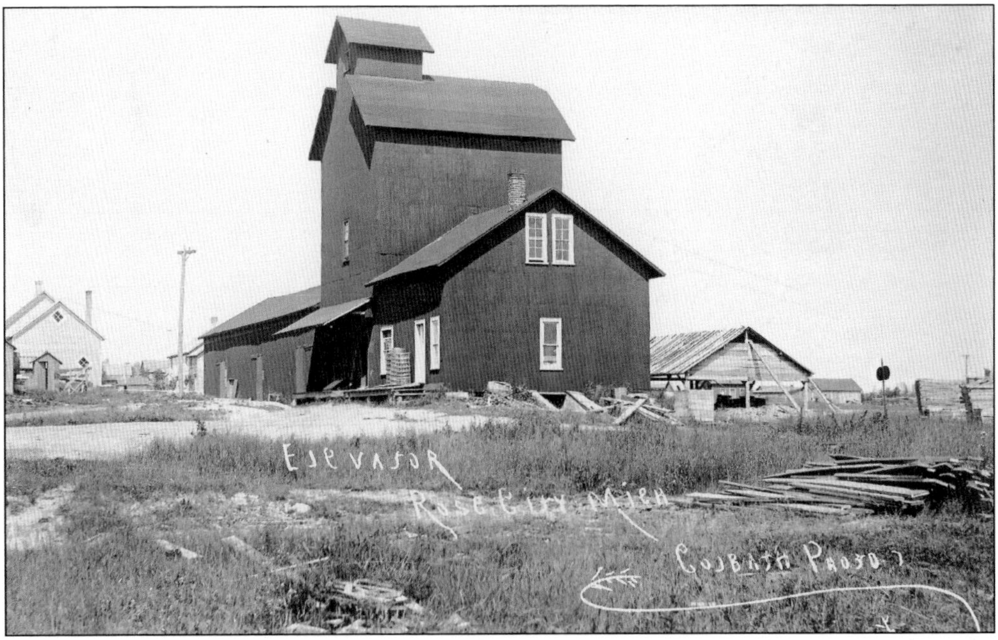

The Rose City Elevator was located east of Bennett Street on Warner Street near where the city garage is today. Farmers from the area brought wheat and other grains there to be ground. The elevator also sold seed for crops or gardens and plows and farm implements. The mill was a gathering spot for local farmers to discuss weather or methods for harvesting.

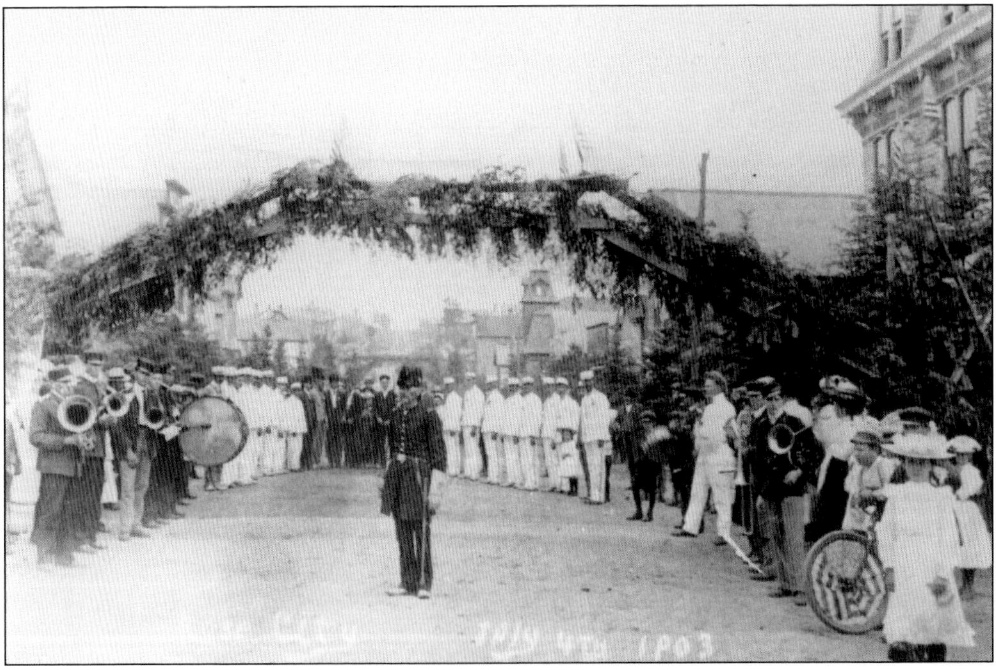

Civil War veteran Seth Rose (1839–1924) was honored on July 4, 1903, by the city. Many of the residents were veterans of the Civil War who received land grants for their service. On March 22, 1898, the new Grand Army of the Republic Post 442 was organized. The post was dedicated as the George R. Muir Post.

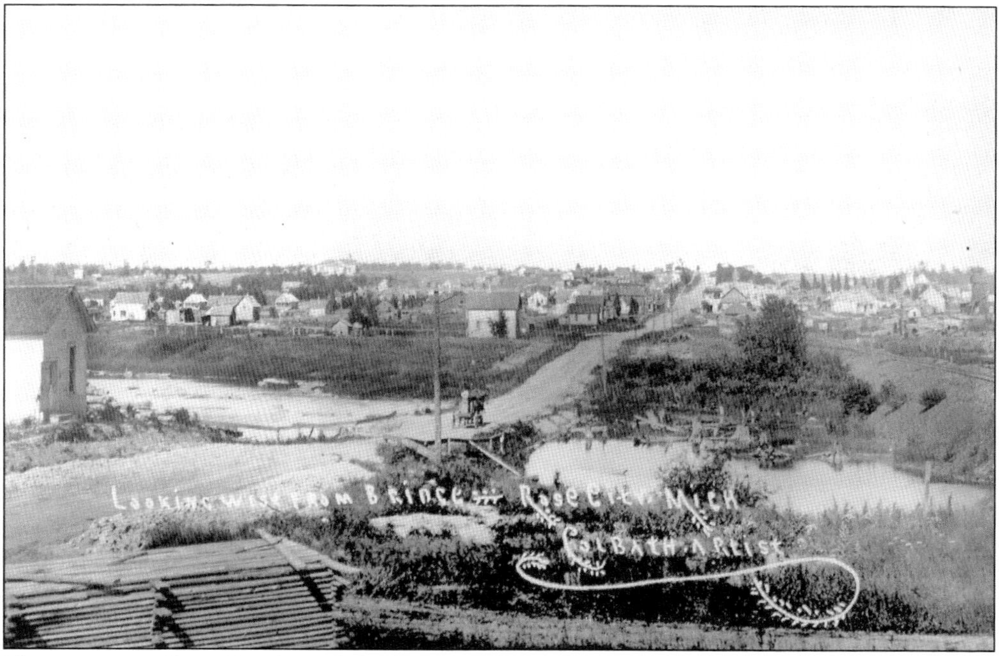

Upon entering Rose City from the east, one can see a panoramic view of the town that reveals many landmarks. Houghton Creek has a new bridge where the Heading Mill processed lumber, and the first house on the left past the bridge is still occupied in 2009. The school can be seen on the left horizon, while the dark-colored Fox Mill is shown in the far right background.

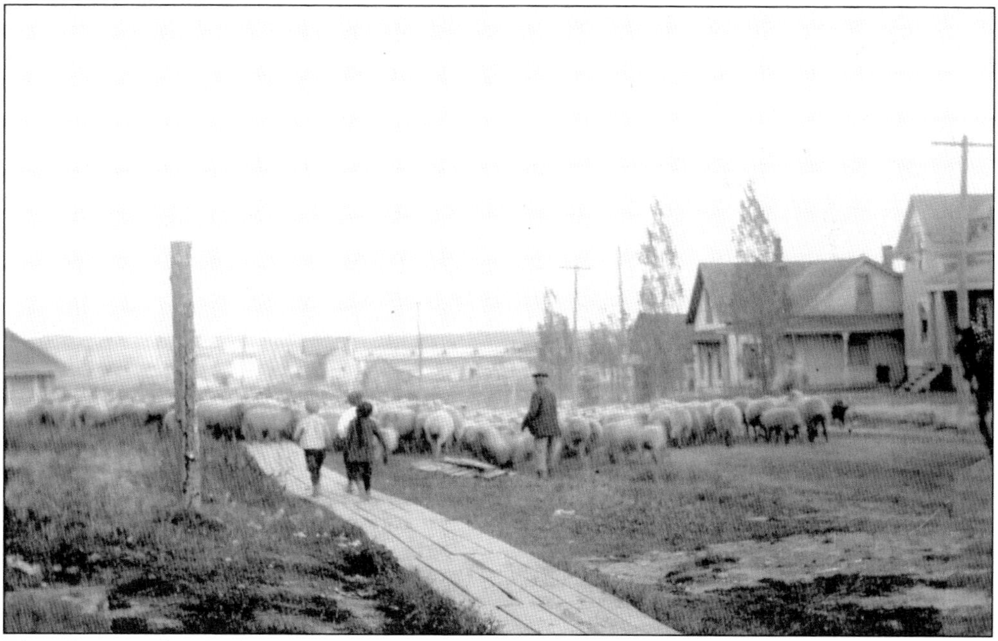

This photograph is looking east on Main Street; notice the sturdy wooden sidewalks. On the left, one can just see the corner of the train depot. The extensive Heading Mill is in the background. The boys are driving sheep to the railroad depot to be shipped to the city.

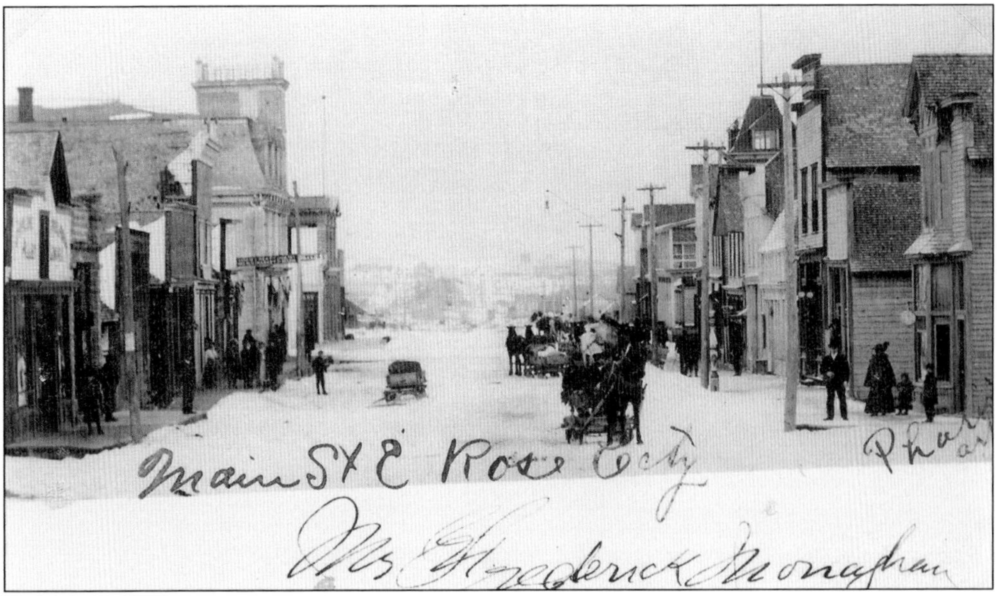

The photograph above depicts busy downtown Rose City during the winter of 1909. On April 3, 1910, fire was discovered in D. W. Benjamin's grocery store, seen in the foreground. Rose City citizens formed a bucket brigade, but the fire raged through the entire block on the south side of Main Street. Despite all efforts, the fire jumped Bennett Street, and the great Houghton House Hotel was soon lost. Flames spread to the north side of Main Street as well. Within an hour, more than 30 buildings were left as smoldering ash and charred timbers.

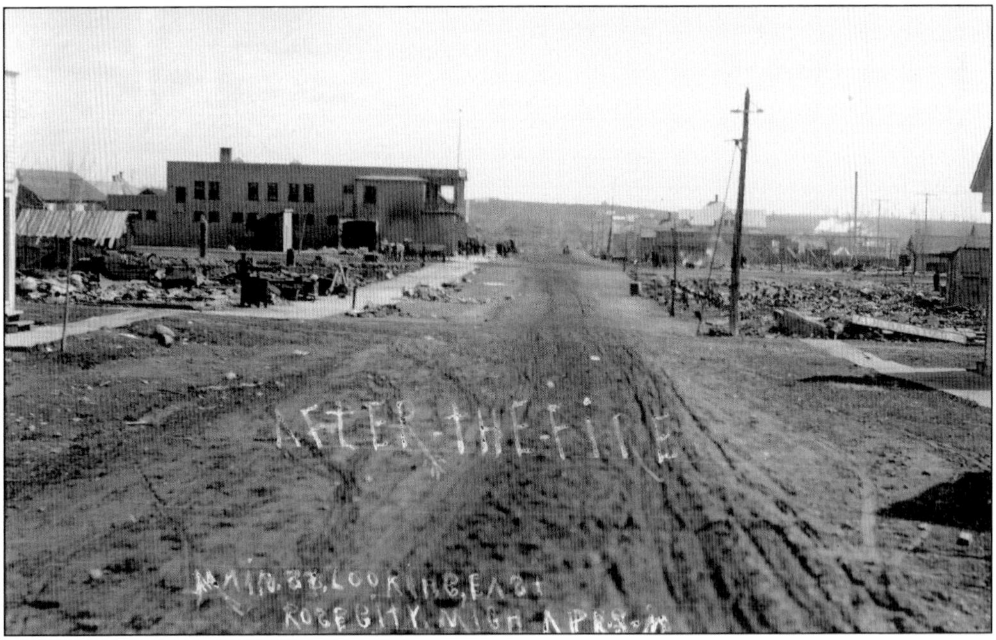

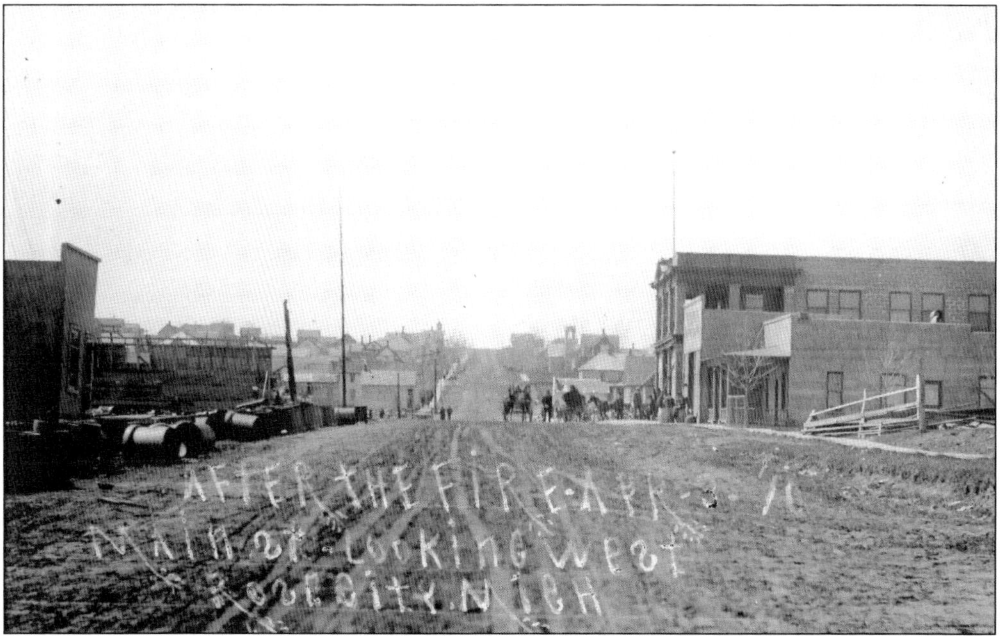

Tired townspeople stand in front of what is left of Rose City after the 1910 fire. After the fire, which wiped out the business district, the only buildings left standing were Bell's Hardware and Naylor's store. The town burned on Sunday and on Monday the city council met and passed an ordinance that only buildings constructed from fireproof materials could be erected in the business district.

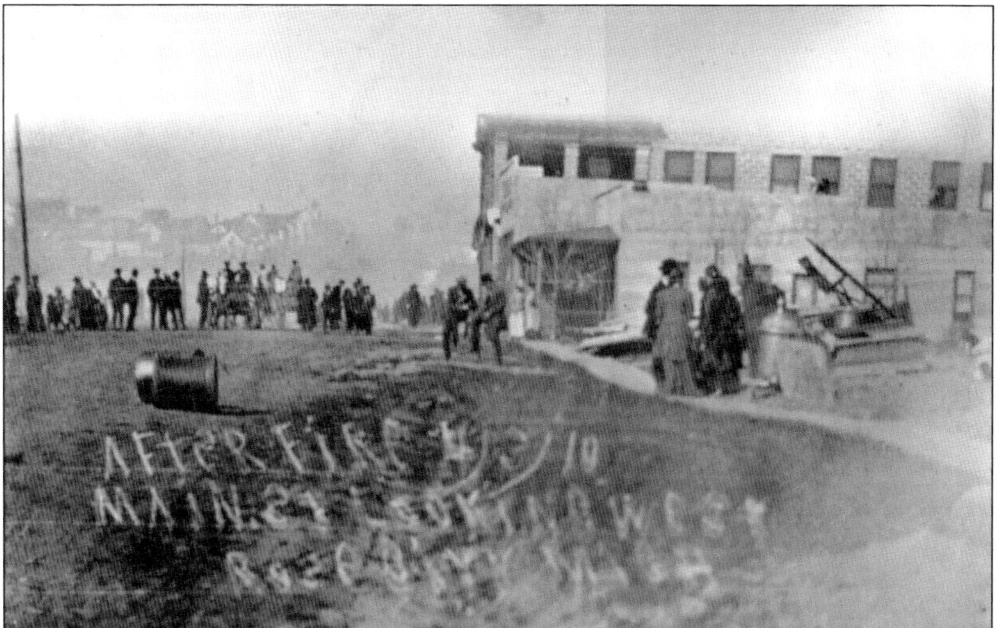

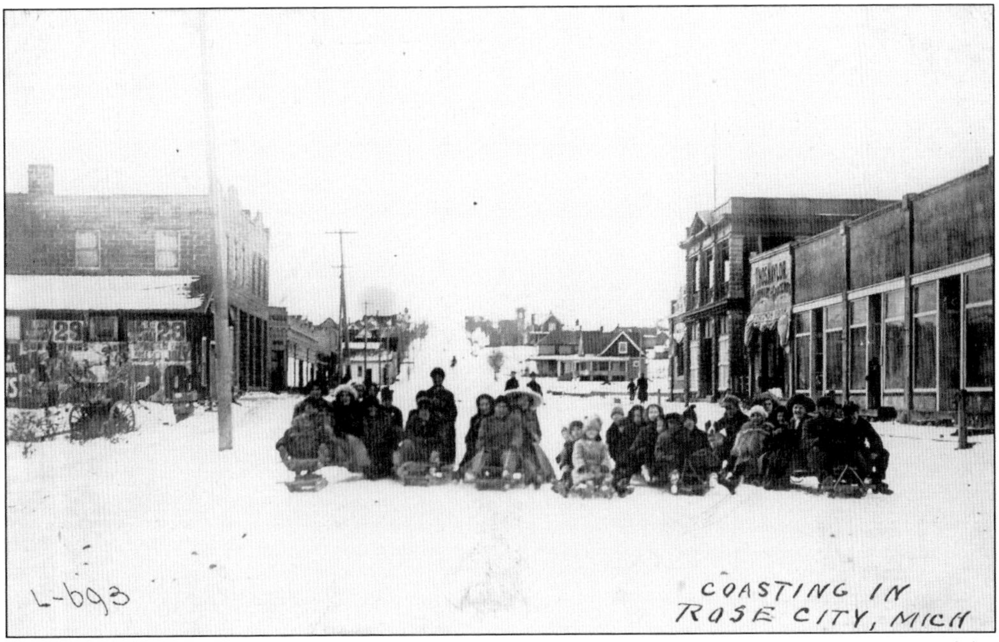

In a happy scene from the early 1930s, sledders pose after an exhilarating ride from the top of the long hill. One person was always posted at the intersection to watch for approaching traffic. One brave youngster in the left front is using a snow ski, which offered more speed but less safety.

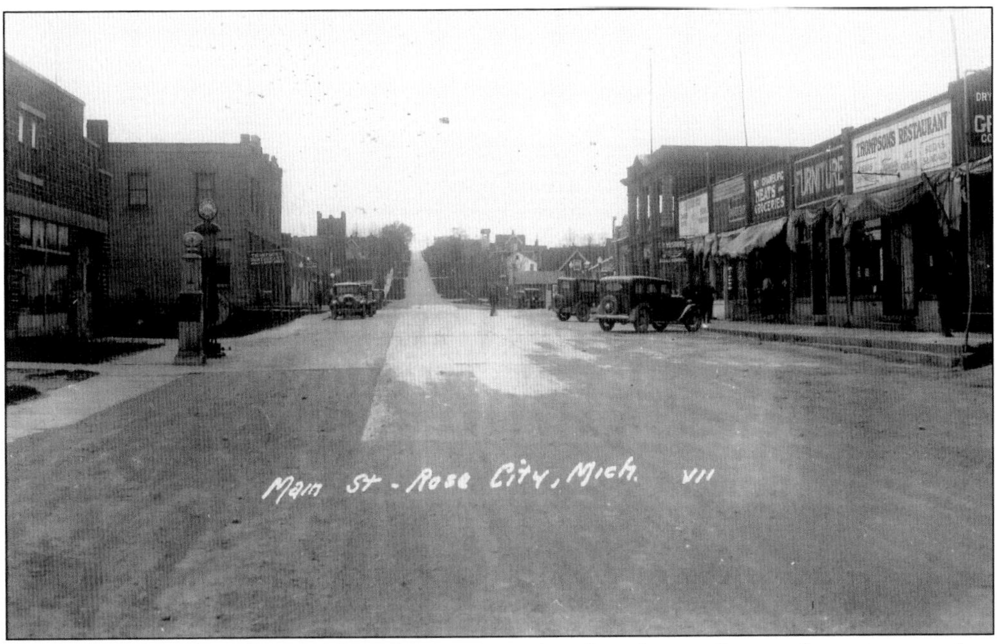

Rebuilt after the fire of 1910, Main Street was widened and partially paved to accommodate automobiles as the horse and buggy disappeared from everyday life. Gas pumps replaced the hitching posts and livery stables. This photograph shows the church towers on both sides of Main Street.

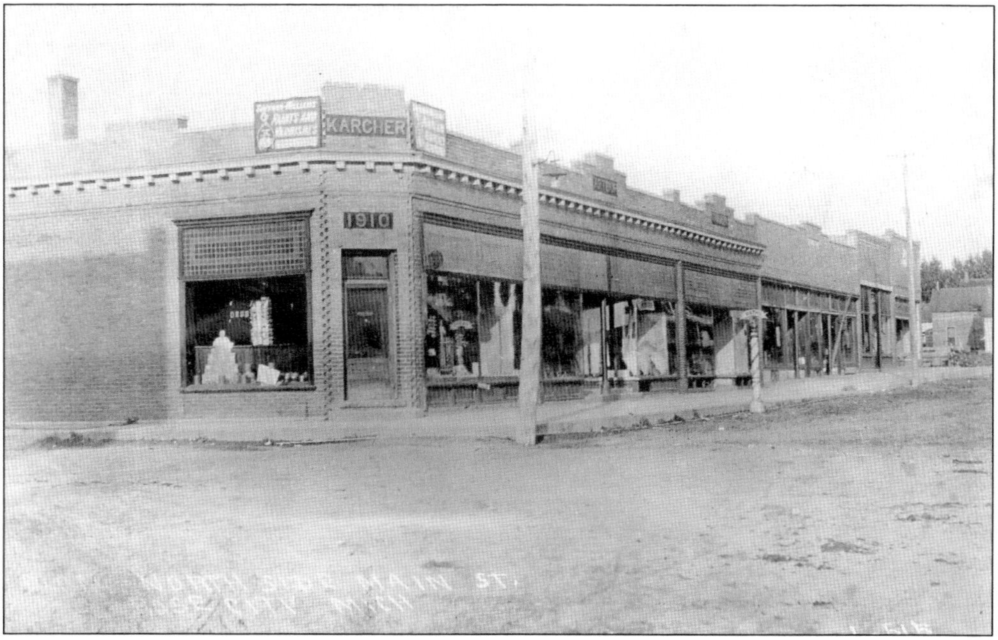

In 1904, Horatio S. Karcher and Dr. Leon R. Ingleright started a drugstore. This partnership lasted until 1910, when E. R. Chapin bought out Ingleright's interest in the business. Clyde Karcher, H. S. Karcher's son, bought out Chapin's interest later. The close partnership of father and son lasted until 1939, when H. S. died following an automobile accident. The original building burned in 1910 but was rebuilt on the southwest corner of Bennett and Main Streets.

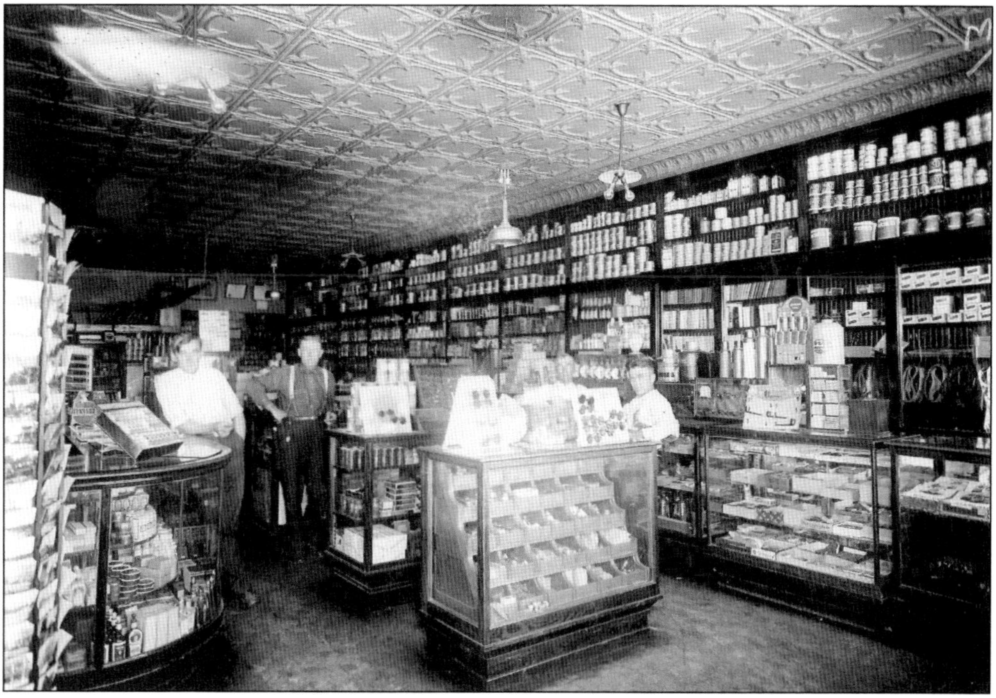

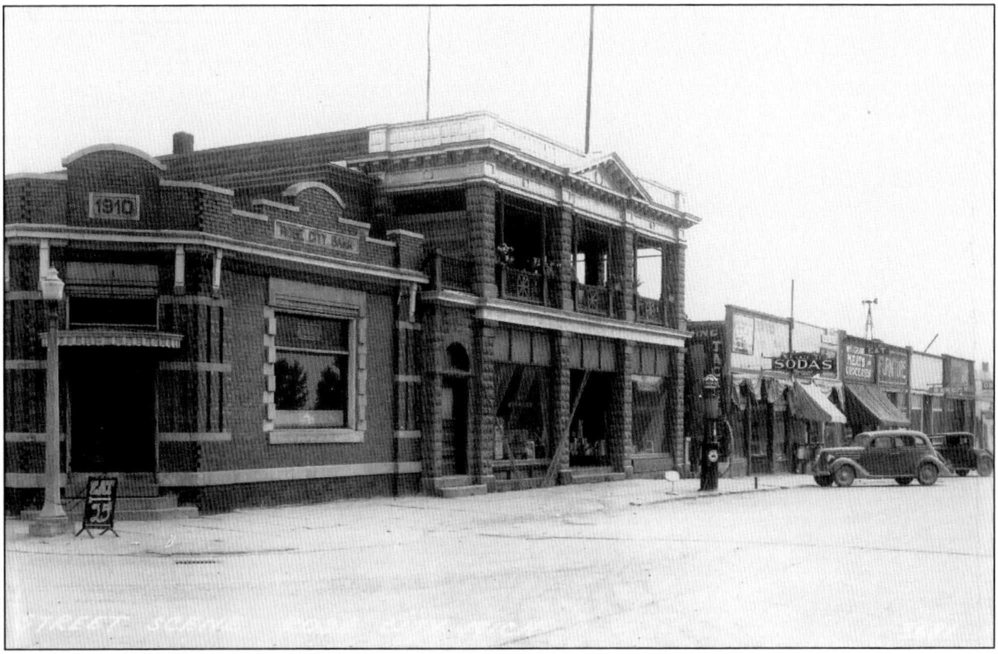

Randall and Bell Hardware, the two-story building in the center of this photograph, was a popular place to purchase anything from a big steel range to a wagon jack, from a tenpenny nail to a carpet tack. This building survived the fire of 1910, but burned in 2005 and had to be torn down.

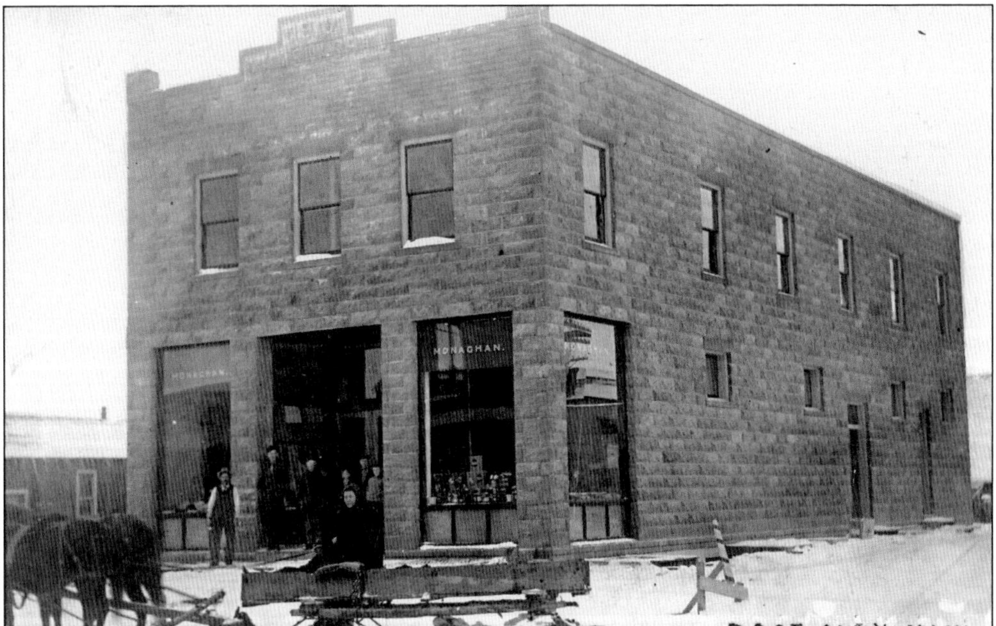

The Monaghan Hotel, on the southeast corner of Bennett and Main Streets, housed Godden's Tavern in the basement, Grawburg's Grocery on the main floor, the Monaghan Hotel, and living quarters. On May 1, 1937, a fire completely destroyed the building. The hotel was never rebuilt. Grawburg's Grocery and Godden's Tavern reopened in other buildings on Main Street.

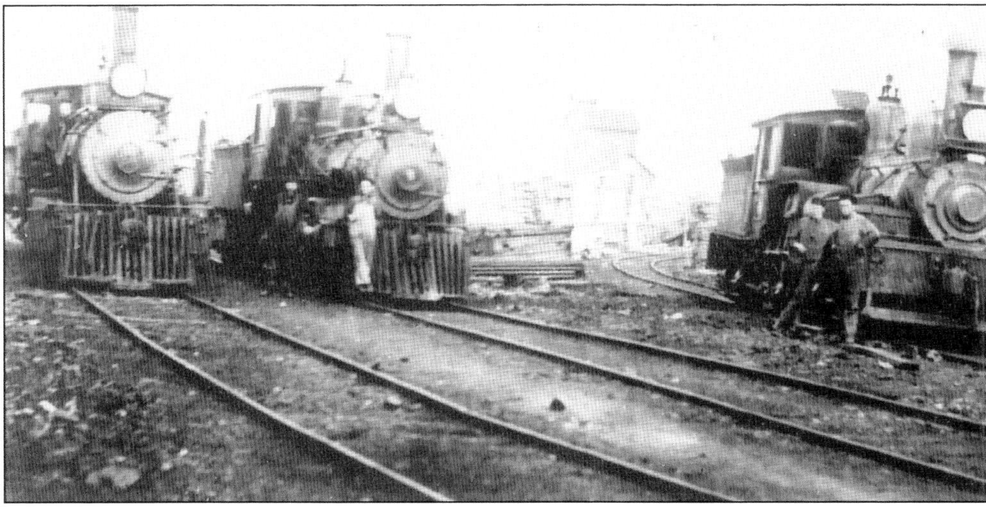

The first train pulled into Rose City on Christmas Day, 1893. People from Ogemaw County now had easy transportation to Bay City and other points south. The rail line was a branch of the Detroit and Mackinaw Railway and served the area until the 1930s. The rails ended in Rose City and never connected the line extending from West Branch. The depot was a bustling place with lumbermen and tourists.

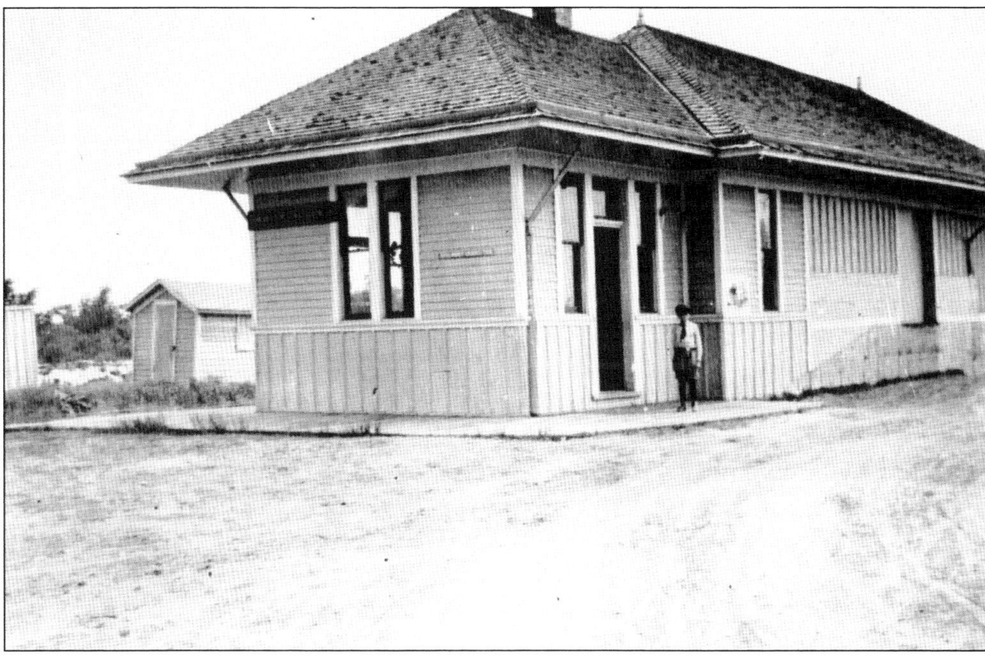

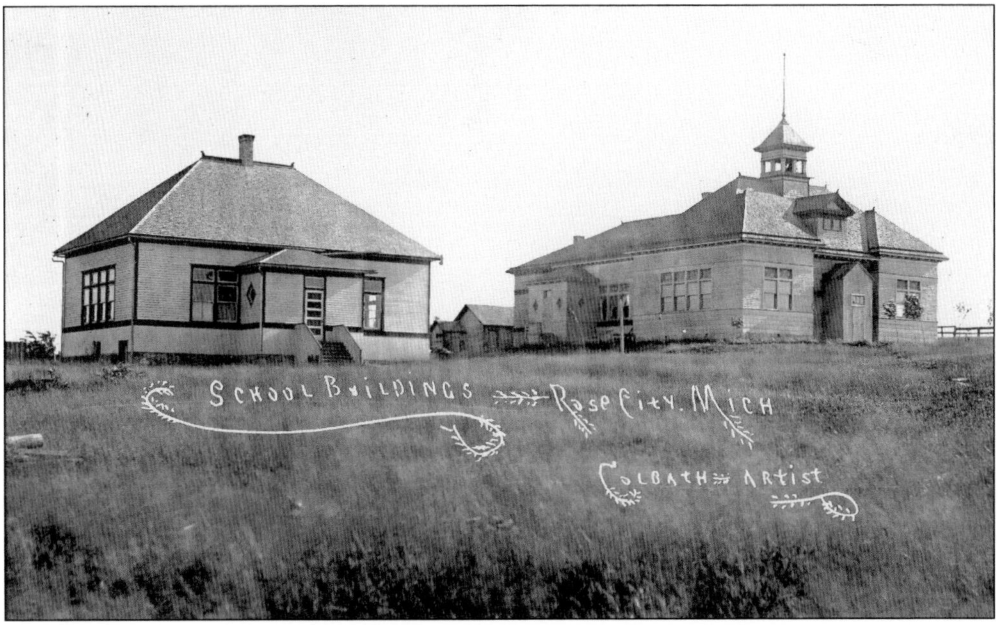

About 1880, a log school was built on the main trail near Churchill. It served the needs of the community for nearly 15 years. A new four-room school (right) was built in 1895 on the hill overlooking town. This building housed 12 grades of students. In 1905, a two-room building (left) was added to the site for the early elementary grades. The building used for high school burned in 1946.

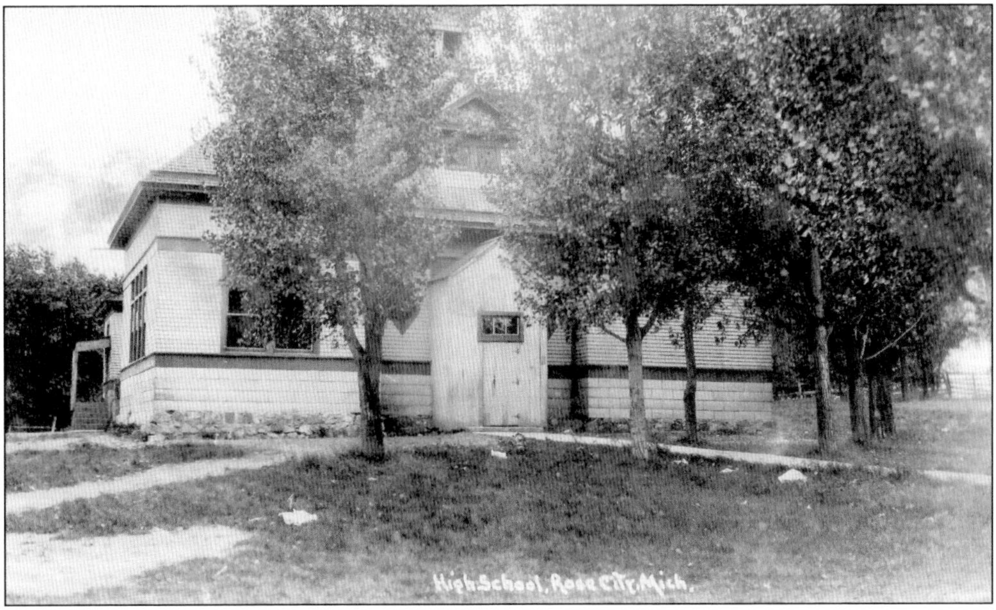

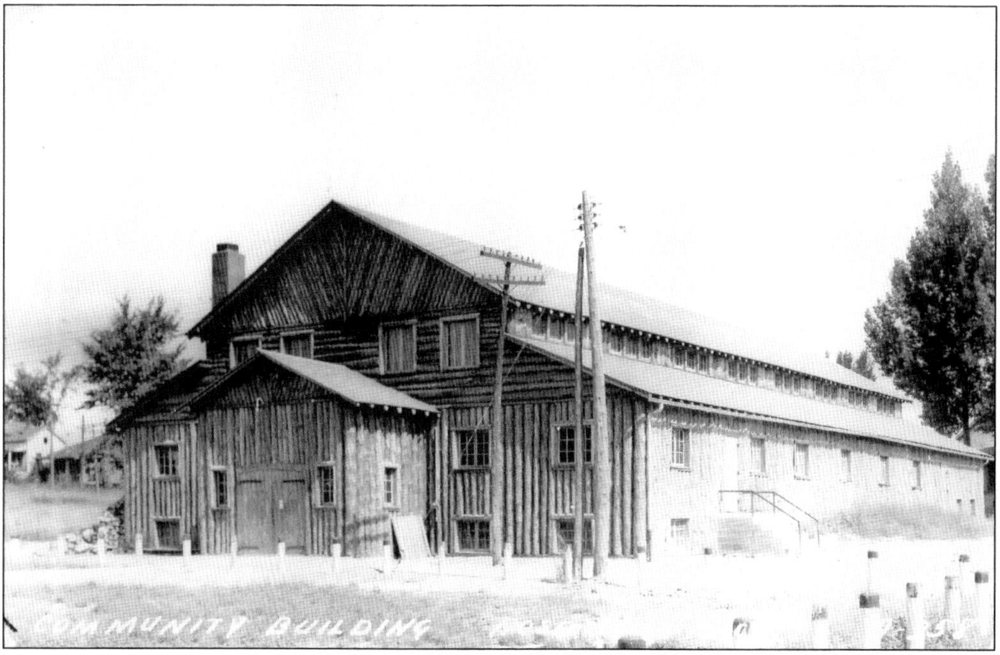

The Rose City Community Building was built during the depression with Works Progress Administration (WPA) funds. It was the heart of the community for many years. In addition to serving as the city hall and town library, the building housed the Roseland Theater and Miss Ruth's Dance School. Countless numbers of hunters were fed in the basement dining hall each November during the 1940s. The building was used as a school for two years, and after the new school was built, the gym and basketball court were used until 1955. The center had seating for about 600 people. The building was razed in the early 1960s.

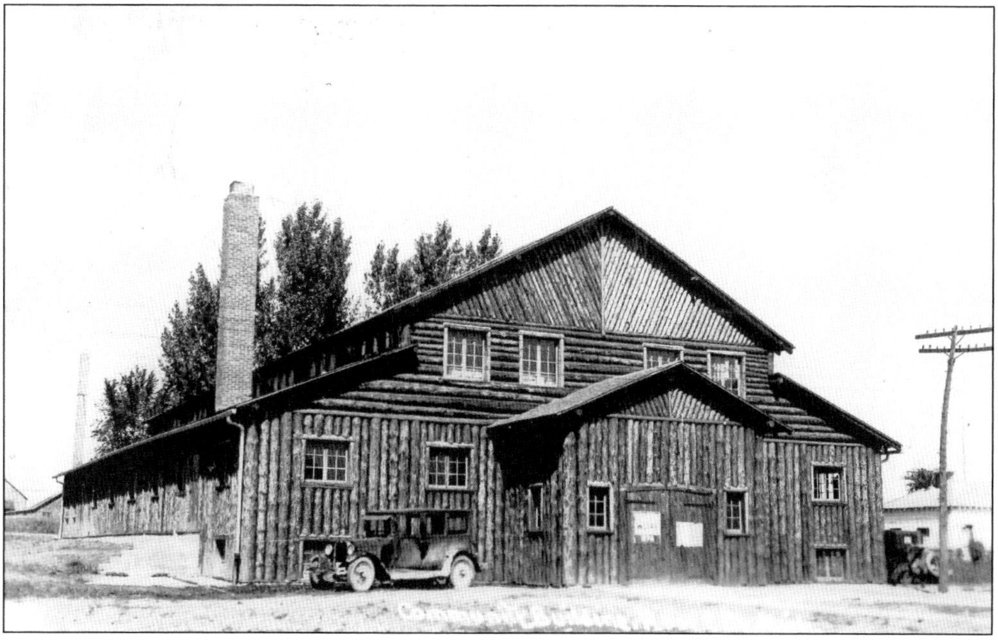

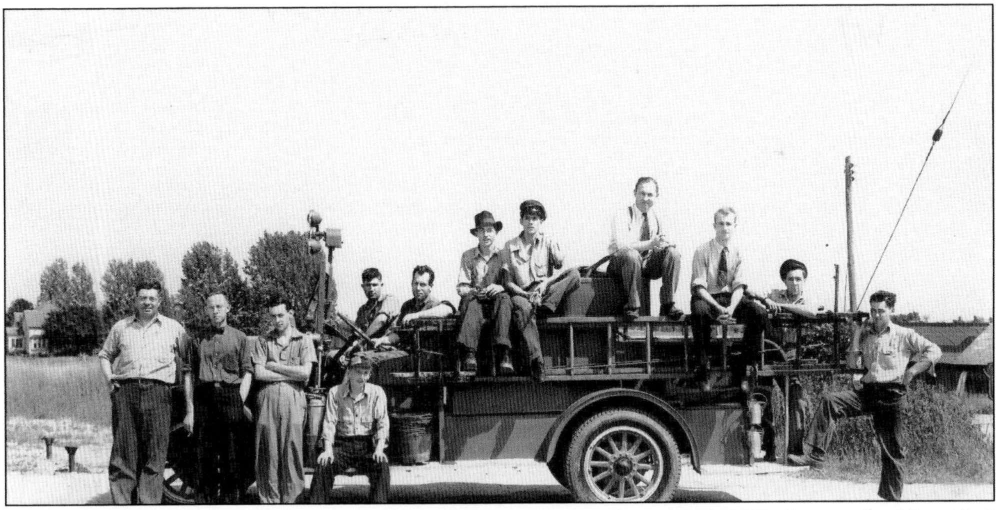

Pictured here is the 1939 Rose City Fire Department and its 1935 REO fire truck. Identified firefighters, from left to right, are (first row, left) Bill Tulloh, Ashley Nunn, Bob Arthur, and Bill Furhman; (second row) Alvin Bell, Oliver Matthews, John Reasner, Howard Eastman, Clarence Cooley, Art Godden, Dick Sanback and Bill Reasner.

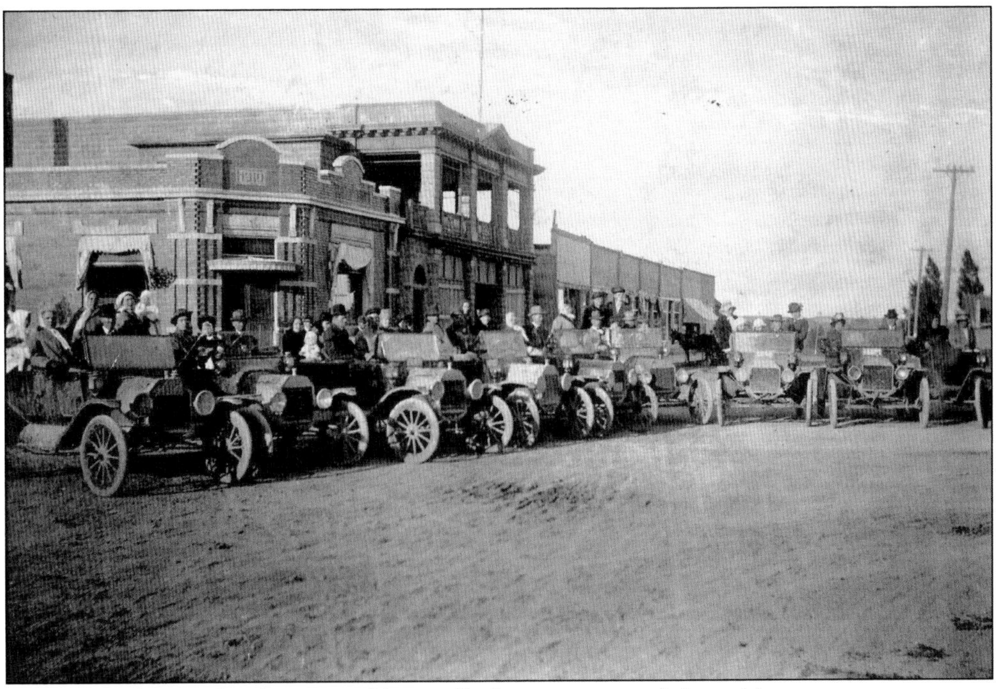

As more and more families were able to afford a new automobile and horses were put out to pasture, small touring groups began to appear. This entourage pauses to pose for a picture in downtown Rose City.

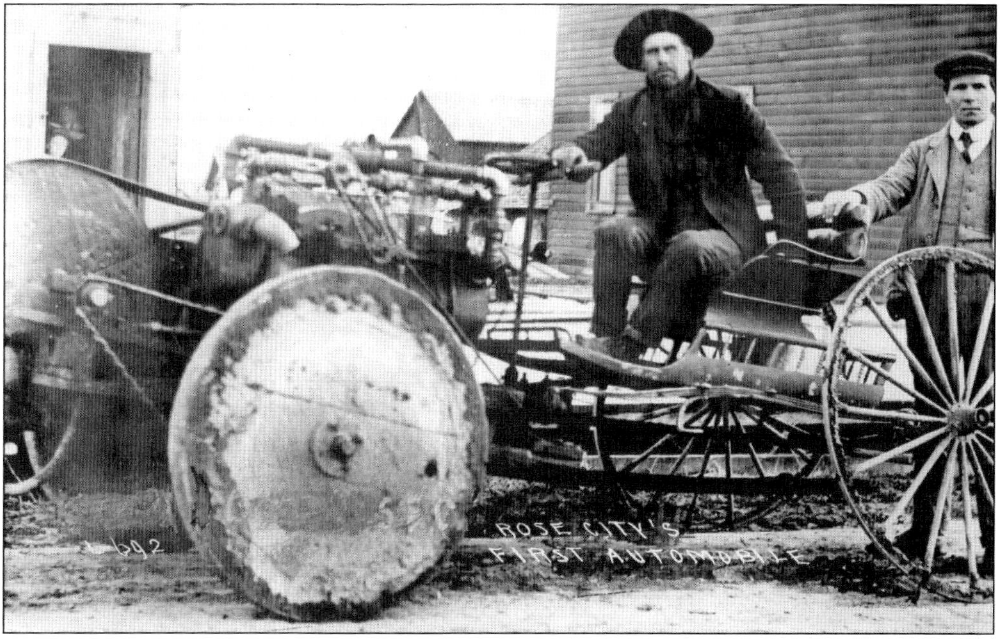

Willard Rose (1872–1926) assembled his first automobile in 1900 and built another in 1902. The automobile was built with a reinforced buggy frame and back wheels. He built his own steering gear and the transmission was created when he connected a chain and sprocket to the right front wheel. Rose was ticketed for speeding numerous times.

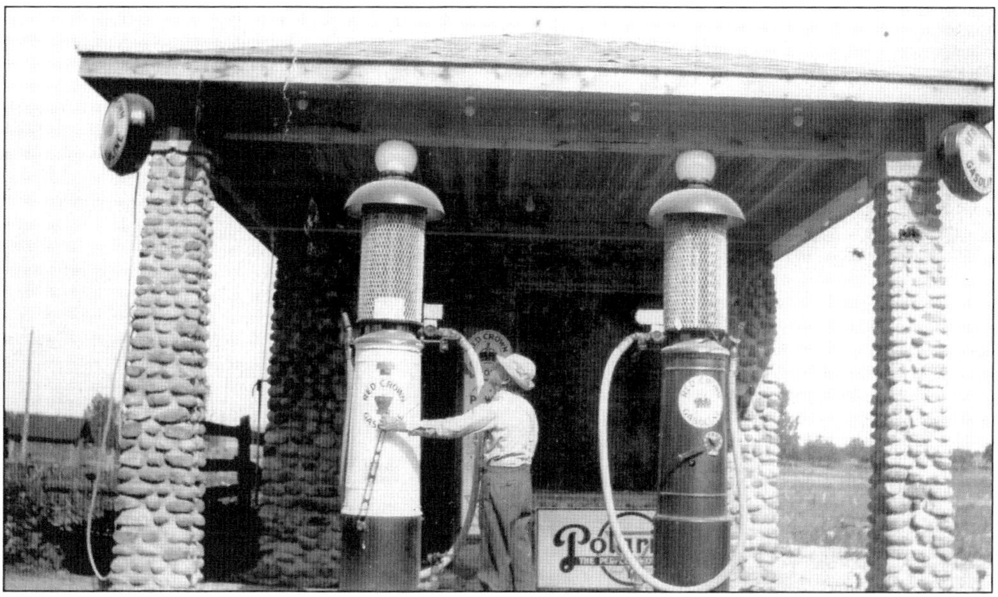

Wesley Chase (1863–1927), an early pioneer settler, stands in front of his Rose City gas station on the corner of Bennett and Page Streets in 1926. Note the early manual pumps with locked handles. Chase was a highly respected businessman engaged in several businesses at varied times. He was also supervisor of Klacking Township for seven years. (Courtesy of the Chase family.)

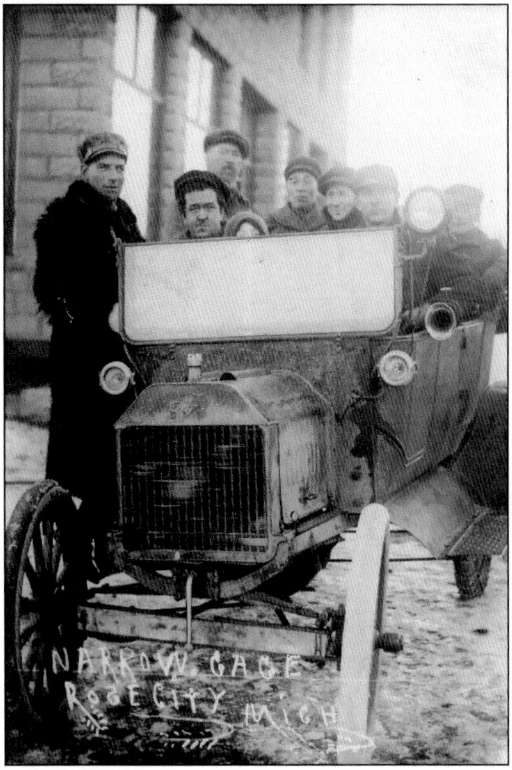

James T. (Tom) Rice demonstrates his new Ford car in approximately 1912. From left to right in this photograph are Harrison Lince, Tom Rice, Jerry Rice, Tom's son, Fred Reetz, Tom Smith, Bill Linton, and Bill Ludwig. Tom Rice owned and operated a blacksmith shop, butcher shop, and pool hall. Later he operated a Ford dealership and garage. Jerry, at the age of 12, demonstrated the Fords to prospective customers.

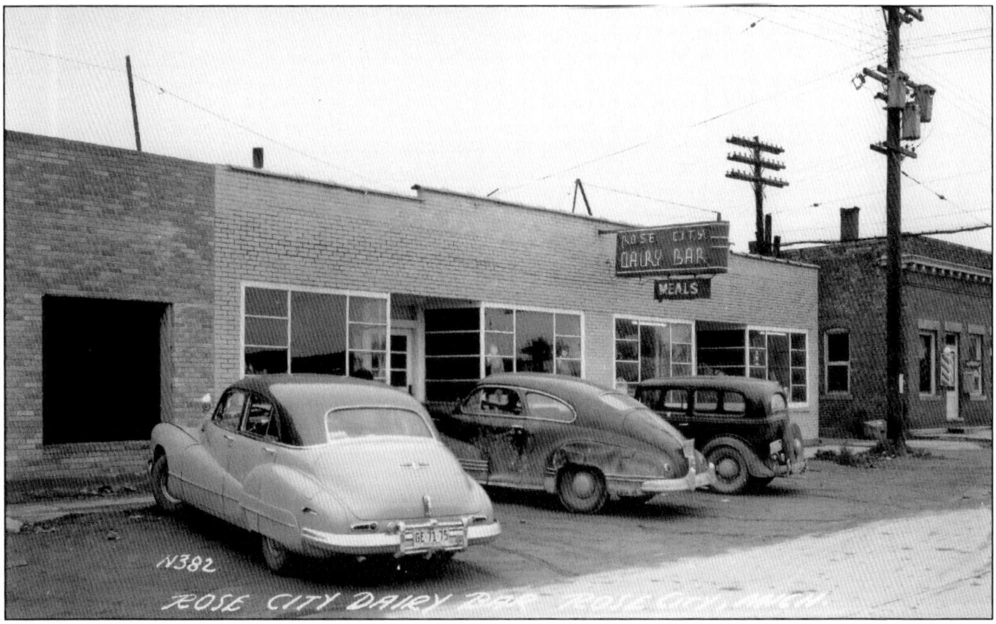

The Rose City Dairy Bar on the west side of Bennett Street was owned by Ernie and Theresa Sherlund. Cooley's Dry Goods Store is on the left; it was owned by Clarence and Roberta Cooley who sold shoes and clothing. The building on the right was owned by Lawson Chambers and housed the telephone office. The office was operated 24 hours a day and the operator hooked up calls with the wire connectors.

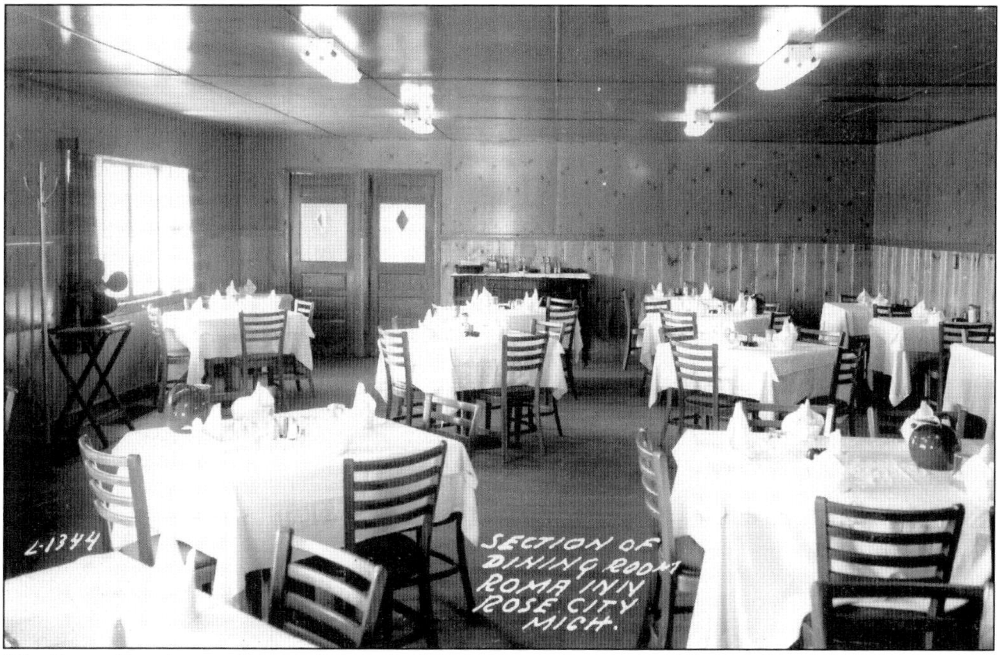

The Roma Inn, located one mile south of Rose City on M-33, was famous for its Italian American foods and was a very popular spot for banquets, wedding dinners, and other group meetings. Besides the fine food and large dining rooms, the Roma Inn had a spacious bar. Built in 1945 by Art Sossee and Joe Falk, it is now called Parr's Pub and is located across from Glen's Market.

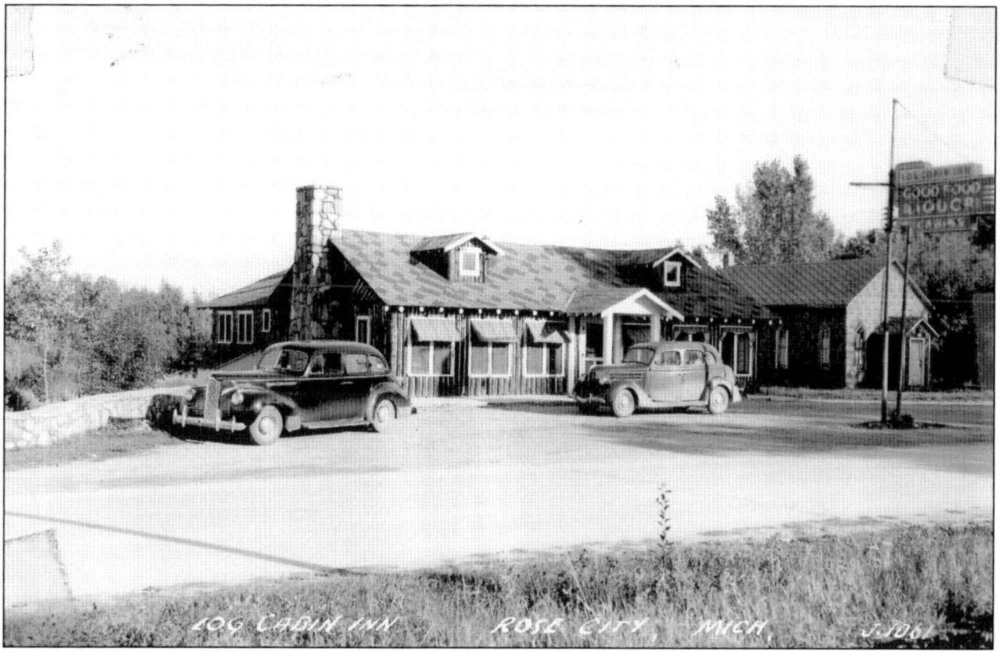

After the repeal of Prohibition, this building was erected by Tex Brown as the Blinking Eye Bar. Lawrence Polzin bought it in 1936 and renamed it the Log Cabin Inn. Upon Lawrence's death, Mrs. Polzin sold it to Leonard Wical in 1955 and he changed the name to Wee-Ona-Bar. It was later owned by Stuart Faull, and lastly by Mr. and Mrs. Tom Burkheiser, who bought it in 1998.

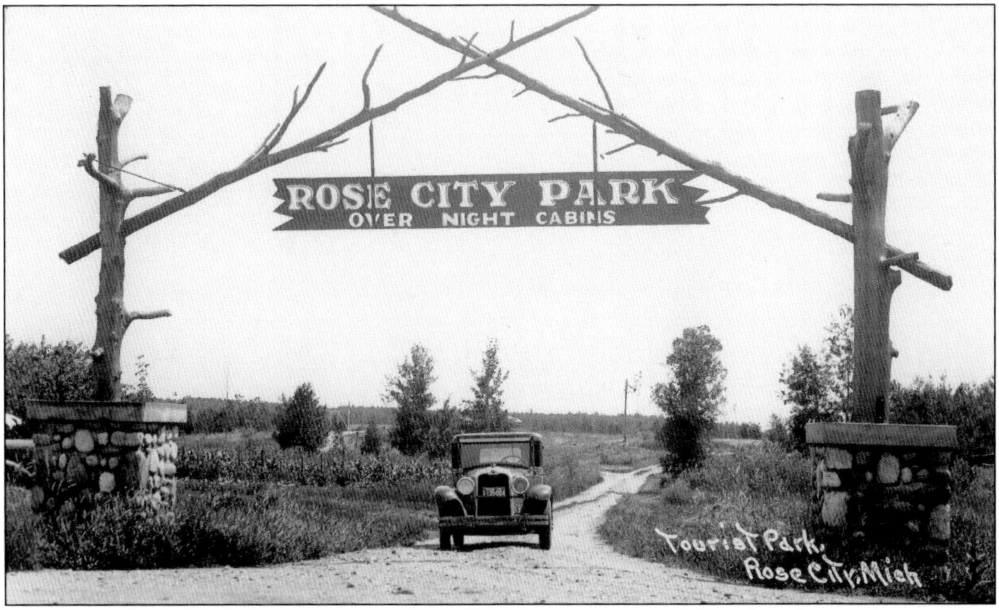

In 1930, automobile pioneer Harry M. Jewett donated 20 acres of land and enough money to build a tourist park in Rose City. The entrance to the Rose City Park is shown above and the same road is used today. By 1931, the people of the community had built more roads, cabins, a ball diamond, and a pavilion. The pavilion chimney was built of stone surrounded by four cooking grills spaced evenly around. The pavilion, still in use today, overlooks Houghton Creek, which runs in a semicircle around the picnic area and provides excellent fishing opportunities. In the 1930s, campers could throw a line in the water from the door of their cabins, which are shown below with the new well in the foreground. (Courtesy of Sharon and Don Alderton.)

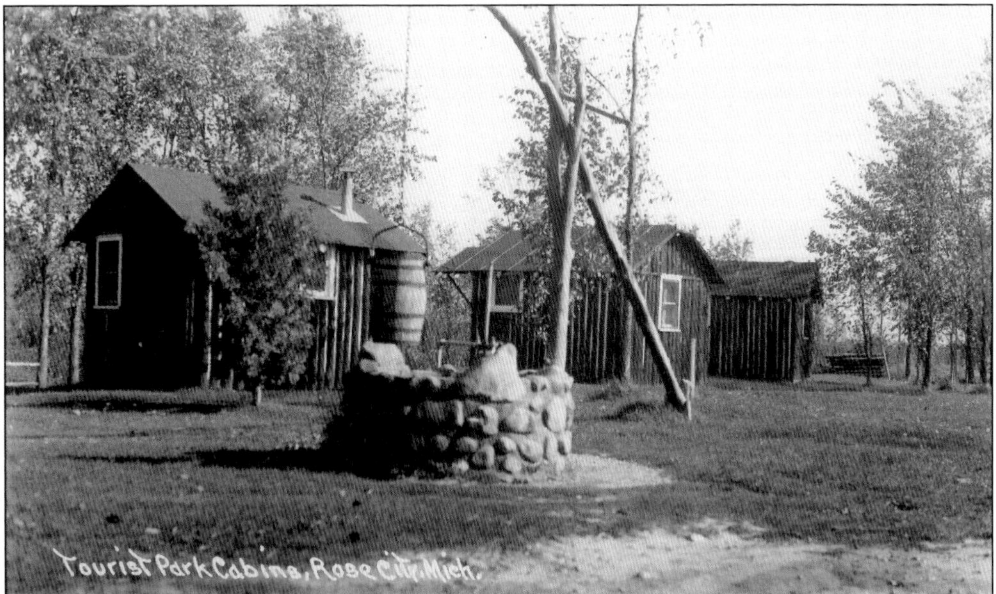

Five

The South Branch, Maltby, and Goodar Areas

Like most of northern Michigan, the South Branch, Goodar, and Maltby areas were first settled by lumbermen. Charles Goodar and Charles Taber arrived in 1878 with a timber contract from the Sage and McGraw Land Company. South Branch, also known as Hunt or Thompson Station, really got its start with this sawmill. As more families arrived, the business of establishing a real town began.

South Branch was first platted on September 20, 1888. A hotel and general store were the first businesses, followed by the Taber and Berry Schools. The post office, Goodar Baptist Church, and the South Branch Community Church soon followed. The population grew to 175 by the early 1900s. The village of South Branch had added a cedar mill, blacksmith shop, shoemaker, wagon maker, a hotel, and other small businesses. At one time, South Branch was home to several saloons.

Goodar was established around Robinson's Mill in 1907–1909. It boasted 25 buildings. Besides the mill, other buildings included two boardinghouses, a general store, and a post office. The general store had everything a lumberman and his family could want, except for liquor. In 1914, the lumber supply became depleted and the mill and many residents moved to Oscoda.

The town of Maltby sprang up around a mill owned by Alvin Maltby in 1889. A school and post office were established in 1900, along with three general stores and Barnaby's Boarding House. Another business, according to Evelyn Berry's account of Goodar Township history, was the Ogemaw Springs Bottling Works, which shipped water in bottles and barrels to Bay City.

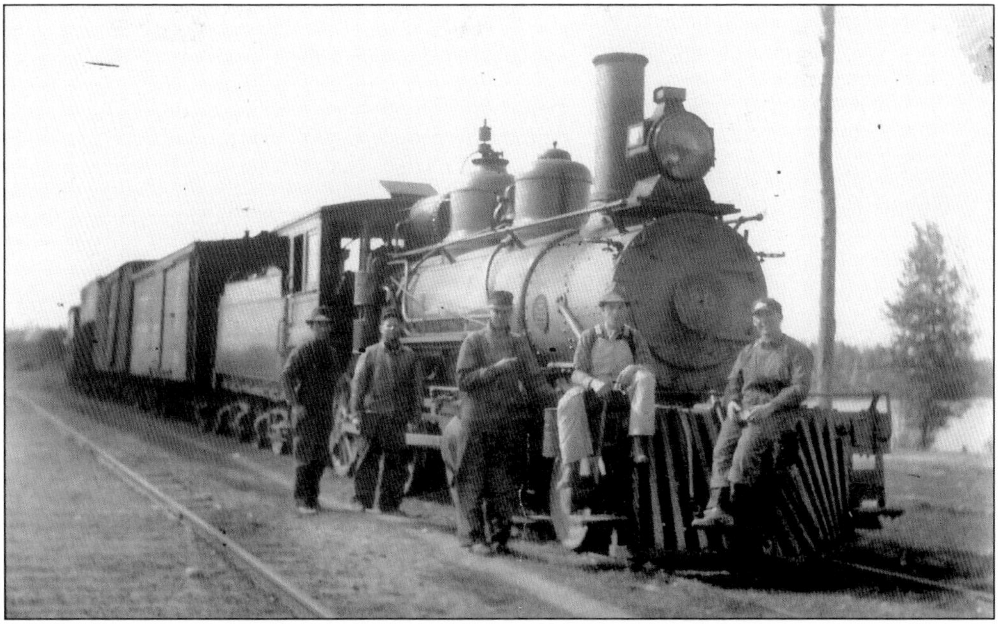

In 1907, Robinson's Mill came to the Goodar area from Grayling. The first action taken by the mill owners was to build a narrow-gauge railway from South Branch to the mill. The engineer in the above photograph is Clyde Taber. Many narrow-gauge lines were extended into the timbered areas for transporting logs. The settlement soon boasted 25 buildings. In the lower photograph, three unidentified men are sitting on a handcar that was used to check the lines and travel from camp to camp. (Courtesy of Beulah Huebner.)

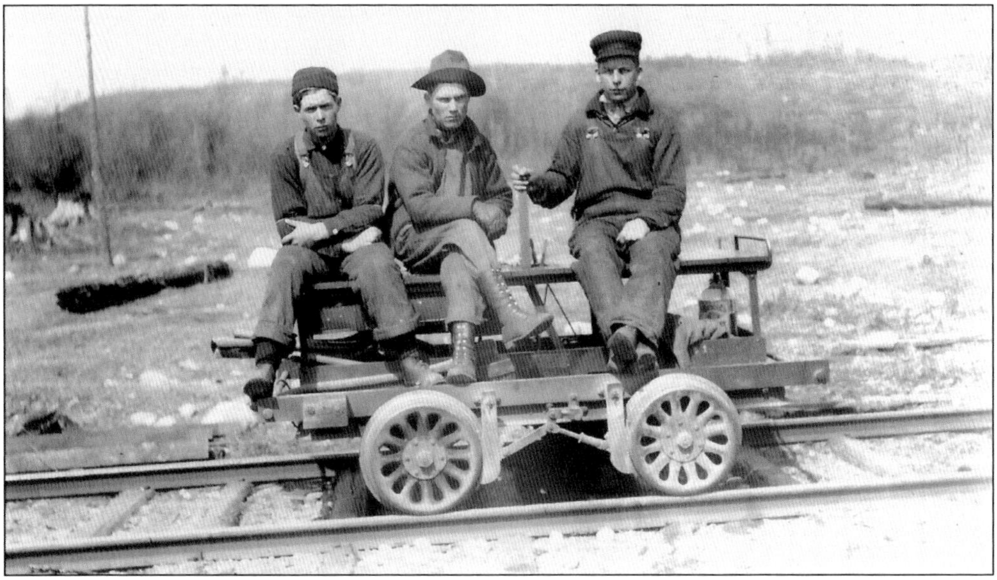

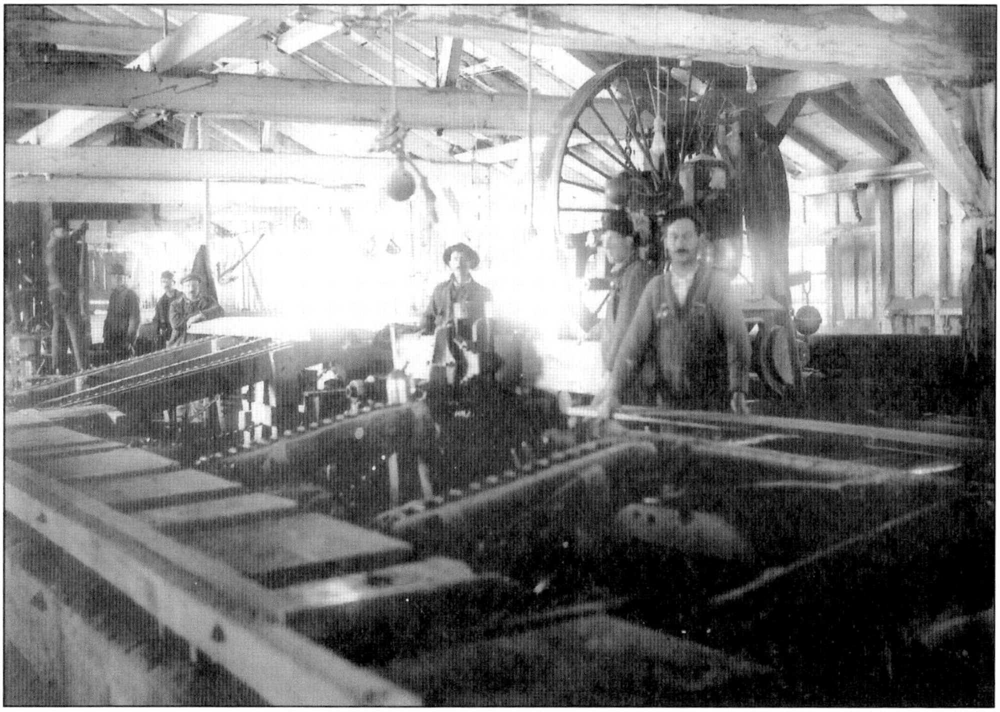

Goodar was one of the final townships to be logged off in the county. Maltby and South Branch served as railroad loading stations for area lumber camps. The town of Goodar was the center of the largest logging operation. The Robinson and Eastman Mills employed about 200 people, both men and women. The women usually cooked in the camps and did laundry. The Robinson Mill (pictured above) also operated several narrow-gauge railways leading to cutting operations in the forests. When the mills were in peak operation, about 200,000 feet of timber was sawed daily. (Courtesy of Beulah Huebner.)

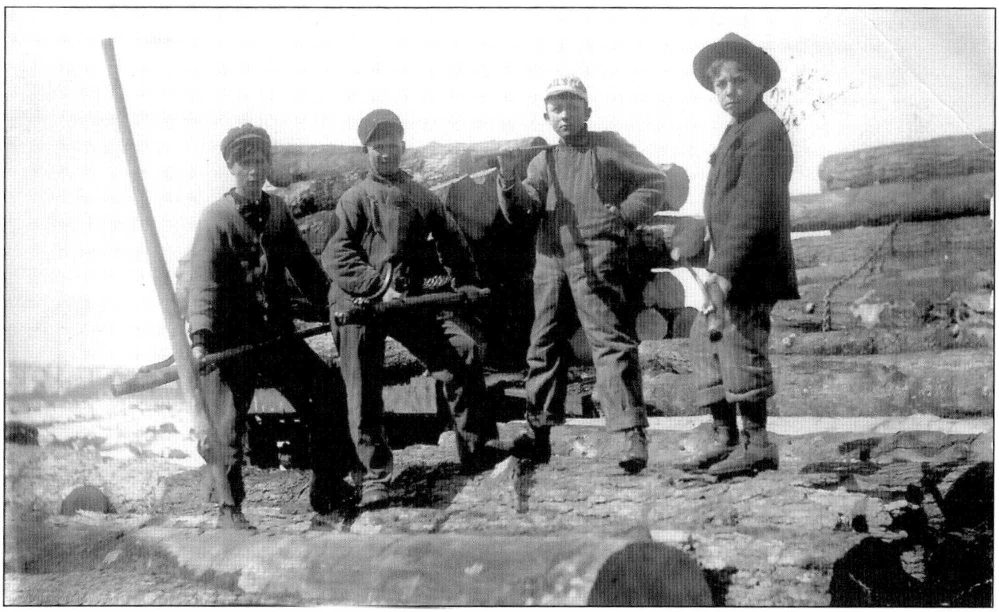

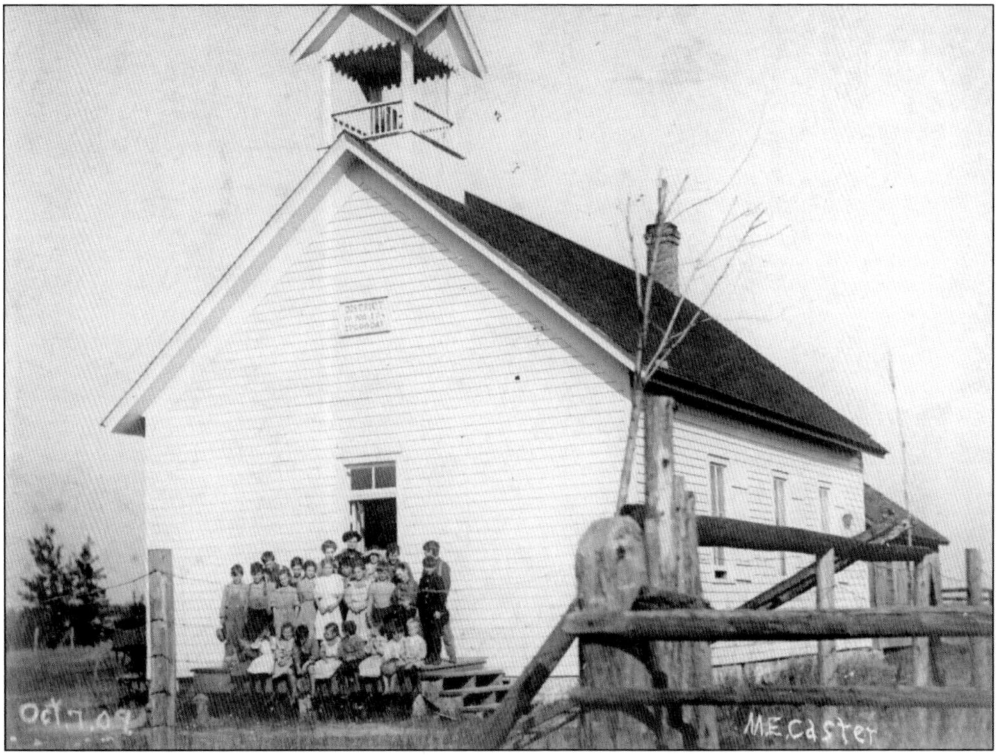

The first two schools in the area were both built about 1888 or 1889. The Goodar School (above) was named for Charles Goodar, one of the very first settlers in the area. He owned and operated the first lumber mill in the community. Sarah Warren McGray was the first teacher. The Taber School was named after Charles Taber, another early pioneer. (Courtesy of Beulah Huebner.)

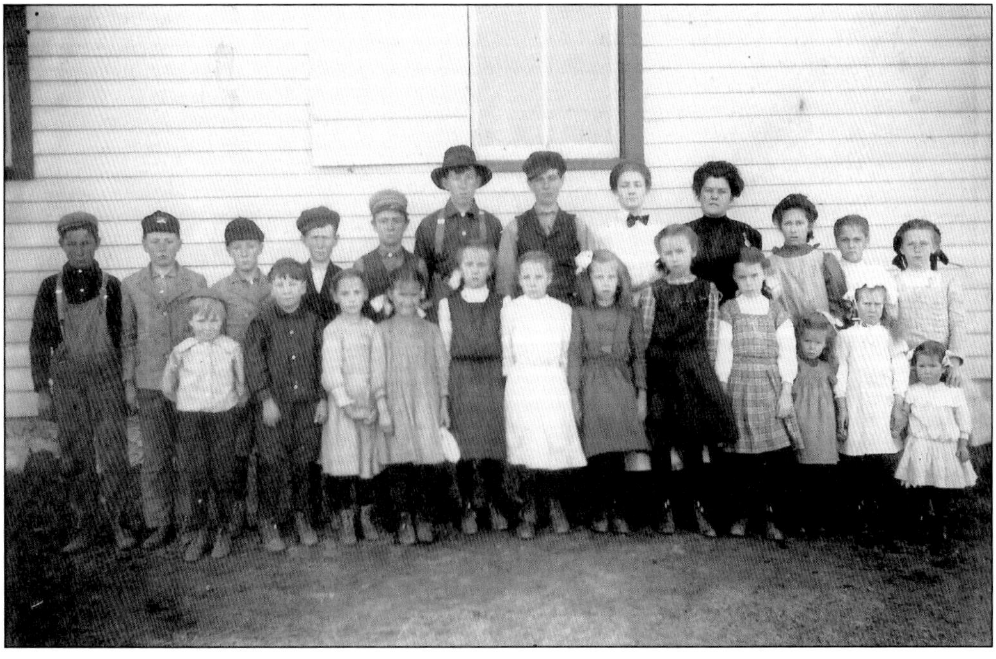

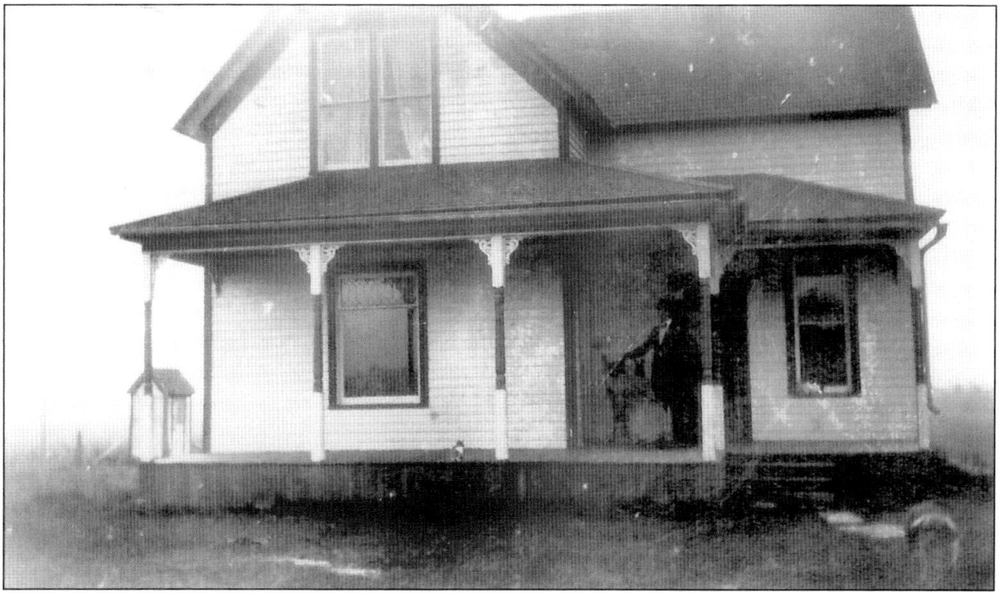

Charles Taber walked to this area from Saginaw in five days, driving his two head of cattle with him. He and his wife Lydia established their home in a veritable wilderness. Charles was employed as a hunter for Goodar's lumber mill. In three months he killed 105 deer and 22 bear. This is a photograph of the Taber home. (Courtesy of Beulah Huebner.)

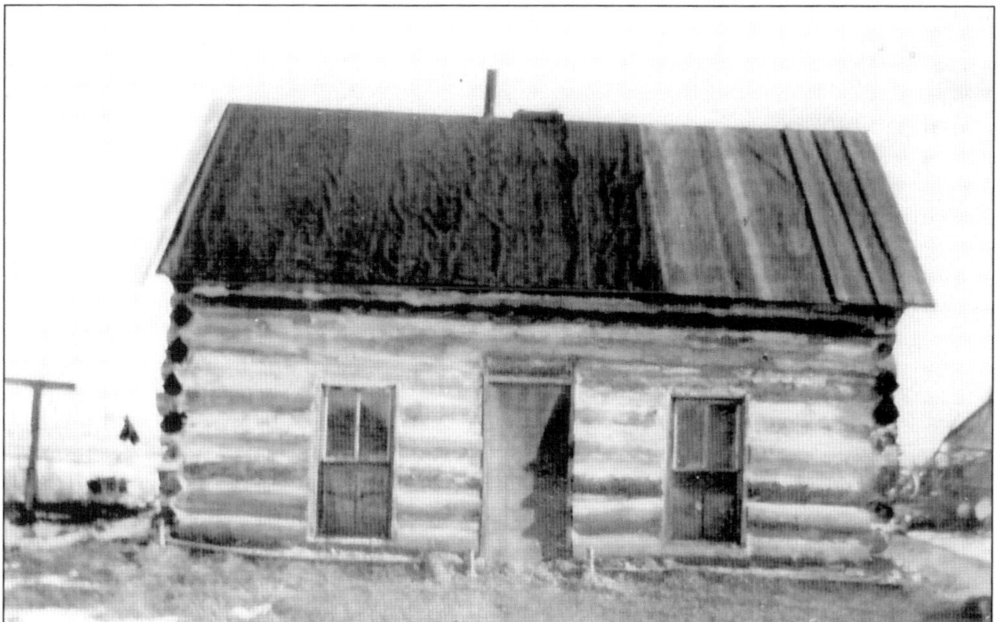

This simple log cabin owned by Hiram and Ida Quigley is typical of the homes in the area of South Branch, Goodar, and Maltby in 1922. Many cabins were made from hand-hewn logs and roofed with hand-hewn shingles, which were often replaced with a tin roof. (Courtesy of Beulah Huebner.)

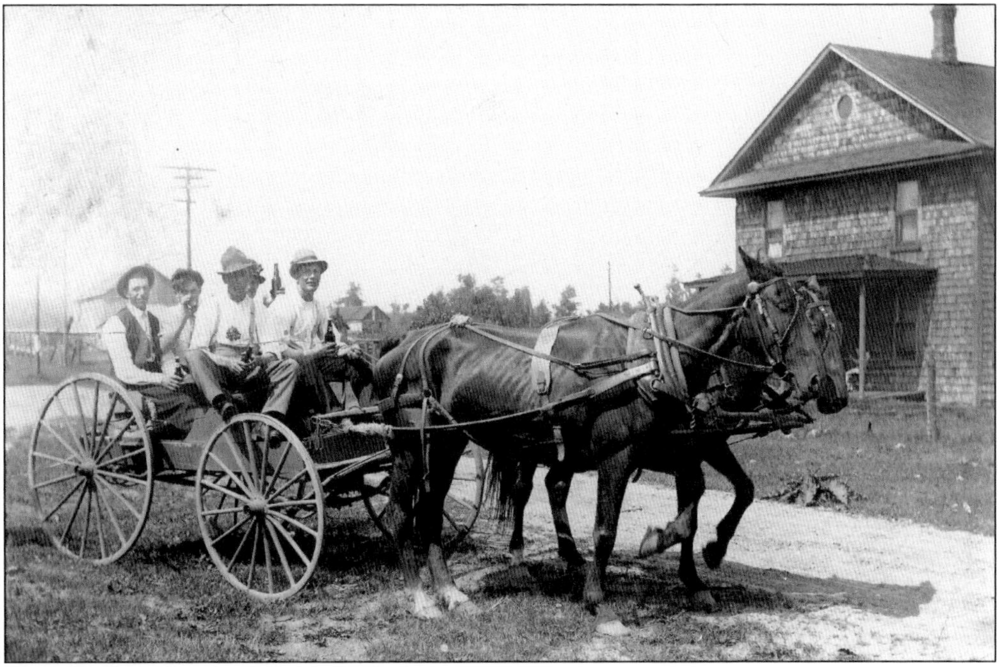

This photograph was taken at the Roy Cline house in Maltby. Frank Thayer lived in the house at the time. The men are identified as Melvin Roe, Joseph Davidson, Ralph Sparling, Charles Harper, and Edward Roe.

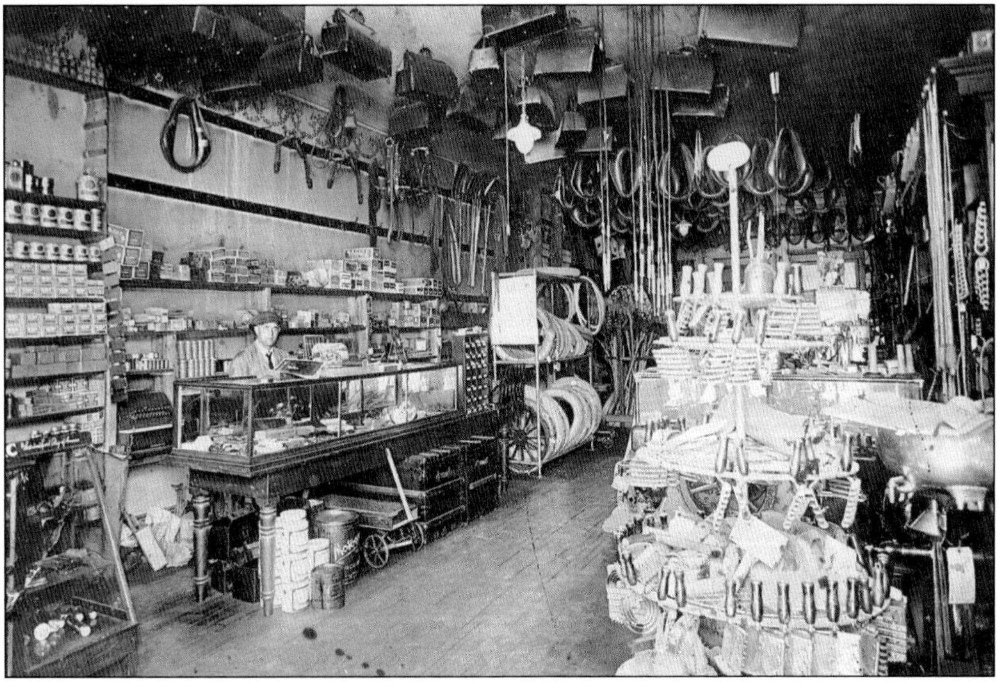

This photograph depicts an interior much like that of a store in South Branch run by William J. Bayne (1838–1904), a Civil War veteran. It is interesting to note that Bayne's property deed forbid the selling of any alcoholic beverages.

Six

The West Branch Area

Capt. S. V. Thomas and Dr. C. L. Nauman, who were associated with the lumber companies in Beaver Lake and Ogemaw Springs, are said to be the first settlers of West Branch. West Branch, like many other communities, was brought into existence by the coming of the railroad and the majestic white pine. In the late 1800s, the Jackson, Lansing and Saginaw Railroad crossed through what would become West Branch on its way north bringing lumbermen and then returning south carrying lumber to the big cities.

In 1905, West Branch was officially incorporated as a city. In 1908, work began on a municipal water supply. Early records are sketchy, but some of the businesses included Tolfree, Livingstone, and Company, a bank; McGowan Hardware; Sergeant Hardware; Maggie and Juggs Saloon; and Mr. Holmes's bar and pool hall. Saloons were the biggest businesses in the early days. At one time there were more saloons than stores. The boys from the lumber camps found West Branch a great place to "let off steam" on Saturday nights.

In the 1930s, an oil boom brought many new faces to the community. Jobs in the oil fields paid well and were plentiful. The oil business continues to this day. In the 1970s, the West Branch Industrial Park and Airport took shape.

With a huge concentrated local effort, Interstate 75 was brought through the county in 1973. This opened the door for more development at the two West Branch exits. Tourism flourishes in this area with the many lakes, rivers, and parks.

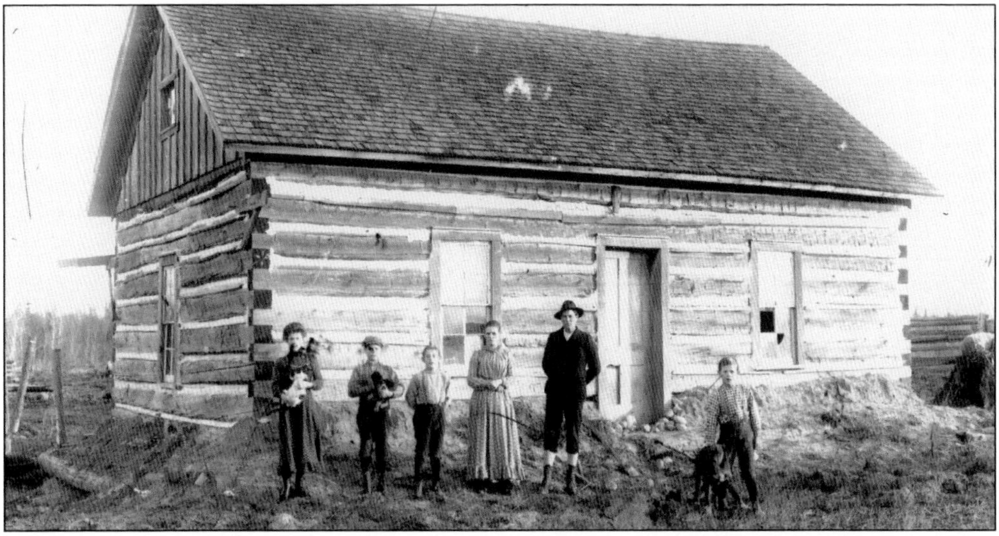

Sturdy log cabins sprang up where logging camps had previously been. After the second phase of logging, which saw the removal of hardwoods, new and more permanent settlers came. Many potential farmers arrived from Canada, as well as other areas, and planted their crops among the pine stumps.

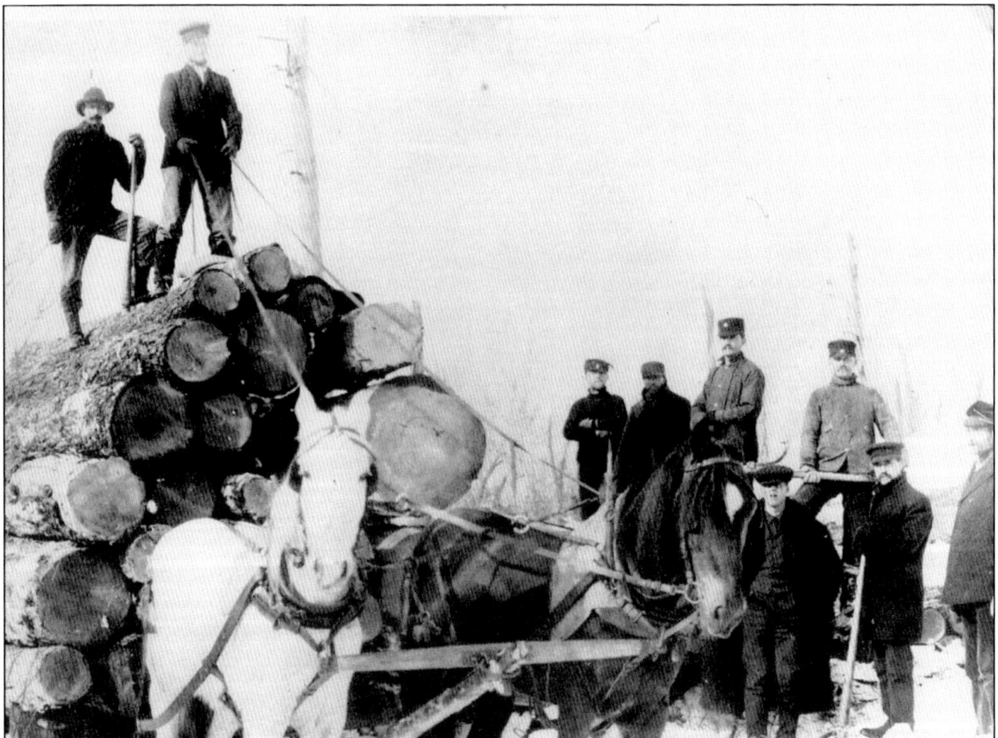

As winter approached, many new farming residents found it necessary to join logging crews to supplement their income and provide for their families. Men would be absent for months, and wives and older children completed farm chores and survived as best they could until spring heralded their return.

John Tolfree and J. W. Livingstone were prominent businessmen in West Branch, organizing the firm Tolfree, Livingstone and Company. Tolfree, pictured in the rear, owned large tracts of timber and farmland and owned one of the first stores in town. Livingstone, front left, operated one of the many saloons.

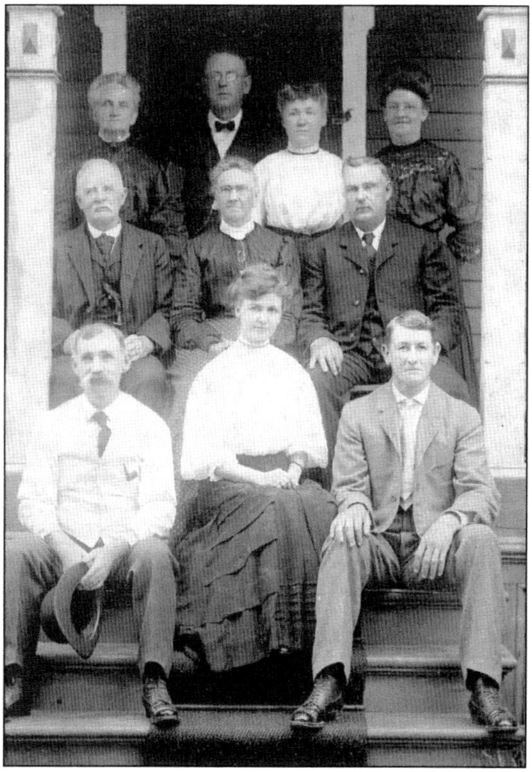

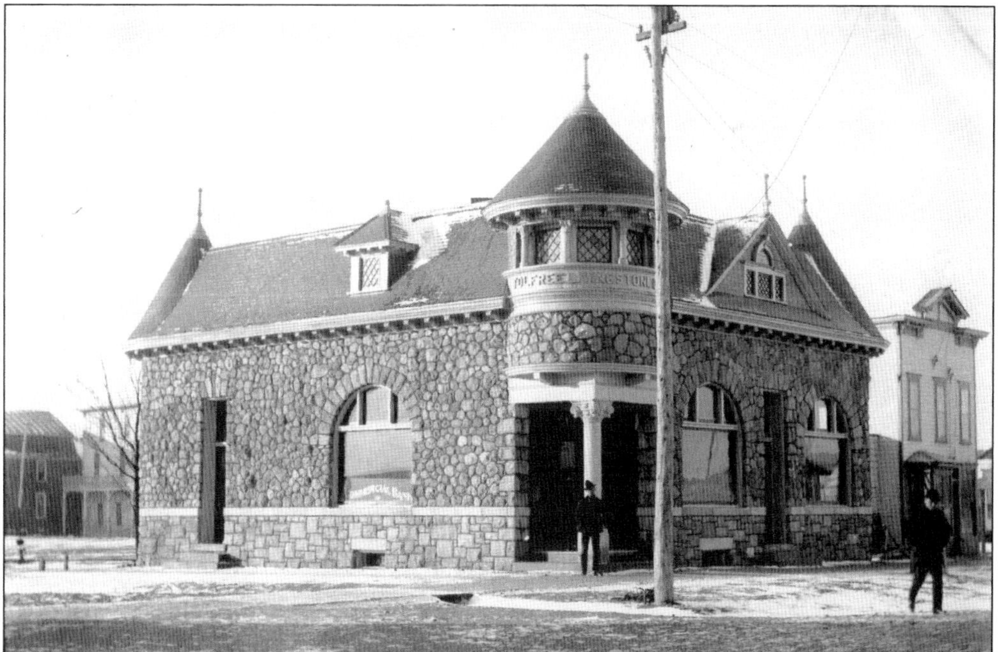

The Tolfree and Livingstone partnership erected a brick building known as the Tolfree-Livingstone Block along Houghton Avenue in 1888. Near the dawn of the 20th century, the Tolfree-Livingstone Bank building shown here was erected just to the west of the existing block.

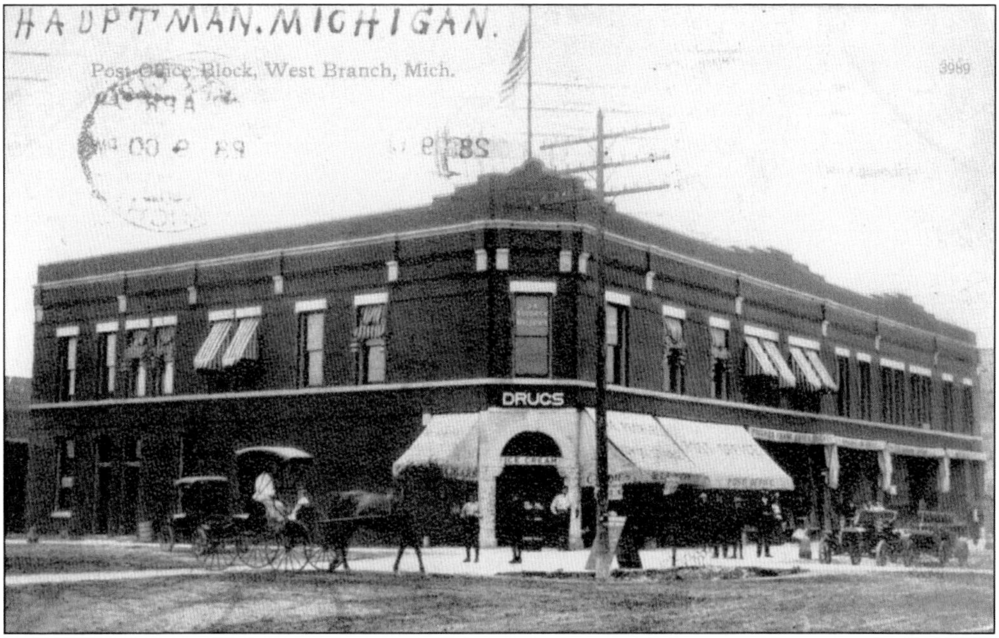

In 1881, it was believed that the area around and west of the railroad tracks would be developed first, thus the courthouse and jail were built there. Weidmann and Wright owned most of the property in that area and land sales could not be secured from them. During 1881, H. C. Ripley offered his lots east of the railroad for sale. Almost 12 blocks were built in that year. This was the closest West Branch came to a boom during the lumbering era. Here are depicted two such blocks that were rebuilt after the 1883 fire.

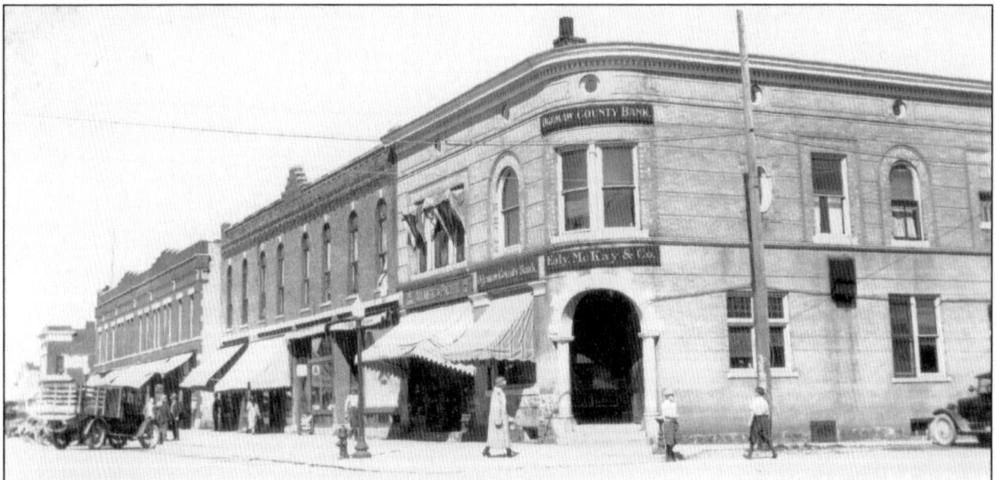

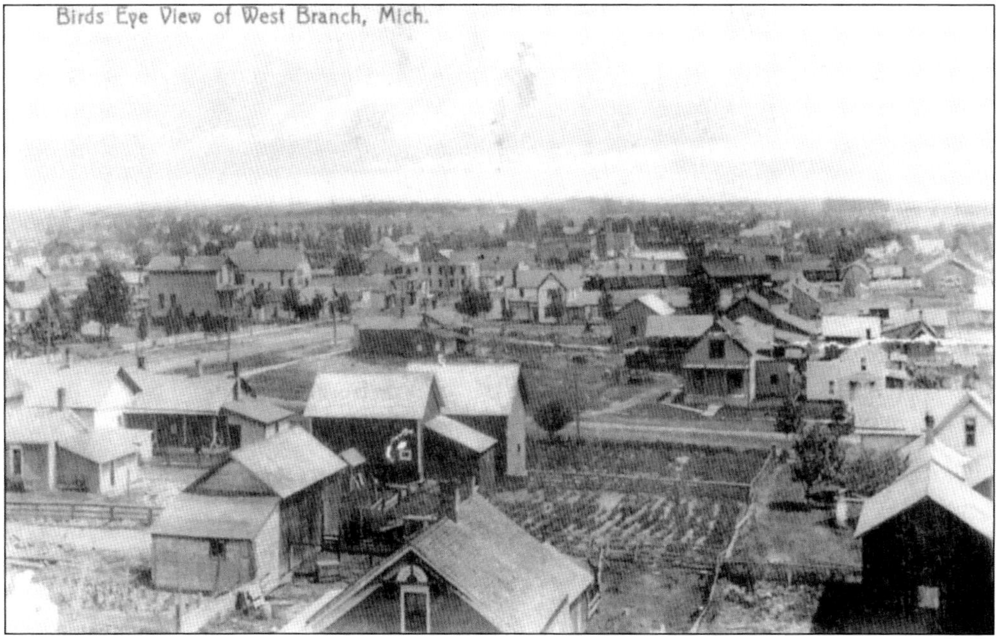

In 1876, after West Branch was named county seat, lumbermen Weidmann and Wright donated land and a building for county offices, a courtroom, and jail facilities. In 1886, improvements were suggested for the facility but before they could be made, the courthouse, jail, and sheriff's residence burned in April 1887. By late 1888, a new courthouse and jail was erected on the old foundations. This is a view from that courthouse. (Courtesy of the Ogemaw Genealogical and Historical Society.)

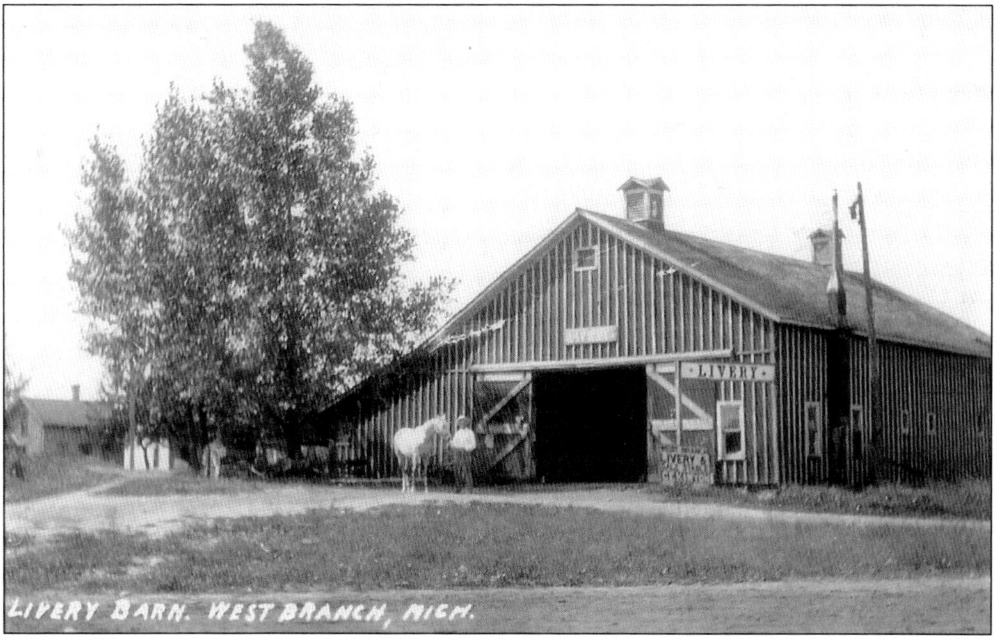

The West Branch Livery, shown here, was located on the corner of Fifth Street and Houghton Avenue, near the railroad tracks. Erected before 1900, it was run by C. E. Kinyon. (Courtesy of the Ogemaw Genealogical and Historical Society.)

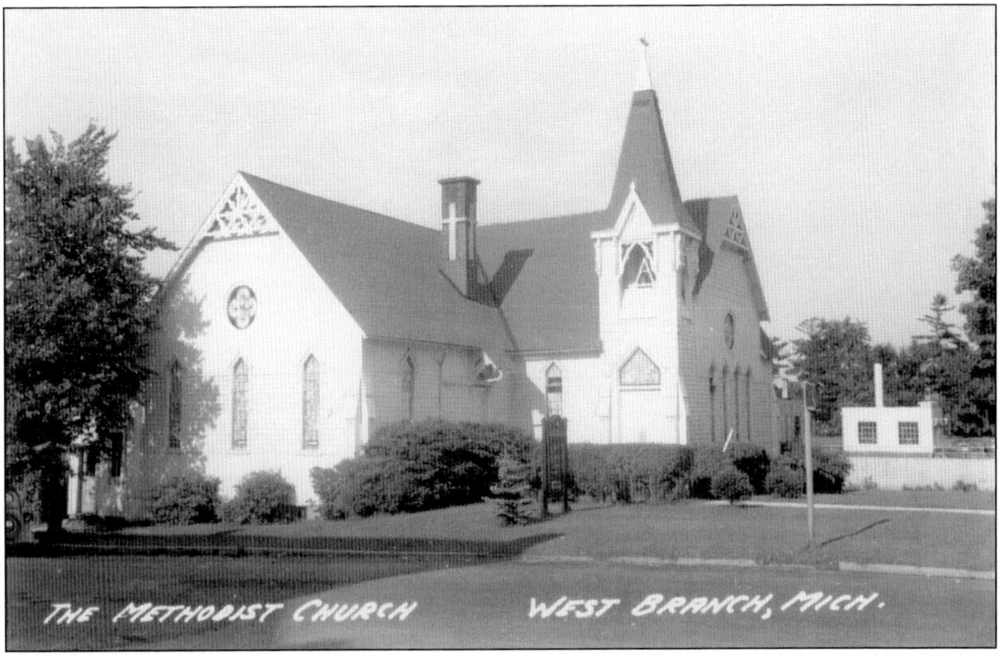

The Methodist Episcopal Church pictured above was organized in 1881 and financed by pledges. The church was erected on the corner of Houghton Avenue and Second Street on land donated by the French family. Now known as the United Methodist Church, the congregation outgrew this church and a new building was erected on the corner of Fairview and State Roads in 1966.

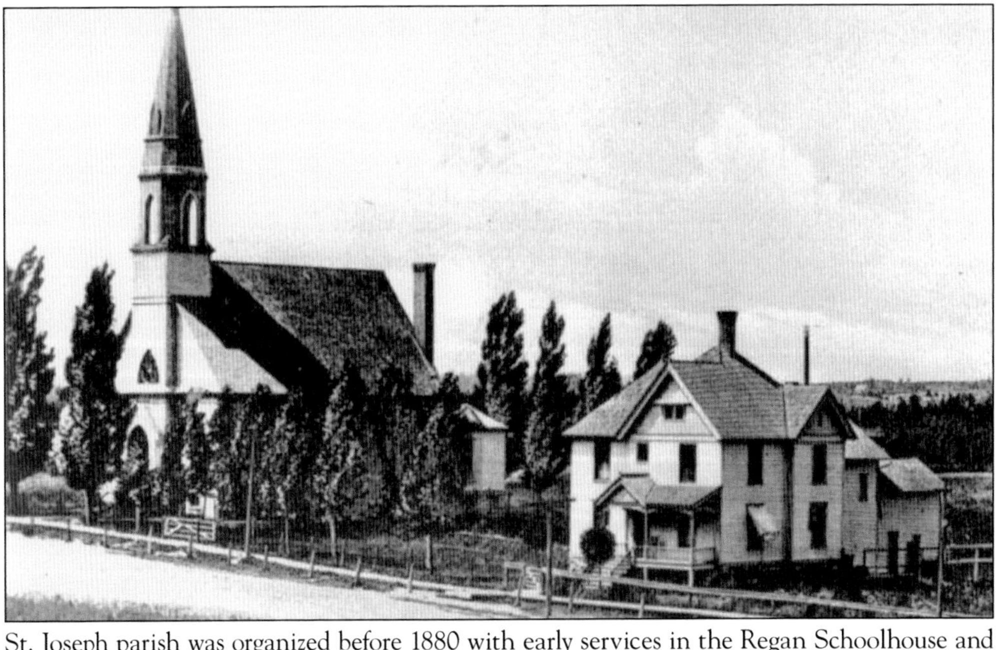

St. Joseph parish was organized before 1880 with early services in the Regan Schoolhouse and West Branch Town Hall. The St. Joseph Church was dedicated in 1891 and the adjoining rectory in 1895. Later the congregation added a school. St. Joseph Church and School, which is located on West Houghton Avenue, is now a prominent landmark in West Branch. (Courtesy of the Ogemaw Genealogical and Historical Society.)

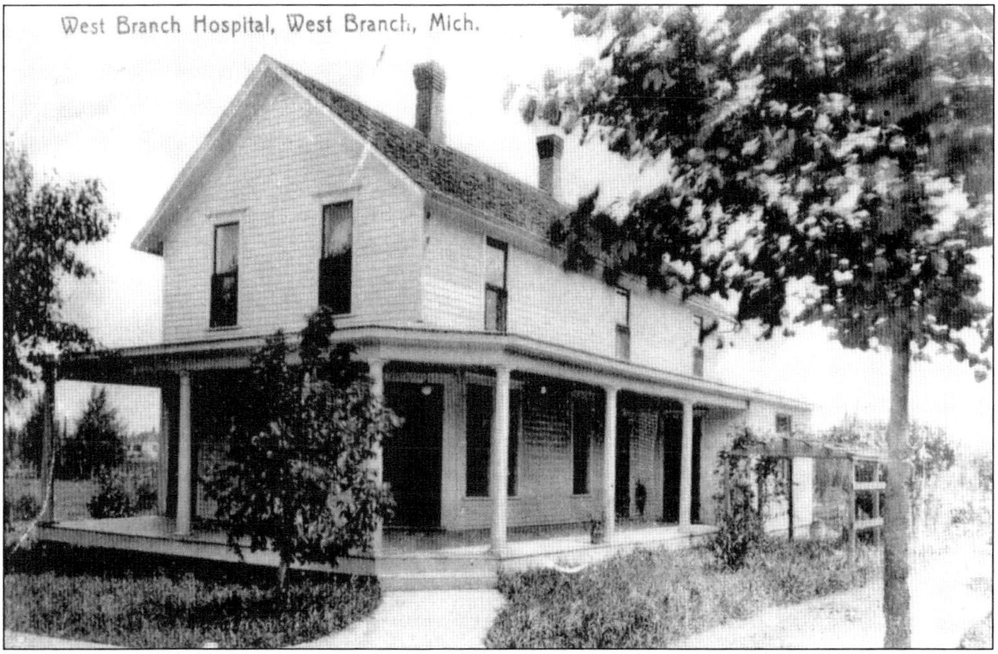

The first hospital (above) in West Branch was a refurbished home. Local doctors could administer relief to patients in a sterile atmosphere and have all the latest medical supplies at hand. The Tolfree Memorial Hospital (below) first opened its doors on December 19, 1929. John Tolfree purchased the property located on Houghton Avenue and donated it to the city. The facility, with additions, serviced the West Branch area until 1999. In 1992, 45 acres were purchased on M-30 south of town to build a larger facility. In January 1999, the new 119,000-square-foot, three-level West Branch Regional Medical Center opened its doors. An adjoining cancer center was dedicated in June 1999.

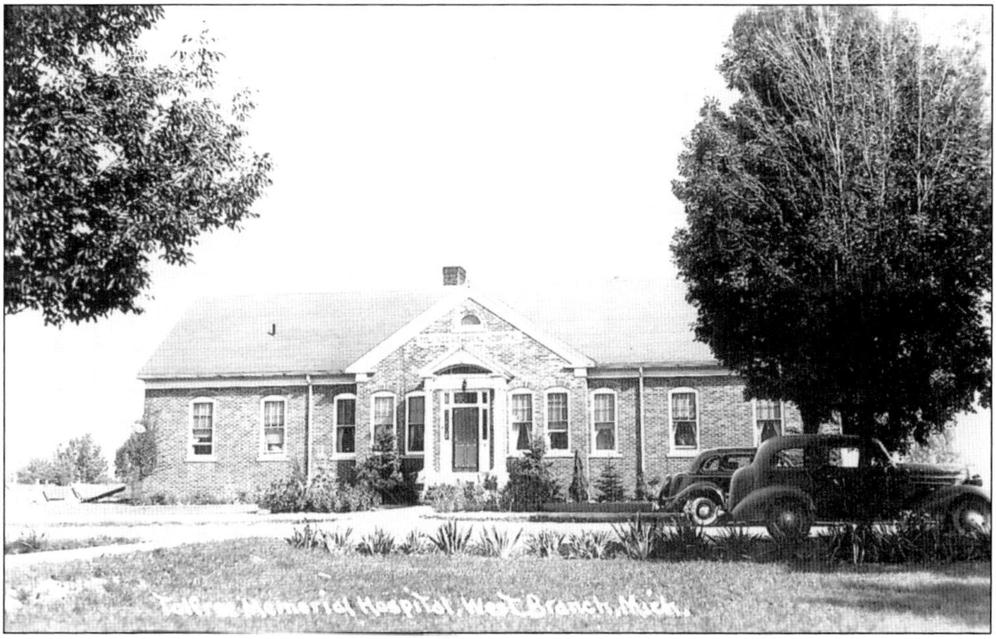

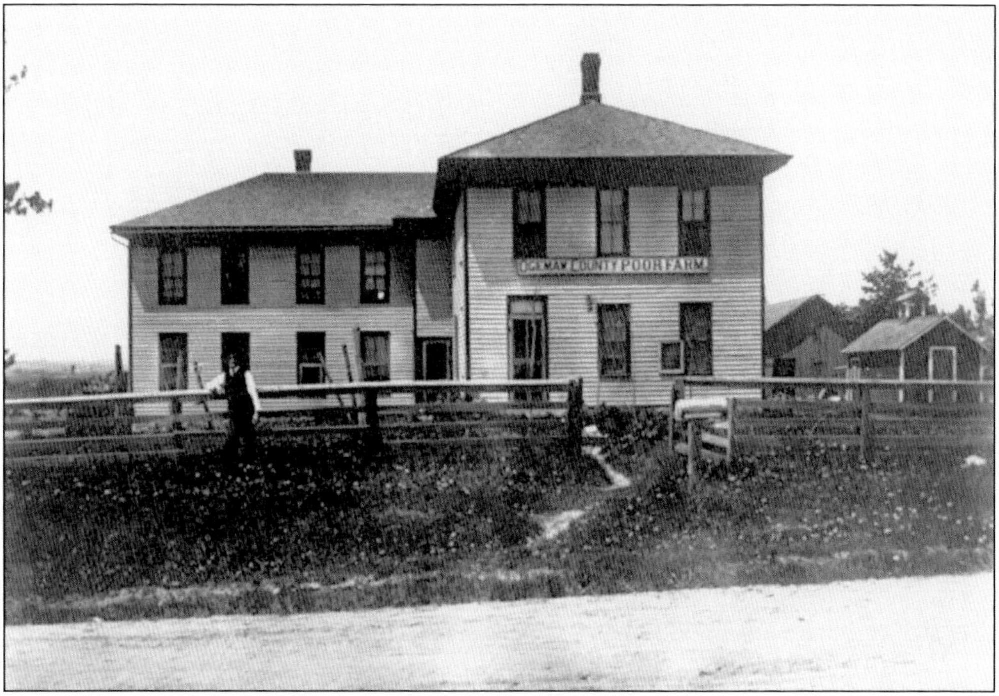

The Ogemaw County Poor Farm, pictured here, was reported to have originally been a boardinghouse in the early 1900s. John Tinning ran the first "farm," where indigent family members could live and work to earn room and board. The poor farm was located on the corner of State and Fairview Roads.

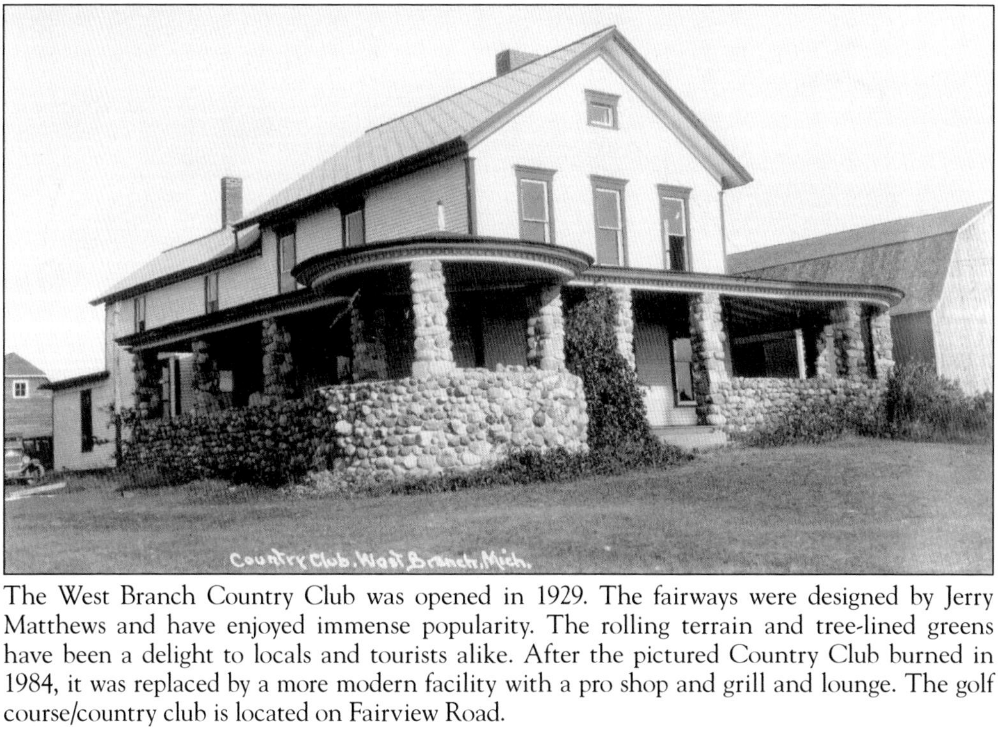

The West Branch Country Club was opened in 1929. The fairways were designed by Jerry Matthews and have enjoyed immense popularity. The rolling terrain and tree-lined greens have been a delight to locals and tourists alike. After the pictured Country Club burned in 1984, it was replaced by a more modern facility with a pro shop and grill and lounge. The golf course/country club is located on Fairview Road.

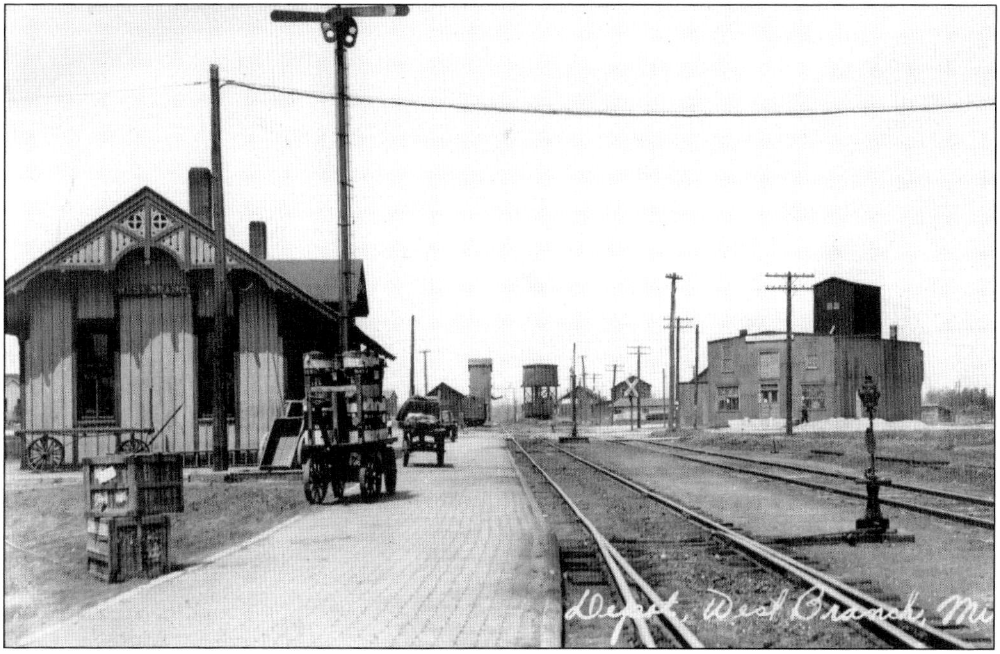

The town of West Branch was first only a rail station for the Jackson, Lansing and Saginaw Railroad. The first depot was built by the tracks in 1872. It is said that John Regan, local lumberman and later horseman, hauled the first freight load. The depot pictured above has been refurbished and now houses the local chamber of commerce and a commercial business.

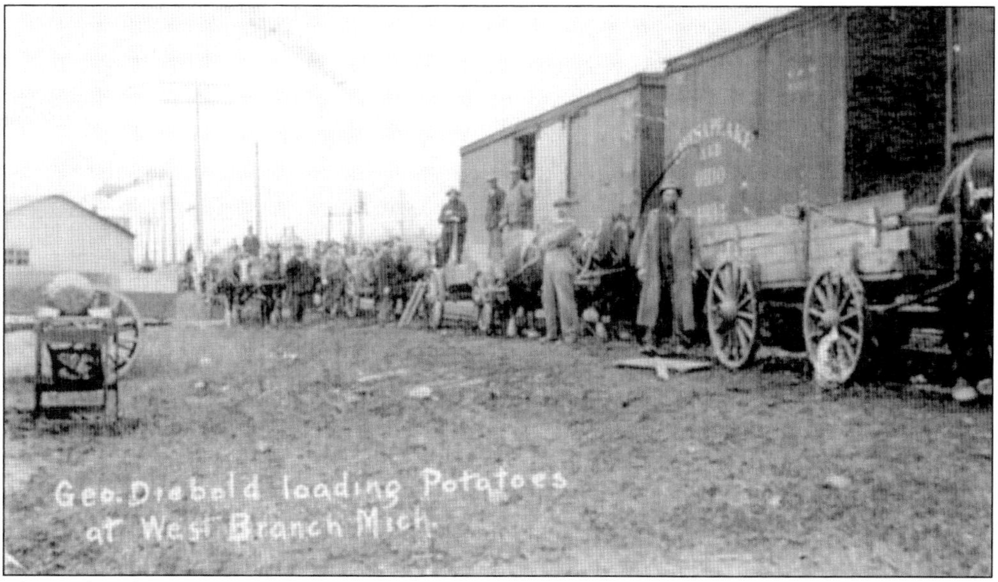

The railroad was an important factor in day-to-day life in early West Branch. Not only did the trains bring in much-needed supplies, workers, and mail, But they also took out shipments of lumber, manufactured goods, and farm products, such as these wagonloads of potatoes for George Diebold.

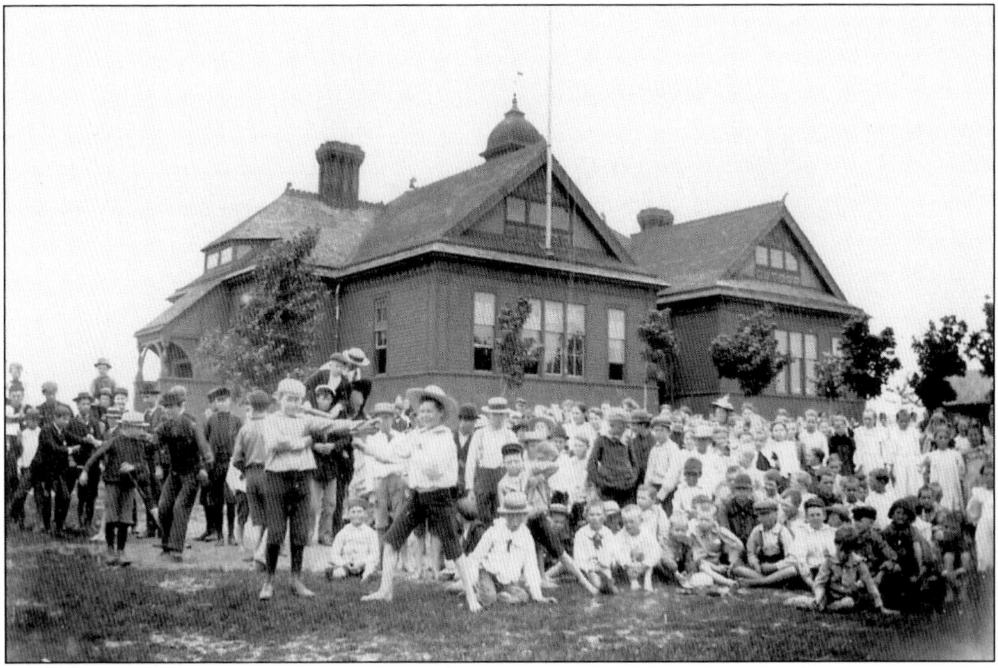

The first one-room school was built on John Tolfree's property where Steuernols is now. It boasted a maximum of 30 students. This building was moved several times and ended up on the north side of present school property on North First Street. It was finally sold to Ronald Goldy in 1955 after being used as a temporary jail, janitor's home, and kindergarten room. In 1886, a two-room frame and brick structure was erected on First Street, and in 1901 it was joined by a two-story high school. The facility is still utilized, with many additions, as Surline Elementary and Middle Schools. (Courtesy of the Ogemaw Genealogical and Historical Society.)

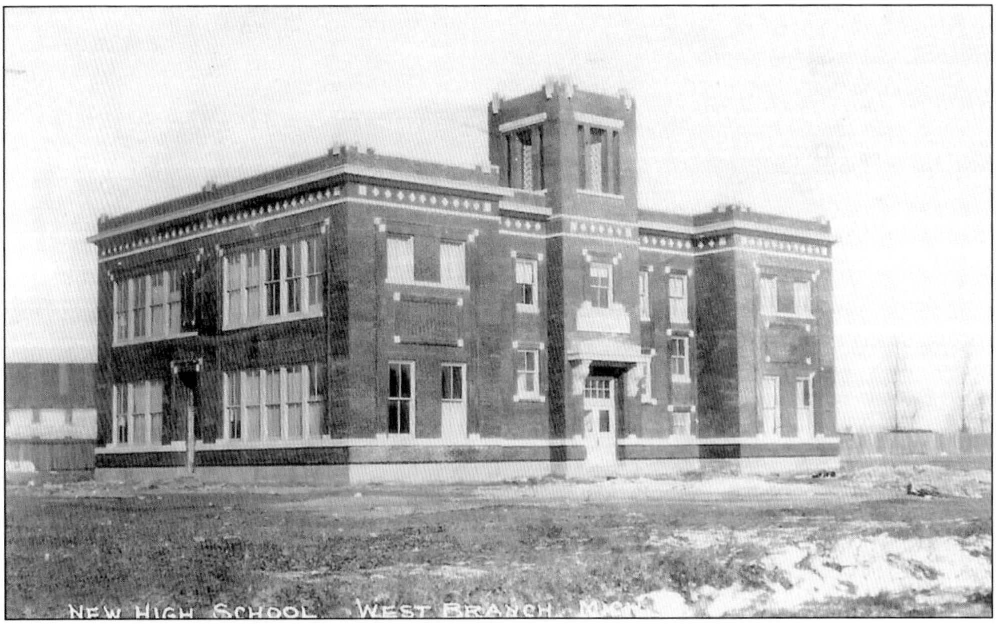

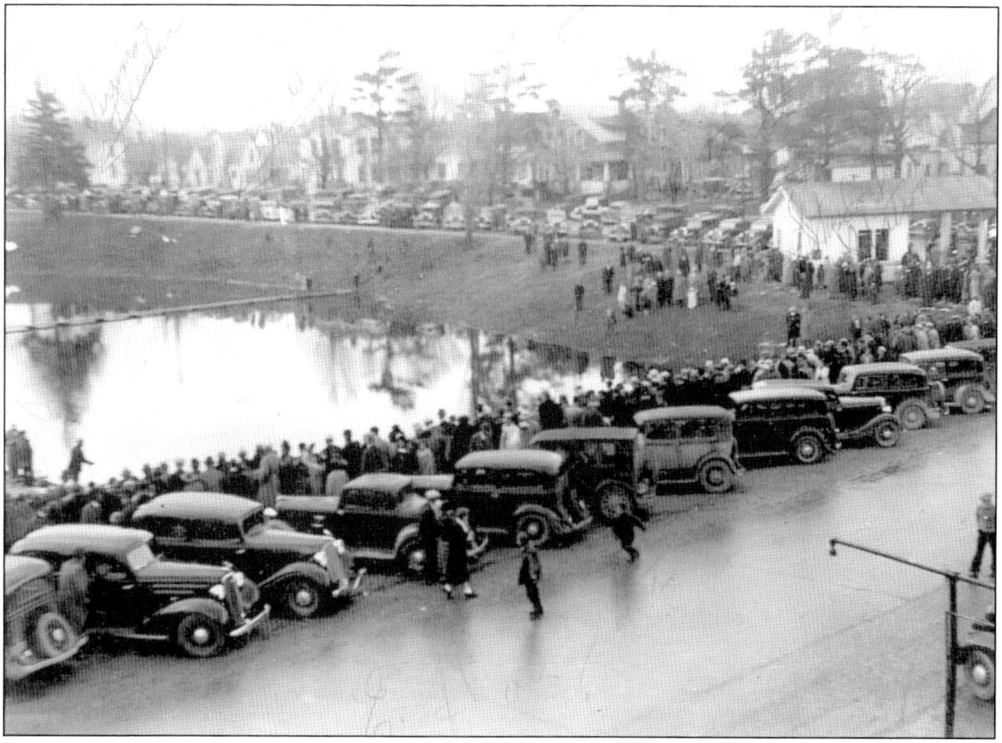

Organizers provided numerous summertime activities including the famous trout festival. The city had a stream but no pond, so a dam was erected on Weidman Creek near the corner of First Street and Houghton Avenue. The photograph above shows the resulting pond for fishing activities in 1938.

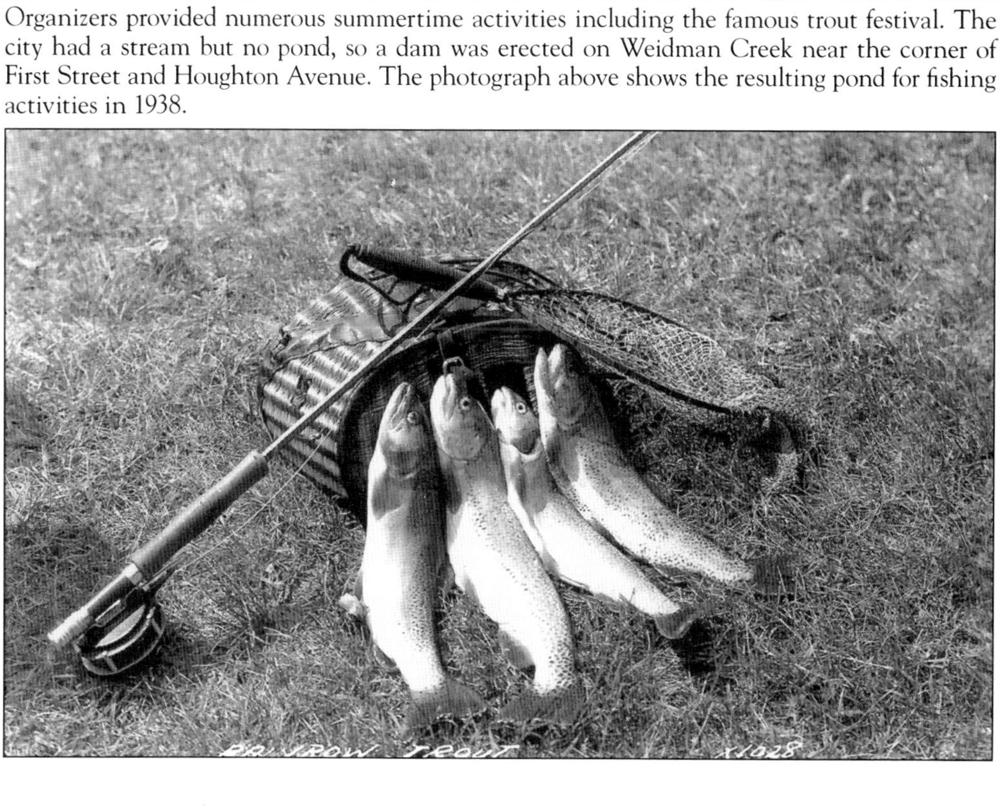

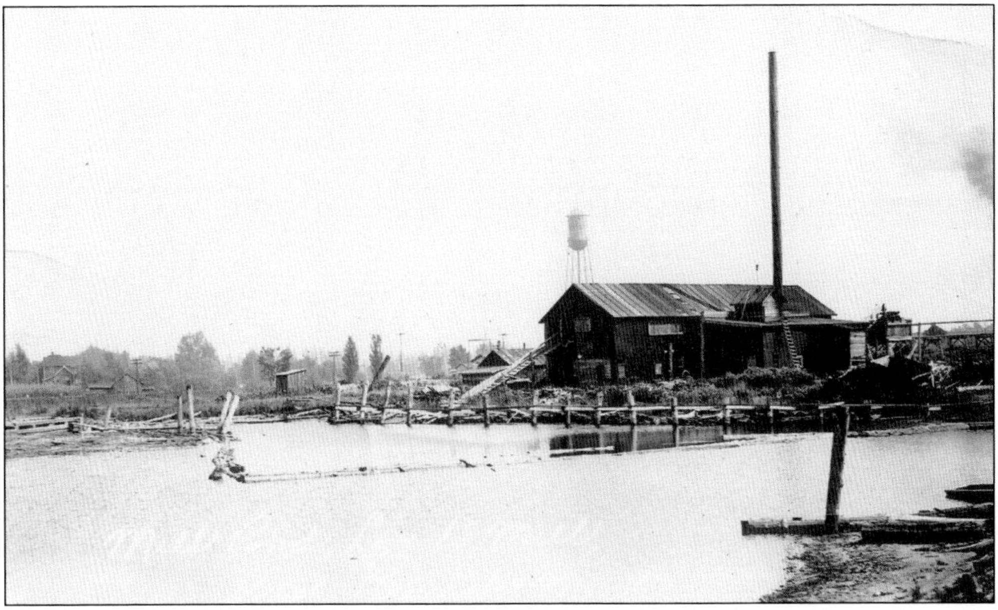

As the great timber was depleted, lumbermen turned to more refined methods. Lumber mills, where logs were sawed into specific size boards, planed, and dried, began to spring up. Water powered many of these mills, by way of waterwheels or turbines. The photograph above is of the Loud Mill just north of West Branch. Note the water tower in the distance. Below, the Cline Mill boasted a crew of 40 men and production of 40,000 to 50,000 feet a day. The West Branch Flouring Mill can be seen on the left. William Hisey began his flouring enterprise here in 1883 and, after a few failures, produced 50 barrels of high-quality flour a day. The four-story mill is still in use today and is one of West Branch's oldest businesses. (Courtesy of the Ogemaw Genealogical and Historical Society.)

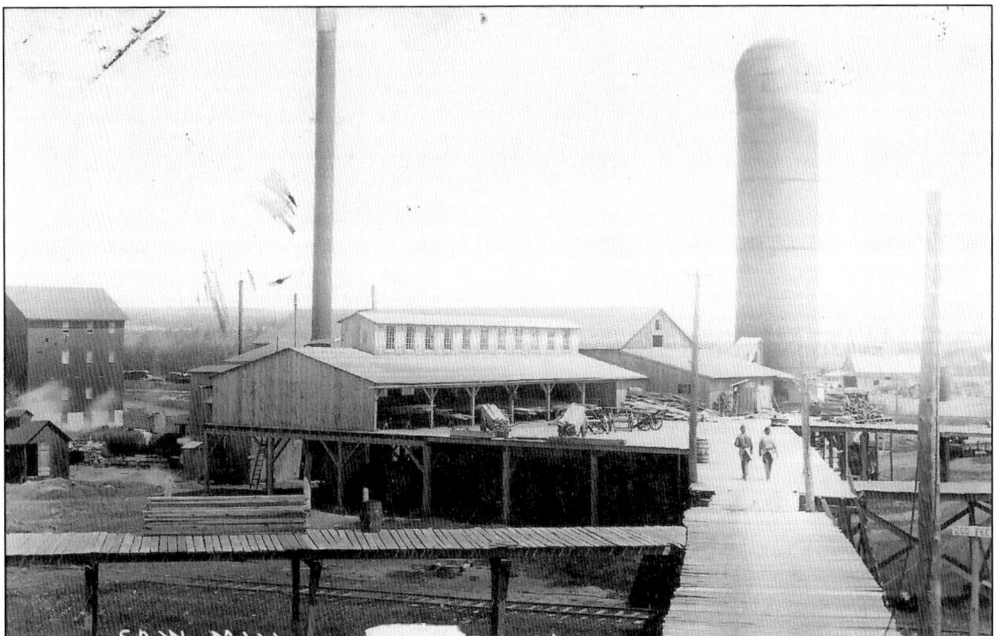

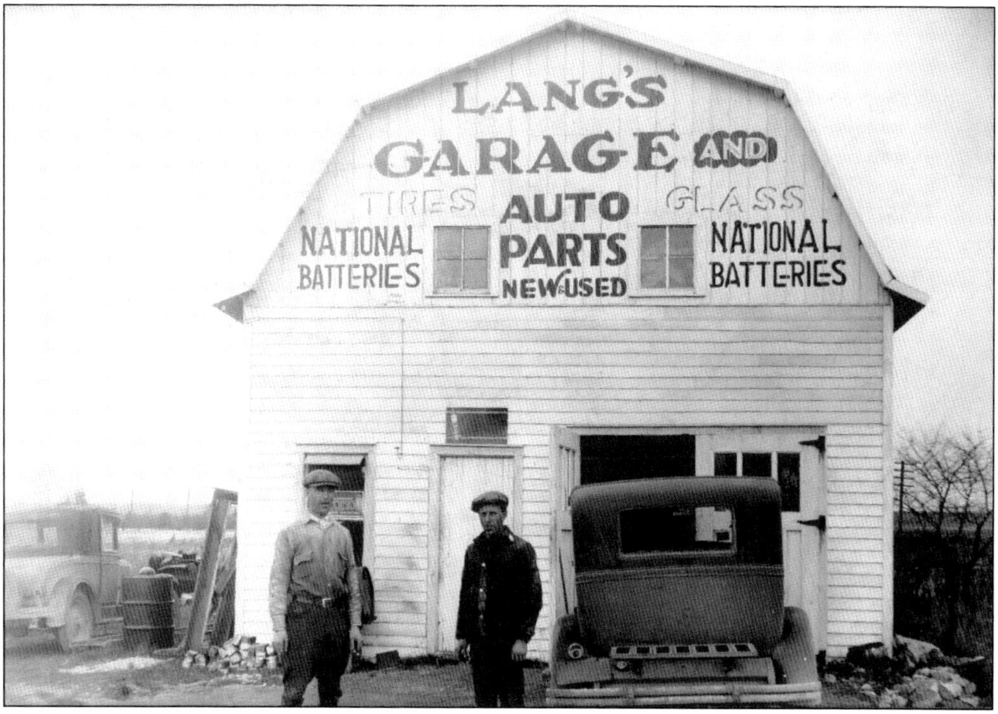

As automobiles replaced horses, mechanic's garages began to appear. This garage, run by Albert and Ed Lang, was situated on Valley and State Streets in 1928. (Courtesy of Bruce Reetz.)

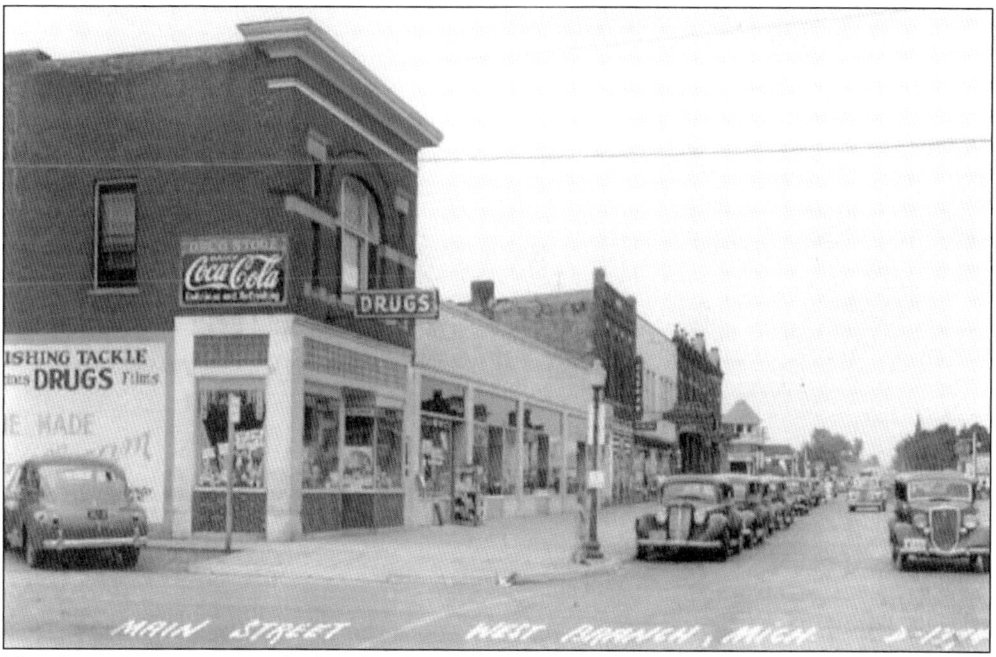

Houghton Avenue was packed with vehicles in this late 1930s photograph. The 100-foot-wide easement has allowed for modern roadway construction and parallel parking. Note that although some buildings have changed, Victorian West Branch was in evidence even then.

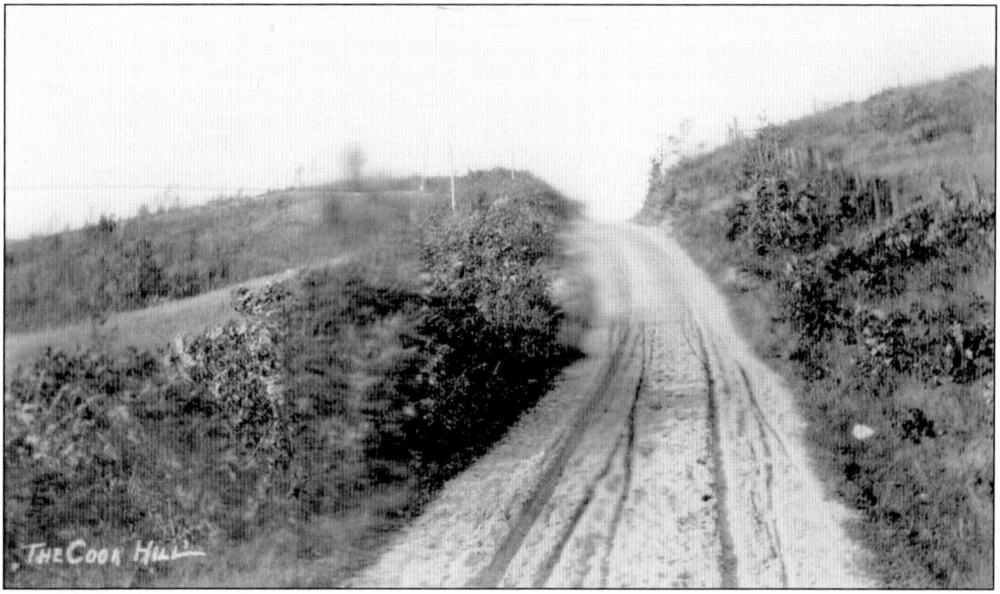

Cook Hill is seen in 1913. A single track is rutted through the sand. The lumbermen have left a sad, desolate view. Today Cook Hill has become a center of activity with shopping centers, restaurants, gas stations, and hotels.

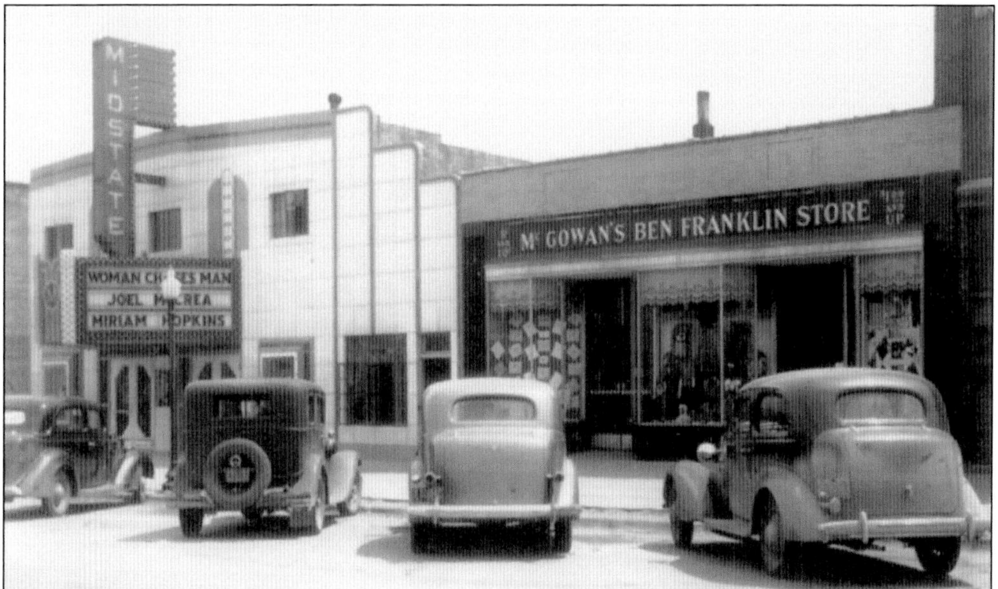

Business was booming along Houghton Avenue with the addition of the Midstate Theater and McGowan's Ben Franklin Store. The theater was a popular place to go for a night at the movies and is still entertaining locals today. The dime store, where farm wives purchased everything from pots and pans to sewing goods, is now closed. (Courtesy of the Ogemaw Genealogical and Historical Society.)

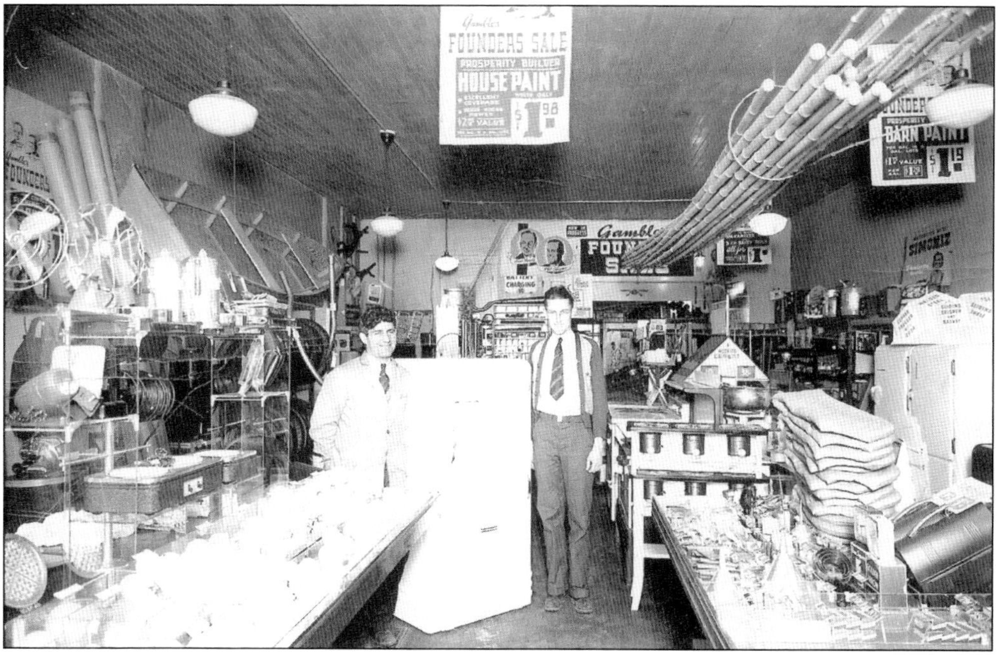

This 1938 photograph shows Stuart Scott (left) and Raymond Yantz pictured inside Scotts Gamble Store on West Houghton Avenue. The store opened in 1937, but moved several times before settling in its final location on the corner of Houghton Avenue and Fourth Street. Stuart Scott died in 1972, leaving the business to son Milford. (Courtesy of the Milford Scott family.)

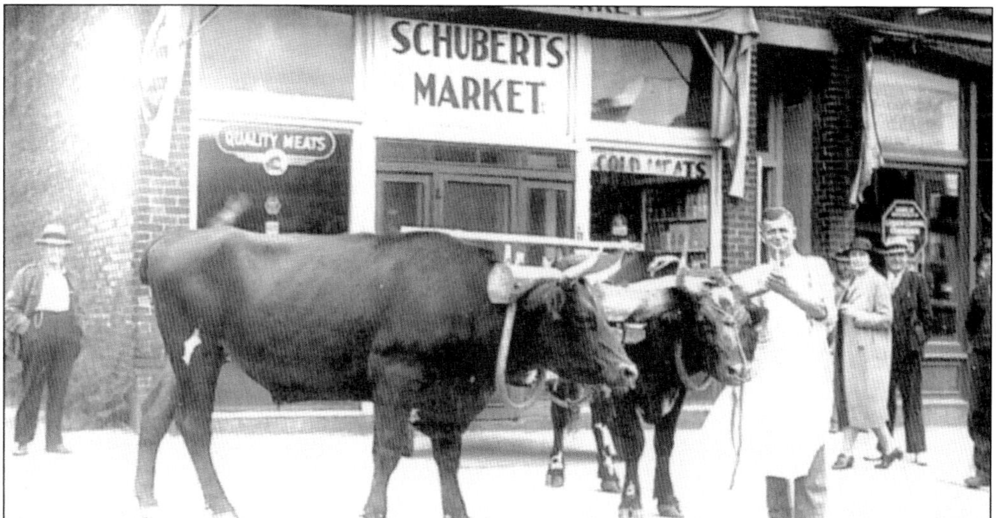

Schubert's Market, owned by Harry Schubert, was located on Houghton Avenue. After his death in 1946, his sons Bob and Russ took over operations. When Schubert's promised fresh meat, they meant fresh meat!

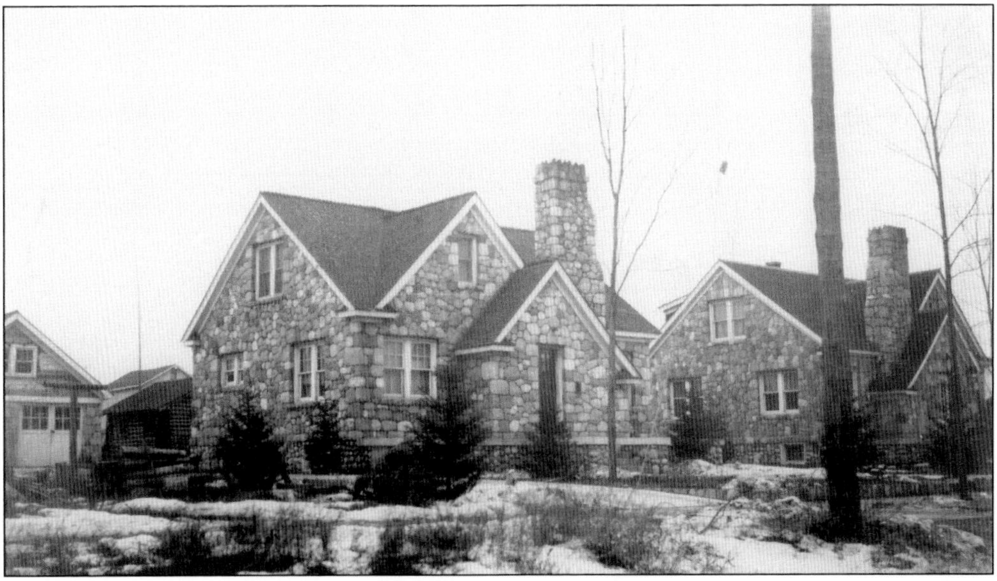

As with other areas of Ogemaw County, West Branch builders found the abundance of glacial rock to their advantage. Beautiful stone-faced homes abound in the area. The houses pictured above were built by the Weiler brothers in the 1930s. The home on the left is now the location of the Ogemaw County Genealogical and Historical Society's Museum.

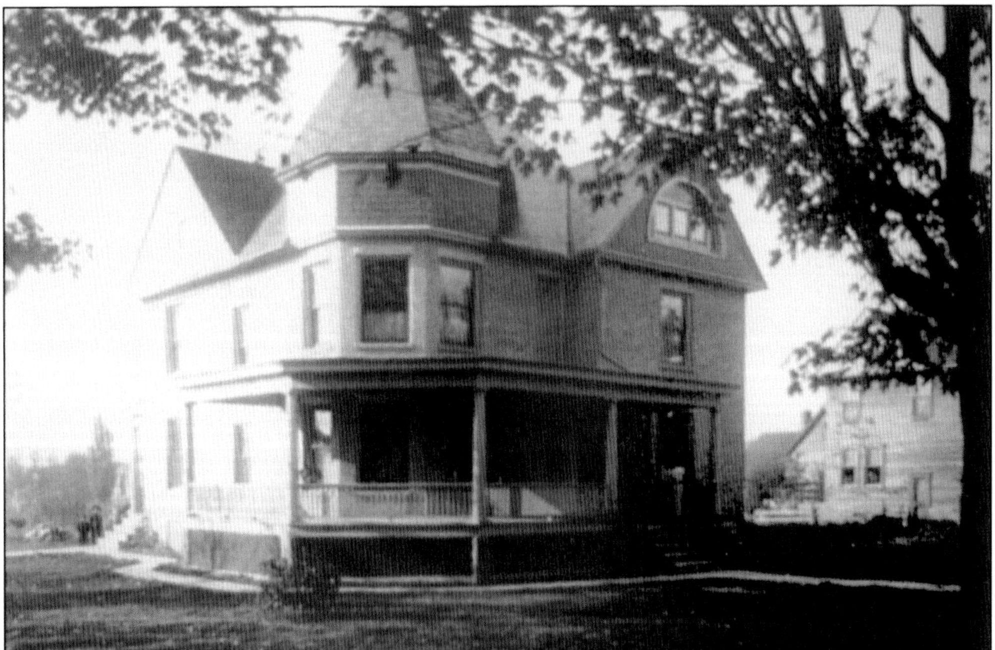

Probably one of the most graceful homes along Houghton Avenue is the Frank Sebastian Smith home now known as the Rose Brick Inn. The home, built between 1906 and 1909, has been restored and opened as a bed-and-breakfast inn in 1988.

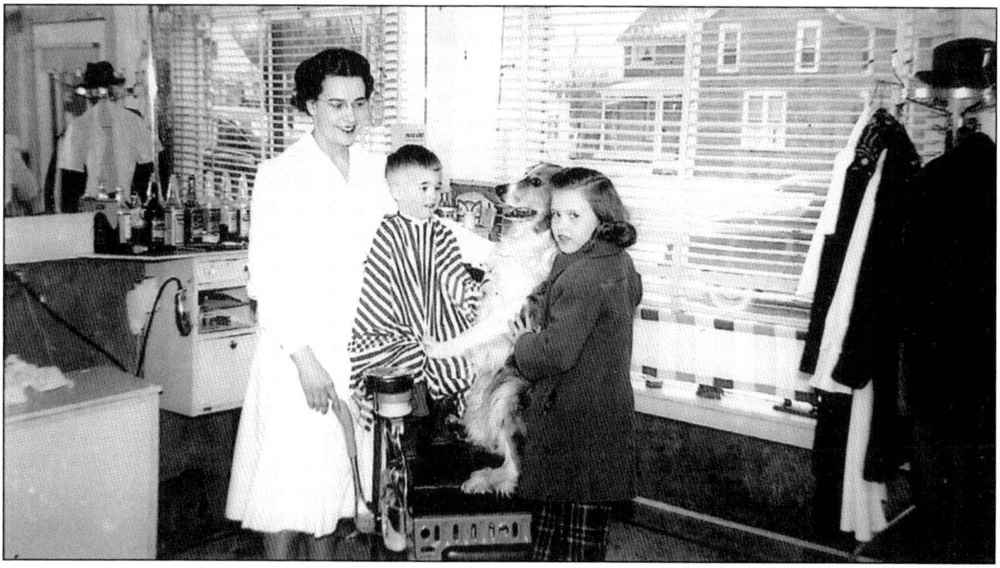

After graduating, Hazel Fach Needham, pictured above, wanted to become a barber. Jim Myas, a West Branch barber, agreed to take her on as an apprentice in 1934. Needham got her license in 1936 and in 1940 she opened her shop. She moved across the street in 1978 to the site on Houghton Avenue, which is still operated by her son Dan. Parliament's Drug Store (below) was begun by Burt Parliament after World War I. It was later purchased by Loren Parliament in 1946. (Above, courtesy of Mary and Gene Densmore; below, courtesy of the Ogemaw Genealogical and Historical Society.)

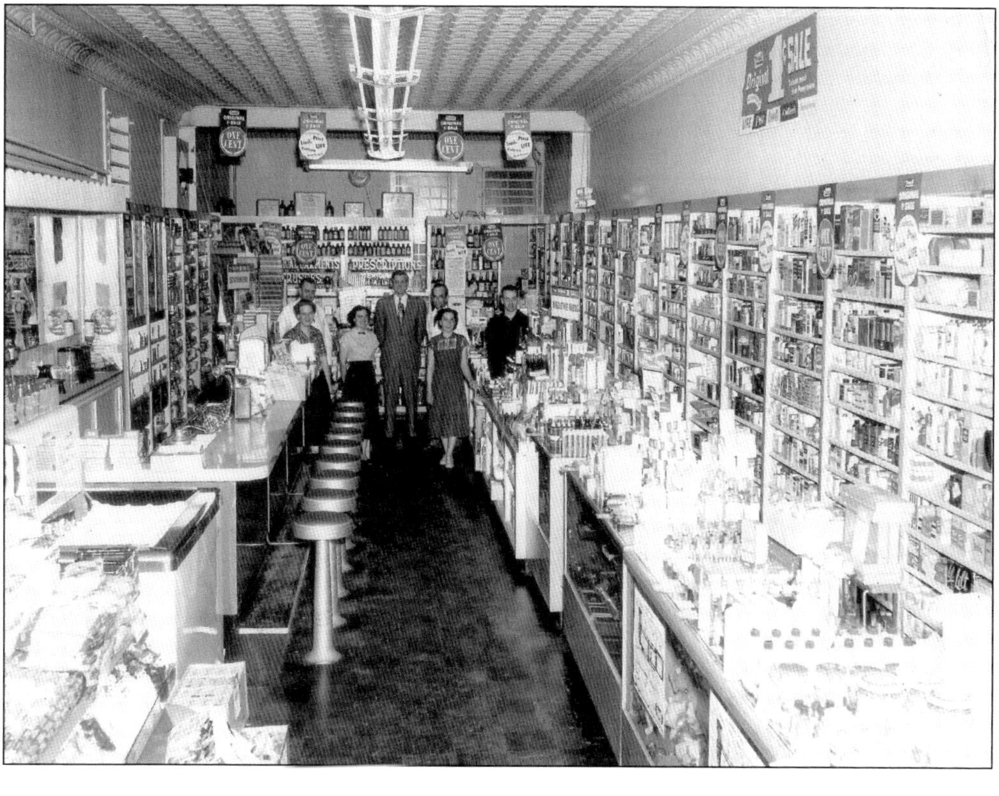

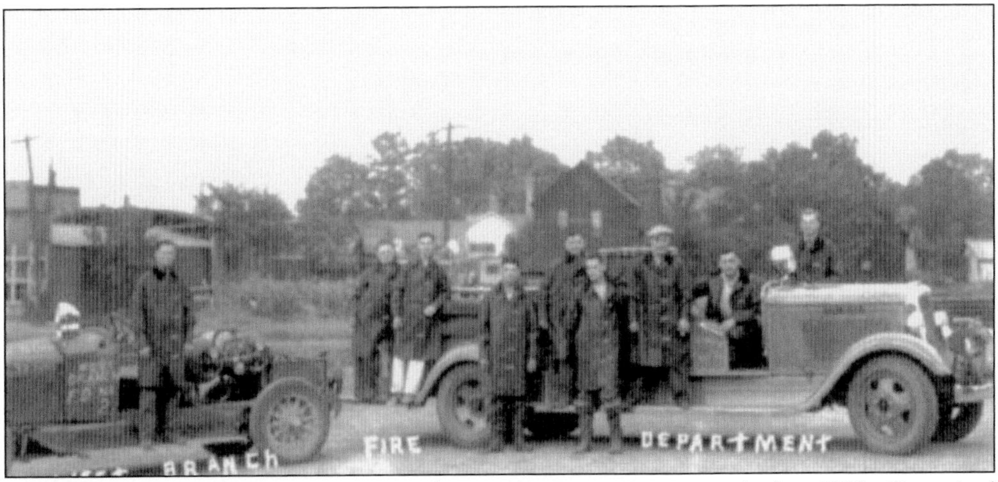

The West Branch Fire Department poses here with new equipment in the late 1930s. Organized at the dawn of the 20th century, volunteers saved many homes from destruction by fire. Sun-dried cedar shakes on roofs made easy tinder for sparks that might fly from the chimney, and the fire call could be heard almost daily. Fire is still a problem in buildings unprotected by firewalls and dry with age.

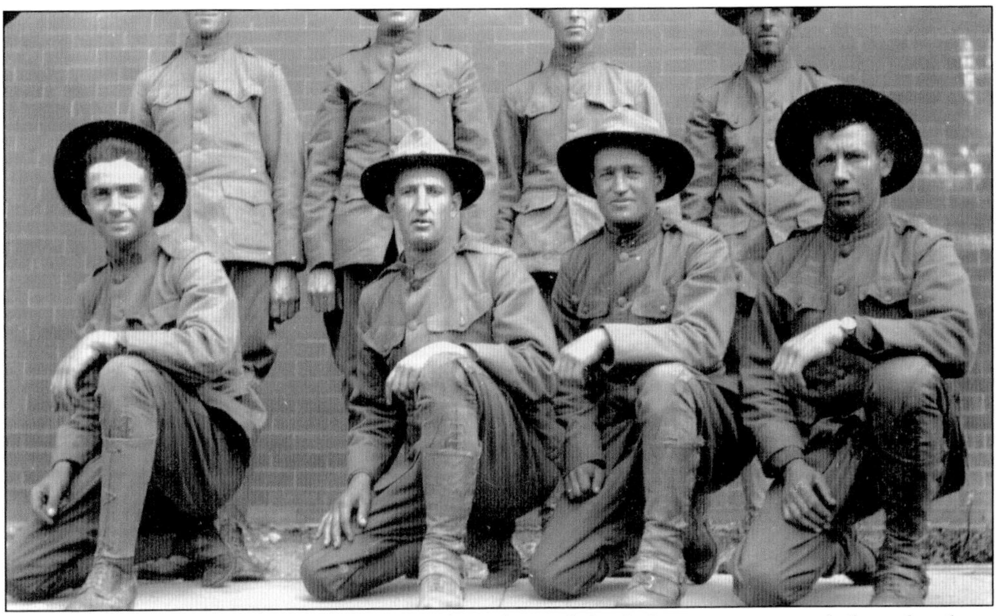

Local men and women have always stood ready to defend their country and their freedom. Civil War soldiers came with land grants in hand and monuments in local cemeteries attest to their numbers. Many wars have been fought since the 1860s, and West Branch natives still stand proudly to serve. Pictured here is one group of West Branch area World War I volunteers, including members of the Polar Bear Unit.

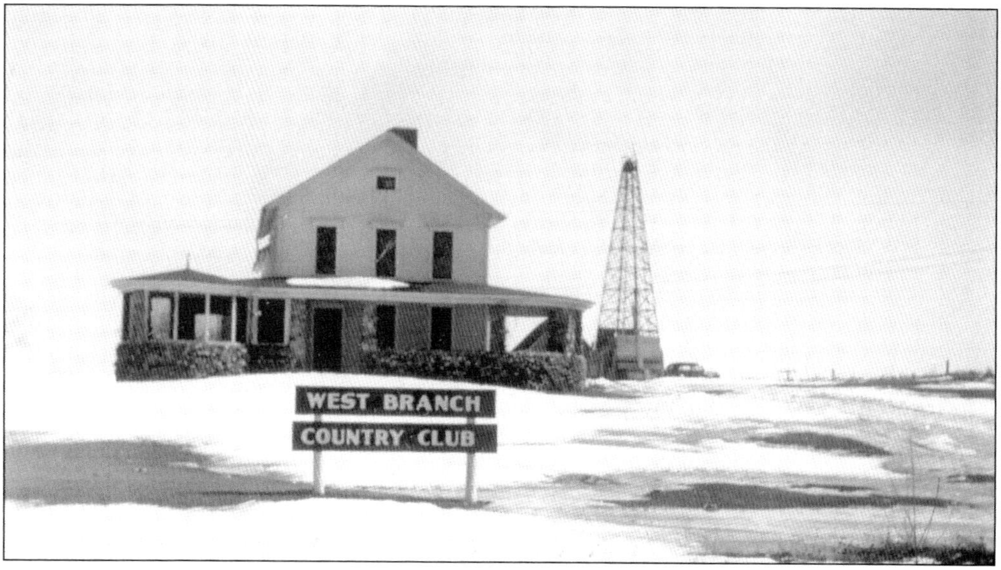

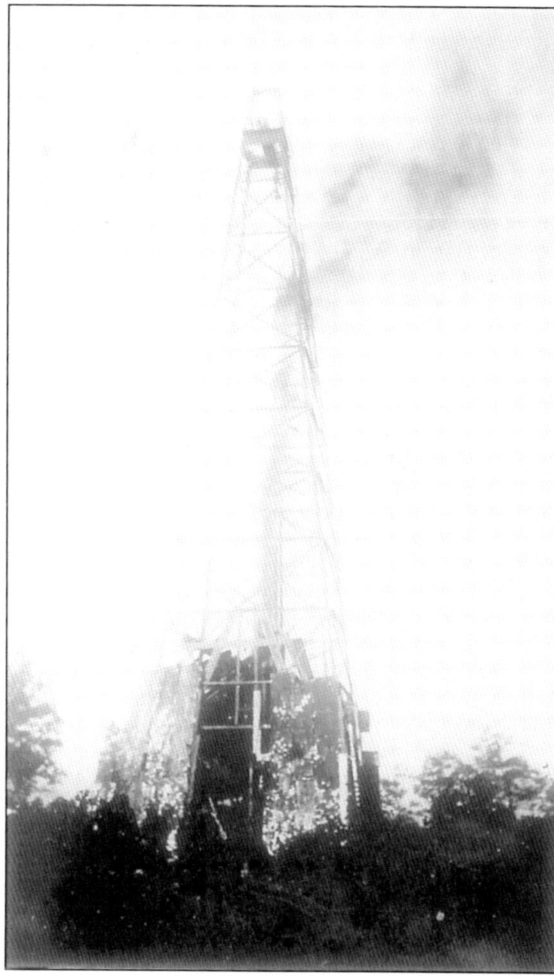

As the Depression era took its toll and area banks closed, oil companies began to appear and the oil boom was on. From the early to mid-1930s, a great influx of oil field workers was seen. Wages of 50¢ an hour took a healthy jump and oil derricks appeared in the most unusual places. Pictured above is the West Branch Country Club on Fairview Road. The building has since burned and been replaced, but oil paraphernalia remains. At right, a local oil well comes in with a black cloud in the sky. (Courtesy of the Ogemaw Genealogical and Historical Society.)

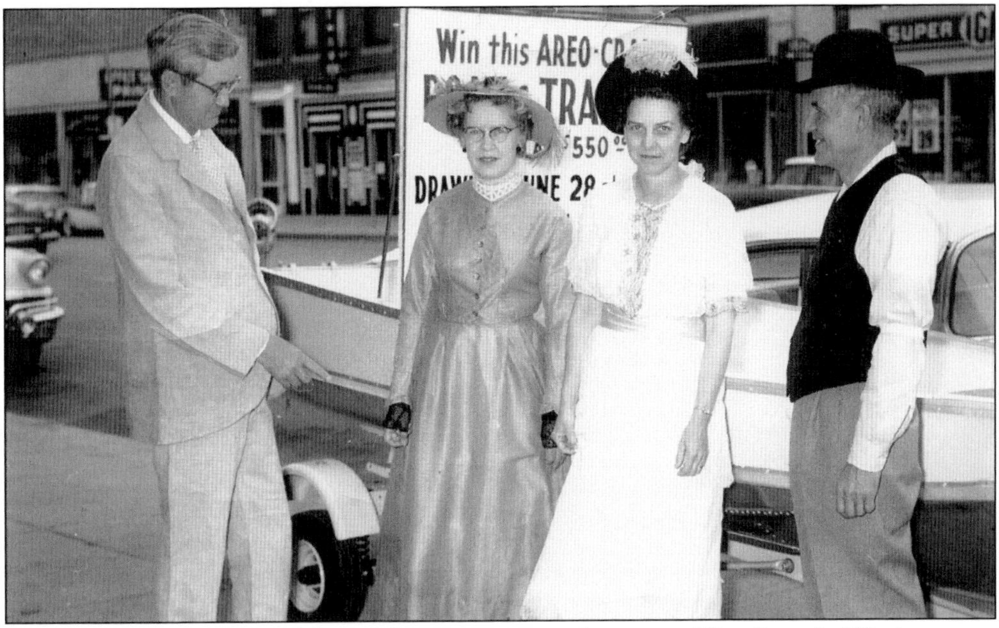

Old-Fashioned Days were celebrated for many years in downtown West Branch. Windows were dressed appropriately and merchants donned their old-fashioned best. Merchandise was displayed on tables on the sidewalks and there were sales galore. Pictured here are, from left to right, Ed and Frances Gould and Cleo and Stuart Scott. The Scotts owned Scott's Hardware and the Goulds managed the Gould Drug Store, which opened in 1939. (Courtesy of the Milford Scott family.)

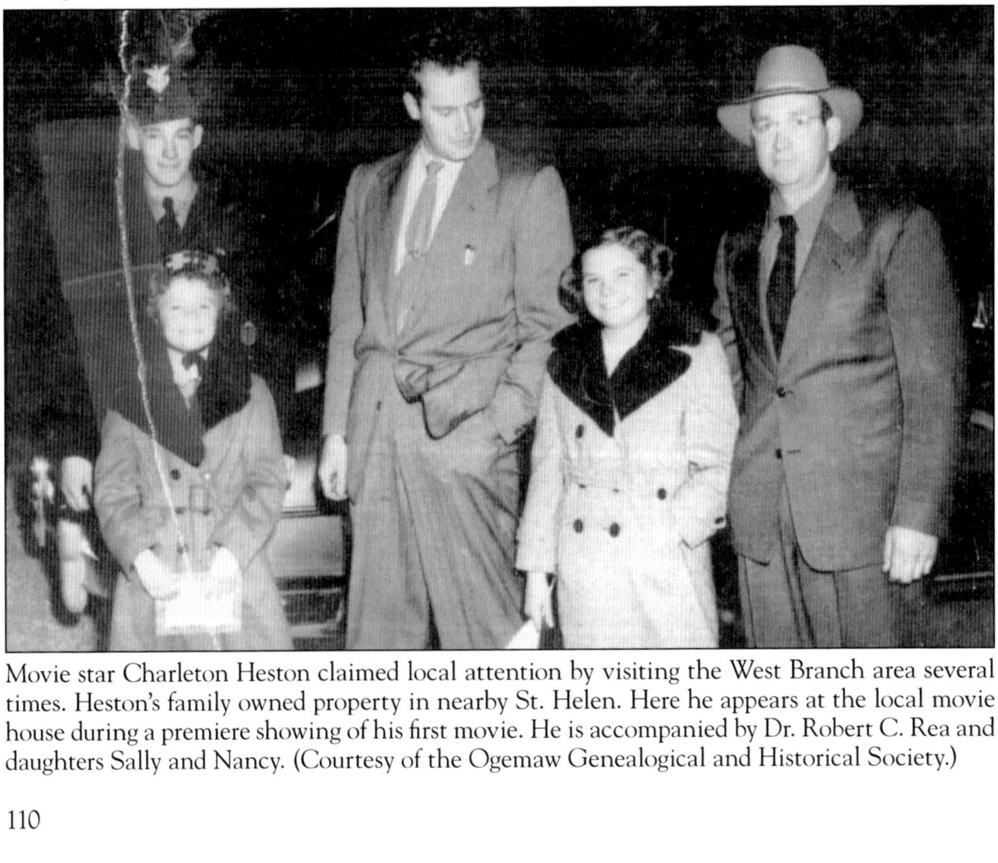

Movie star Charleton Heston claimed local attention by visiting the West Branch area several times. Heston's family owned property in nearby St. Helen. Here he appears at the local movie house during a premiere showing of his first movie. He is accompanied by Dr. Robert C. Rea and daughters Sally and Nancy. (Courtesy of the Ogemaw Genealogical and Historical Society.)

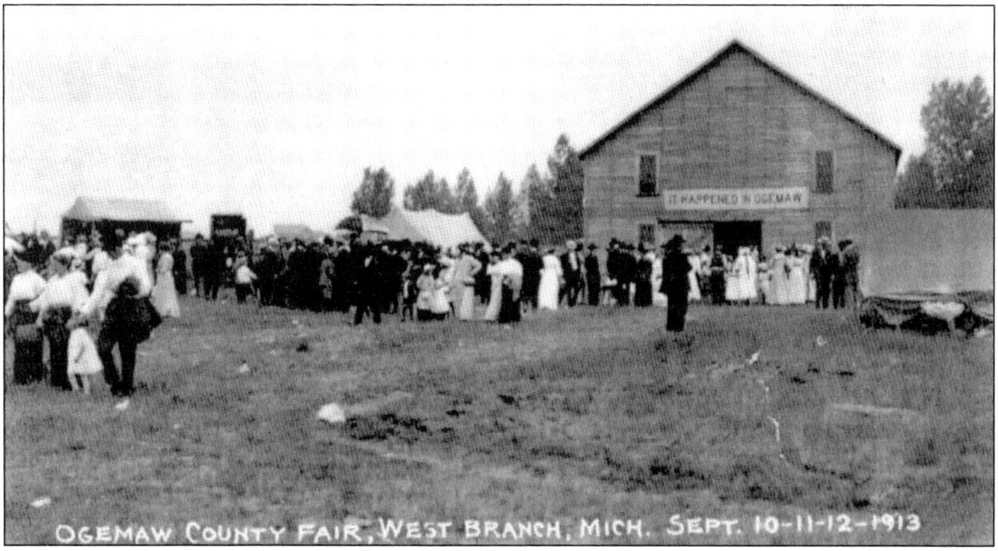

The Ogemaw County Agricultural Society was organized in 1885. The society purchased 20 acres north of West Branch on Fairview Road and held the county fair there. The event of the year was to spend the day at the fairgrounds. Pictured above is a postcard titled "It Happened in Ogemaw," dated September 10, 11, and 12, 1913. Eventually, the 20 acres of land was not enough on which to promote area agriculture, so the agricultural society purchased a large tract on Rifle River Trail, south of M-55 and east of West Branch. The grounds have been improved over the years and Ogemaw now boasts one of the best fairs in the state. Pictured below is the West Branch Livestock Yard, which now utilizes the original 20 acres owned by the agricultural society.

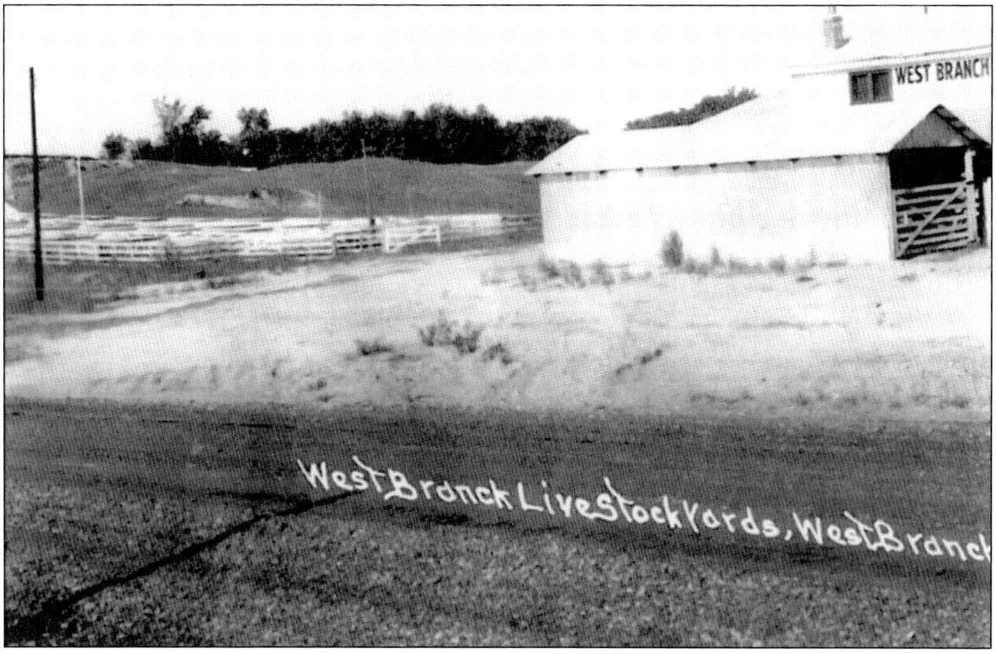

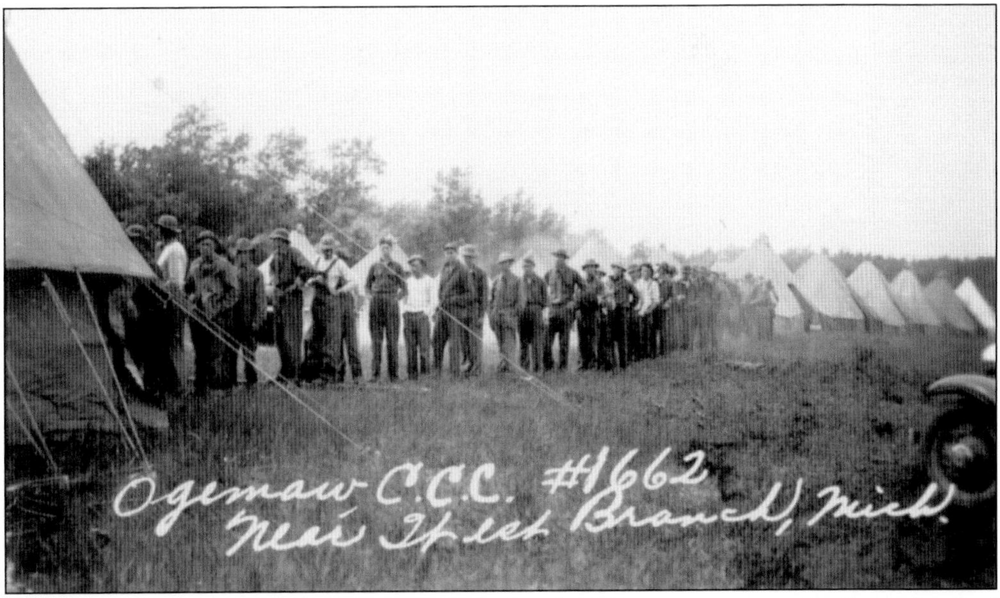

In 1914, the Ogemaw State Forest was established and 4,160 acres were set aside. Forest fires had taken their toll and reforestation had not taken place naturally. Under the direction of forestry superintendent Grover Zettle, fire towers, headquarters buildings, roads, and communications plans were formed. By 1930, the Ogemaw State Forest had grown to 255,340 acres in Ogemaw, Roscommon, Gladwin, and Arenac Counties. In March 1933, Pres. Franklin D. Roosevelt laid out a plan for a Civilian Conservation Corps (CCC), which would provide employment for the nation's youth and income for their families. CCC Company 1662 was organized in July 1933, and was assigned to Camp Ogemaw, near Ambrose Lake. The CCC boys greatly advanced reforestation and firefighting efforts before the camp closed in 1942. Below is pictured the Ogemaw Game Refuge near Clear Lake. Families have enjoyed animals there for many years.

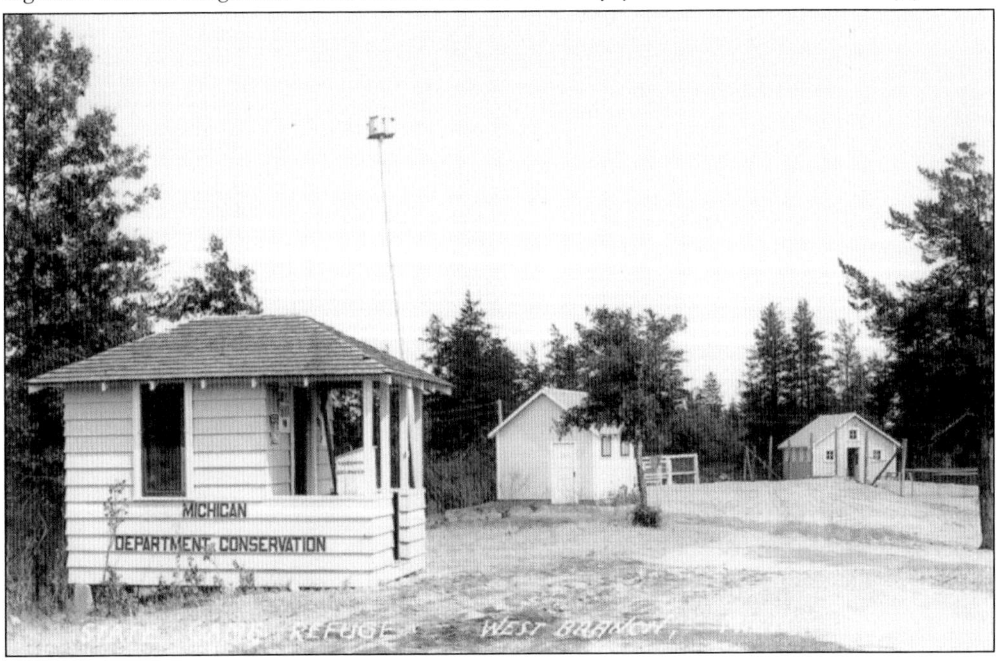

Seven

Gone but Not Forgotten

Because the lumber camps depended upon the fine timber that was found in this county, many small settlements grew quickly but disappeared as the lumber was removed. Some settlements were just a speck in time and little is known about them. Few photographs remain. The following images were taken in Ogemaw County, but not necessarily of the specific area mentioned, unless otherwise noted. The little settlements were very important to the area's history. Many are still known by their original names, such as Nester Corners, Greewood, Ogemaw Springs, Damon, and Campbell Corners, as well as others. The names are still recognized today, although their buildings have all but disappeared. Others remain only as a name on an old plat map or in the minds of some older citizens.

Most of the settlements consisted of a mill or two, lodging for the lumbermen, and perhaps a post office. Some were large settlements like Ogemaw Springs, which at one time consisted of several saloons, a church, school, general store, and several grocery stores. In 1880, Beaver Lake was said to be the largest settlement in the county. Beaver Lake bragged of three hotels, several general stores, a drugstore, many saloons, a blacksmith shop, a church, and a school. Damon was once a bustling town and a hub for supplies to the lumber camps as far away as Roscommon and McKinley. Damon is now called the lost city, having been given that title in James Oliver Curwood's book *Green Timbers*. Damon is no more lost than any other place in this chapter.

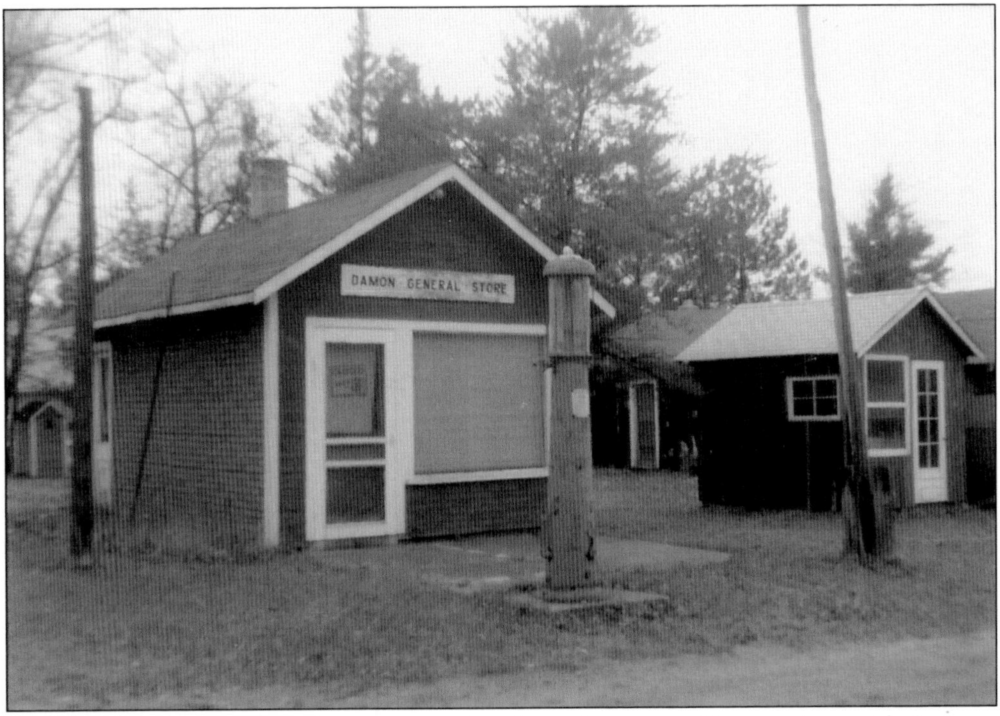

Once a thriving community, Damon is now listed as a ghost town. Damon, along with Ogemaw Springs and Piper, was one of the earliest settlements in Ogemaw County. When the timber was removed, the area reverted to the State of Michigan for nonpayment of taxes. Although some pioneer farmers tried to raise crops in the area, the sandy, infertile soil soon was abandoned. The area today is mostly state and national forest land, with summer cabins and a few permanent dwellings. The above photograph depicts all that remains of the city of Damon. The cabin below was a home on nearby Turney Ranch Road. The cabin shows what the homes in the area looked like during the lumbering era.

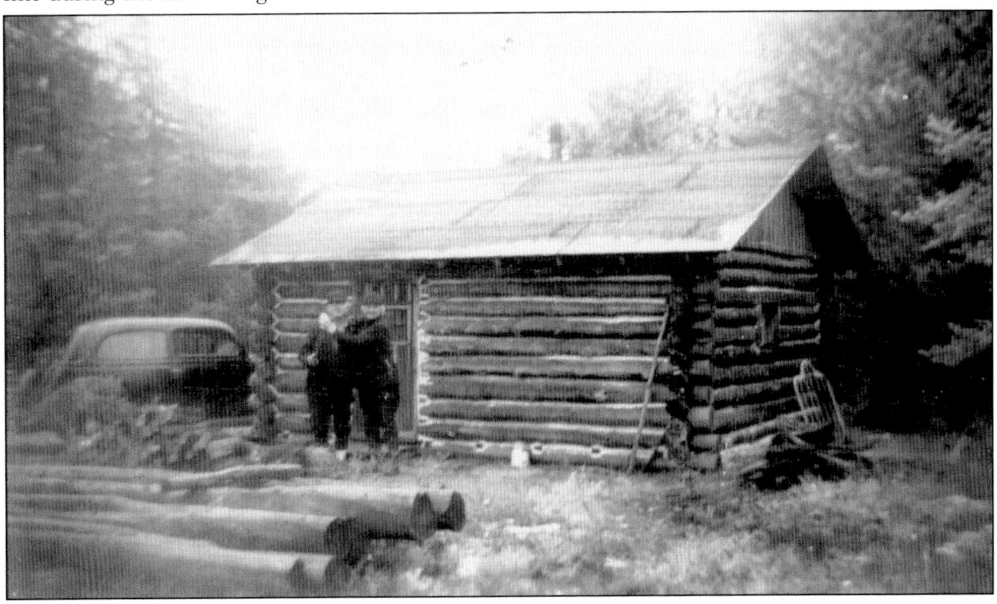

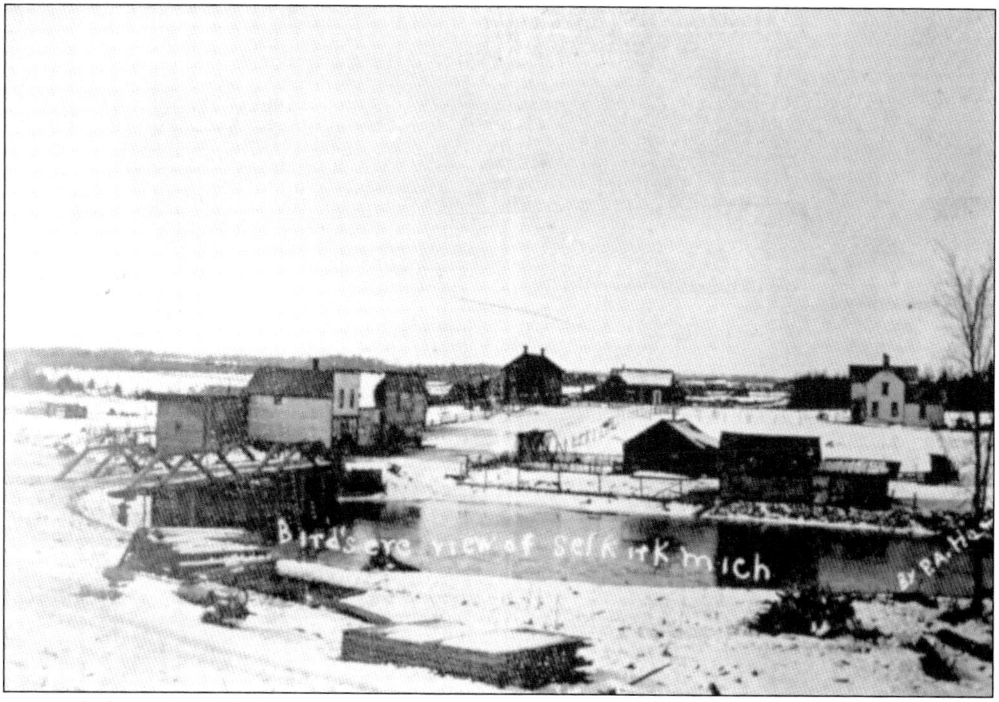

Located along the Rifle River near the intersection of an old Native American trail and the Tawas–Manistee State Road is the settlement of Selkirk. Because of its location, the community developed early into a lumbering and stopping place for travelers. A general store, blacksmith shop, hotel, and post office soon appeared. The Peters brothers built a large sawmill just north of town in 1903. This 1905 view above, looking west from the top of cemetery hill, shows the Carscallen Store, post office, town hall, Rifle River, and the bridge crossing it. Also shown is the Peters Brothers' Mill, just across the river to the right of the bridge. (Courtesy of Ardath Church.)

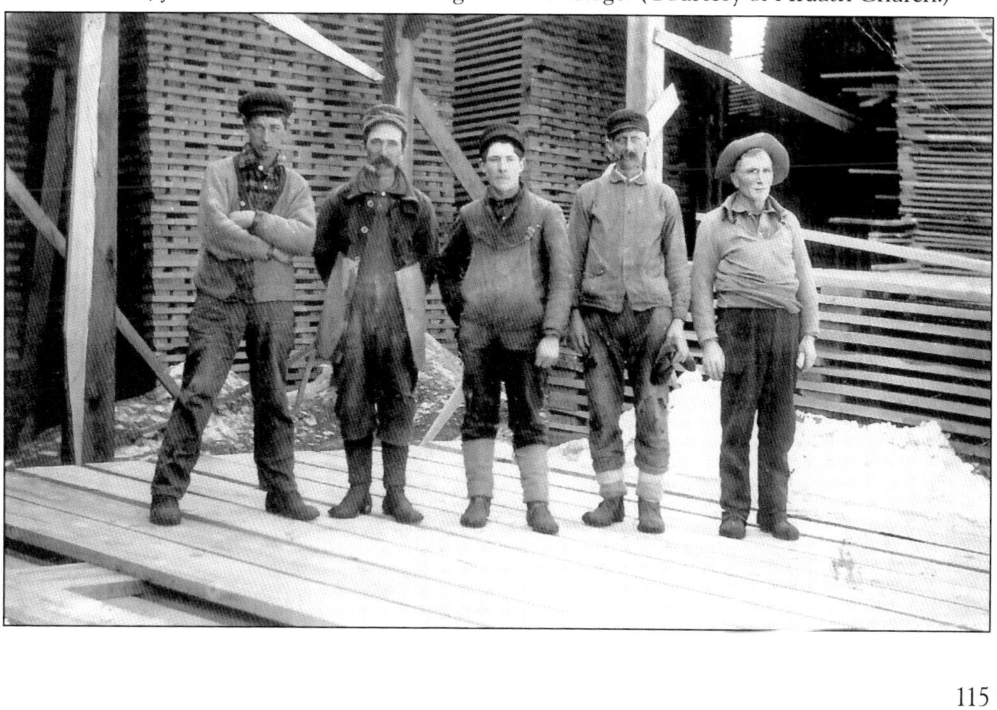

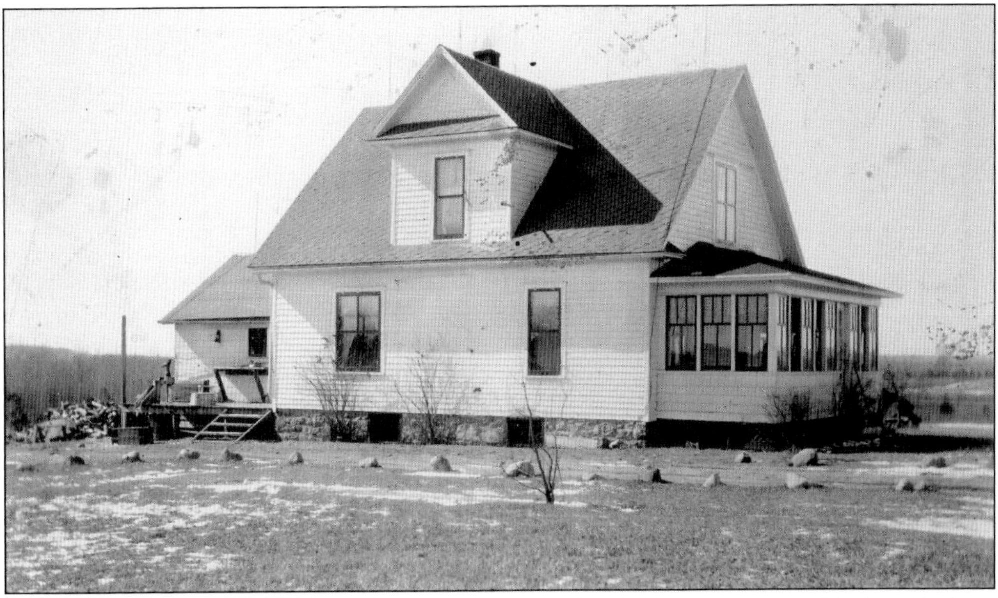

This photograph is of the Ernest Thompson house in 1926. Thompson was a blacksmith, later becoming an automobile mechanic as the times changed. He owned a small airfield at the corner of Gerald Miller Road and State Road. (Courtesy of the Ernest Thompson family.)

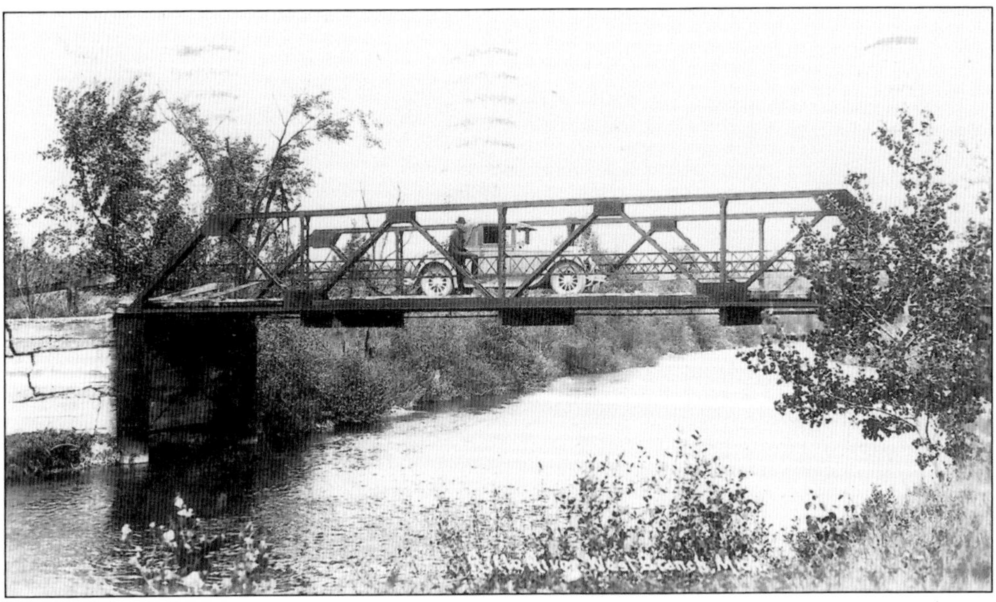

The first bridge was built in Selkirk in 1879. Early bridge construction was of cedar posts driven into the soil of the riverbank. These pilings were lashed together and provided a stable base for crossing the river. This bridge was used until 1904 when an iron bridge similar to the one above replaced it.

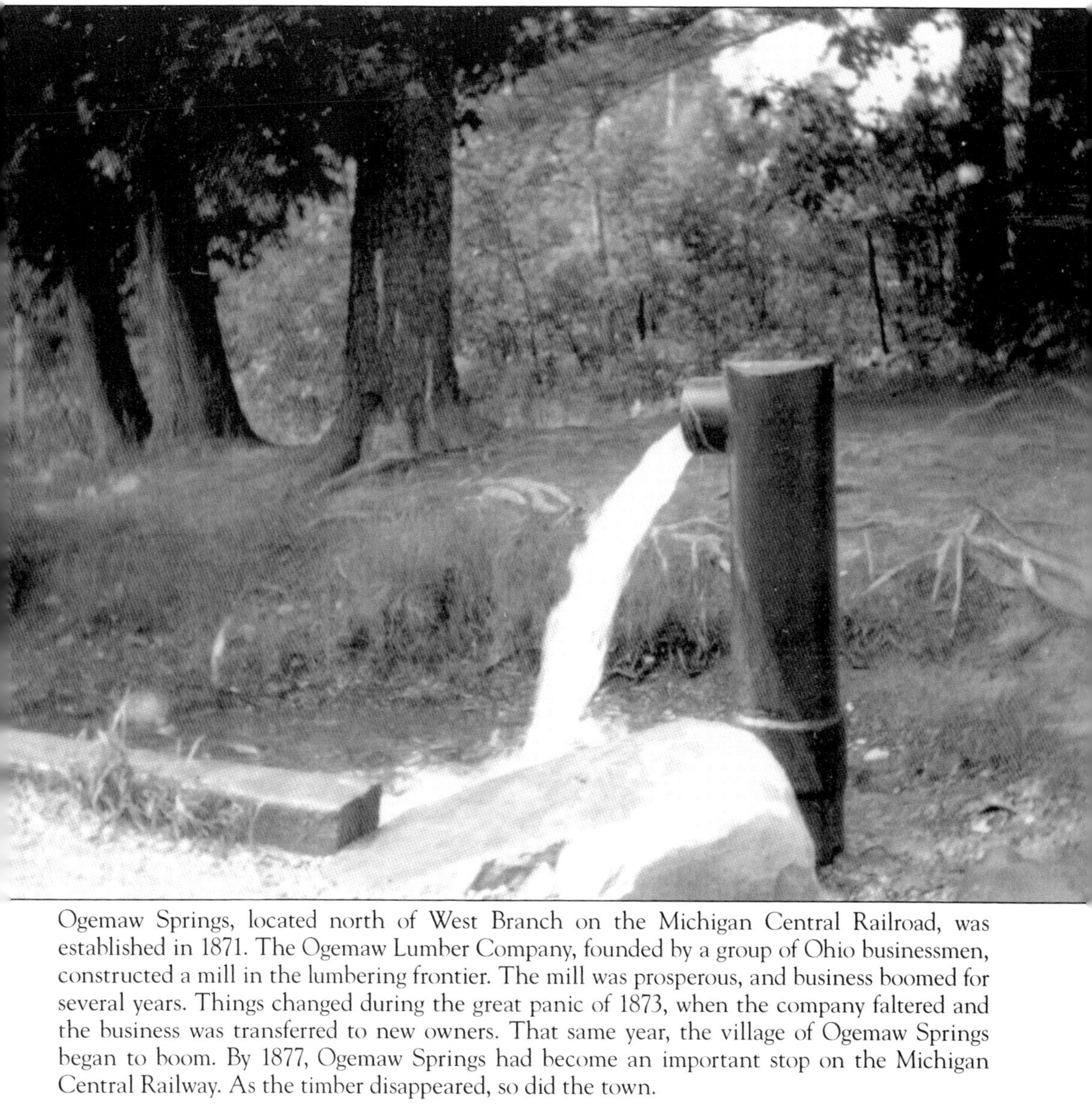

Ogemaw Springs, located north of West Branch on the Michigan Central Railroad, was established in 1871. The Ogemaw Lumber Company, founded by a group of Ohio businessmen, constructed a mill in the lumbering frontier. The mill was prosperous, and business boomed for several years. Things changed during the great panic of 1873, when the company faltered and the business was transferred to new owners. That same year, the village of Ogemaw Springs began to boom. By 1877, Ogemaw Springs had become an important stop on the Michigan Central Railway. As the timber disappeared, so did the town.

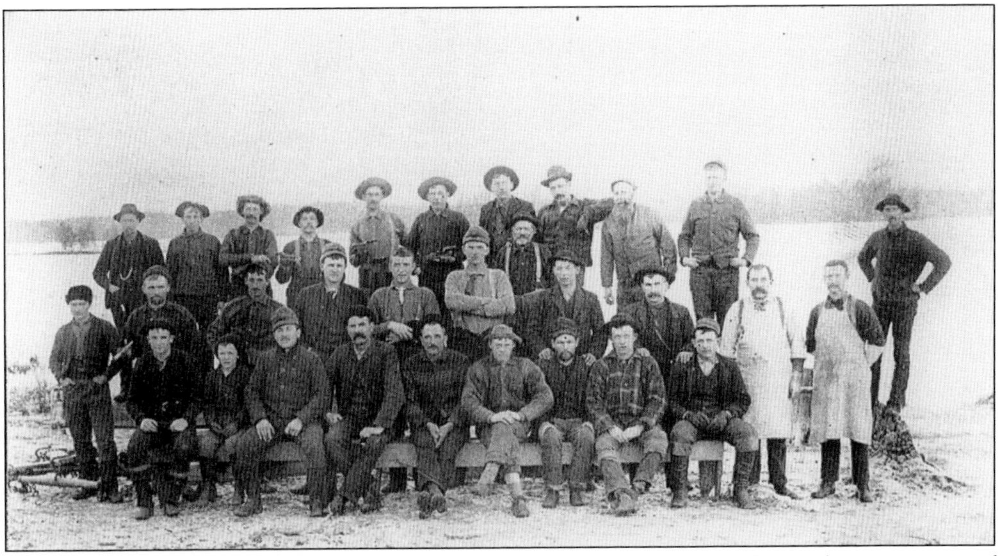

The above photograph is believed to be of a lumber camp located in Clear Lake. It was one of several camps in the area. The fine timber drew many lumbermen to the northwest corner of the county. The villages of Piper, Damon, and Beaver Lake were nearby. Today Clear Lake is a resort area with several restaurants, a hotel, a fire department, and a convenience store. (Above, courtesy of the Rose City Antique Mall.)

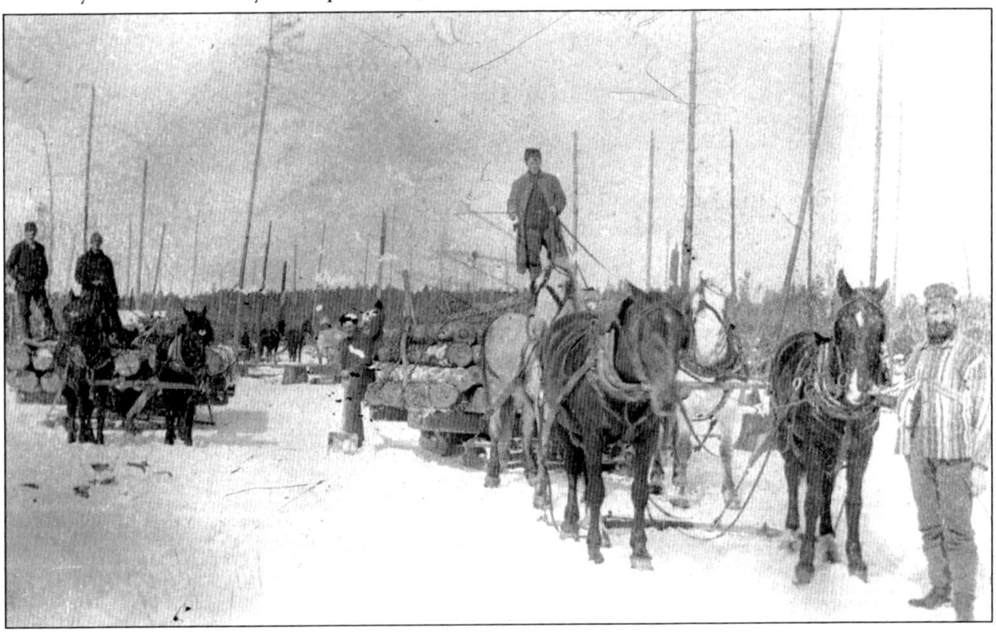

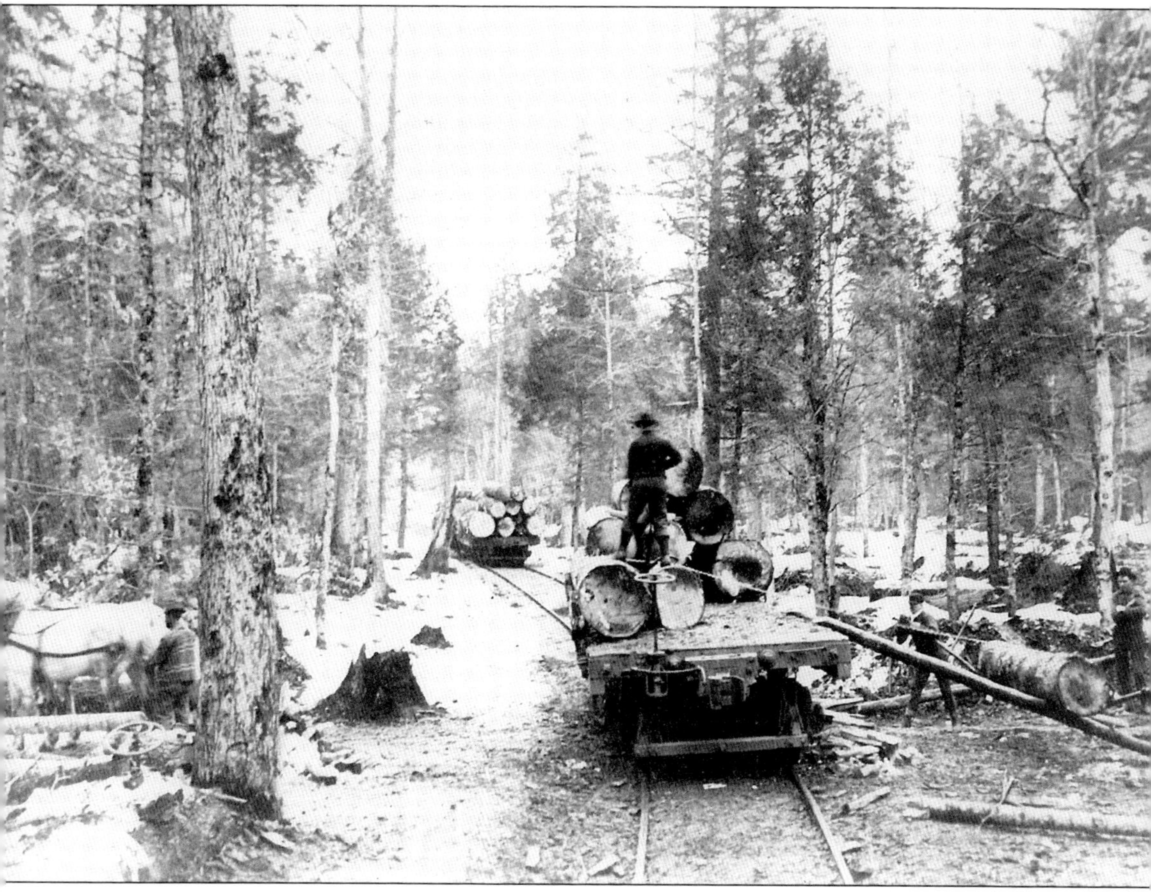

Beaver Lake was located in Foster Township, in the northwest corner of Ogemaw County. The community was settled in August 1872. It was described in the 1889 Industrial Edition of the *West Branch Times* as a clean, thriving, modern mill village. Dr. H. B. Kiehle had his headquarters here, traveling to other communities within a 40 mile radius to tend the sick. The daily stage ran from Beaver Lake to Piper. In 1877, with a population of 50 residents, Beaver Lake had a station on the Michigan Central Railroad. A sawmill and shingle mill shipped shingles and lumber regularly to markets down state. Near Beaver Lake is Preachers Hill, home of African American Preacher Brown and his family during the lumber days. The cemetery, a testimony to the struggles in a difficult era, has only one stone remaining.

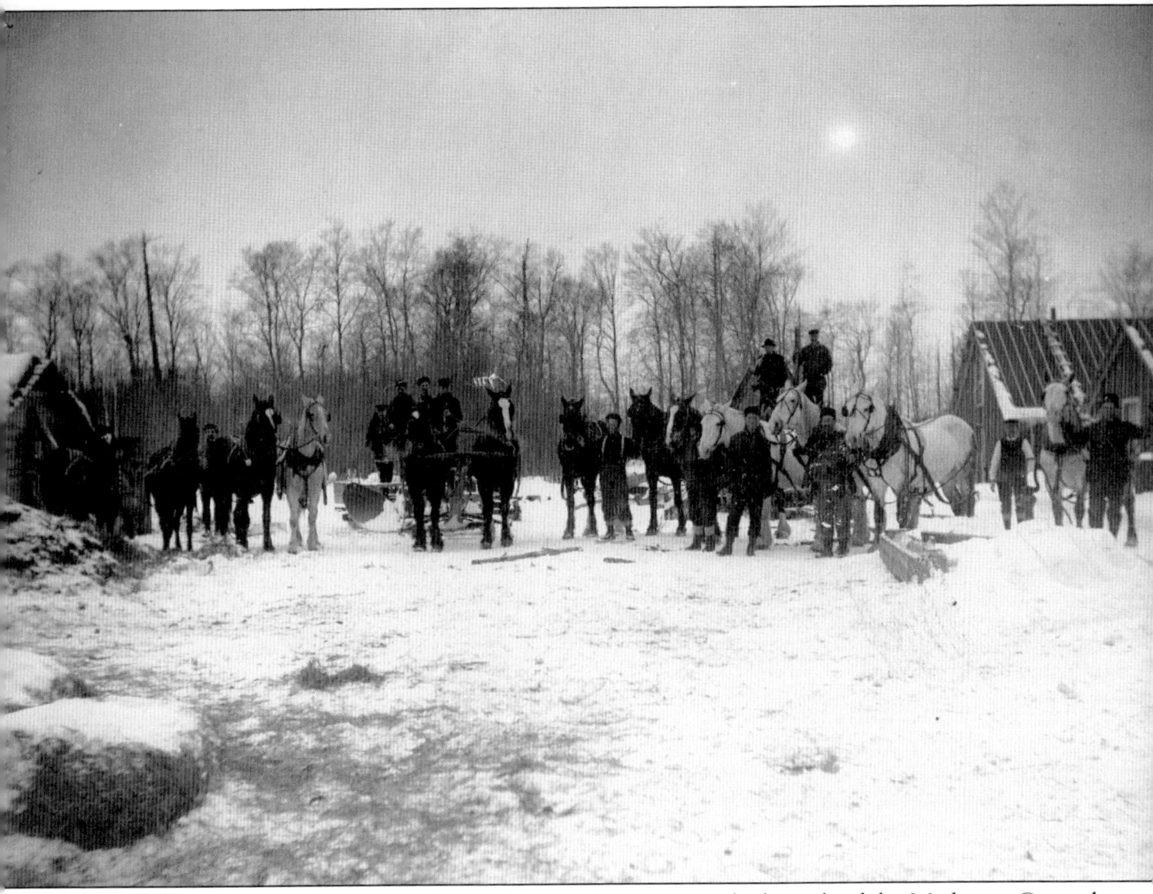

In 1882, the town of Piper was founded along the Beaver Lake branch of the Michigan Central Railroad. Almost seven miles northeast of Beaver Lake, it was located on a hill near Clear Lake. In 1881, F. M. Thompson had a planing mill, sawmill, and general store in the area. In addition to Thompson's Mill, Jacob Phillips and Company set up a shingle and lumber mill. In 1877, the population was 125 and growing. Piper consisted of a ball field, a roller-skating rink, a general store, church, school, and other places of business. Within 10 years, 50 million board feet of lumber was cut in the area. In March 1892, 10 years after its founding, the post office closed and the village became deserted.

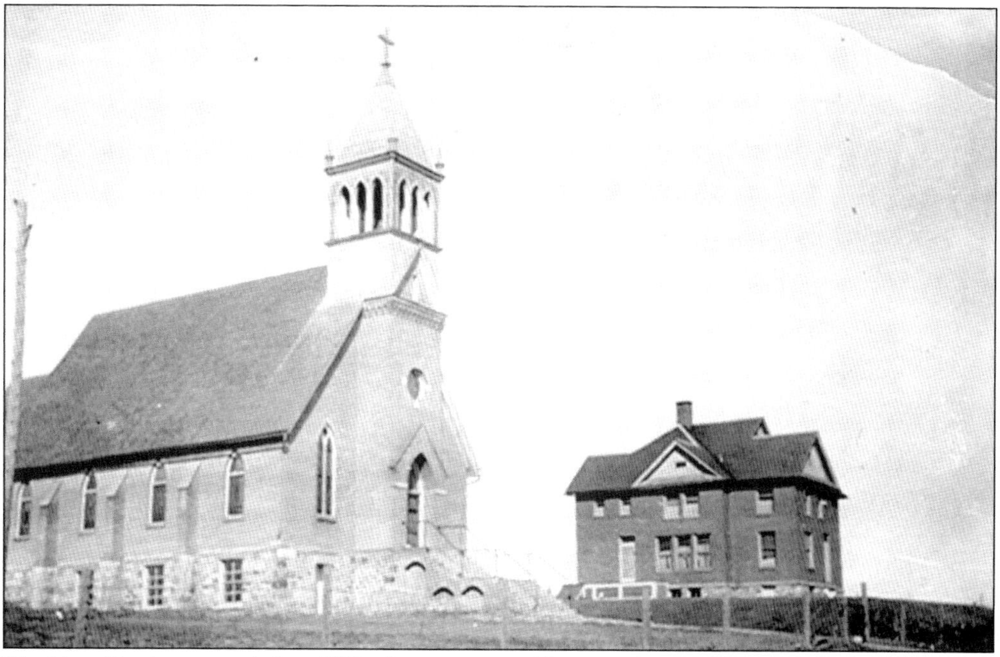

Klacking Creek was settled in 1872 when a group of farmers came to this area. Many of German heritage, these new residents included John Klacking, Christopher Reetz, Conrad and Eustace Meir, John Hacht, John Smith, Horace Sherman, and others. Religion was of supreme importance, and soon mass was being celebrated at the home of William Meir of nearby Campbell Corners. When the home became too small, the services were moved to Sherman School. In 1903, five acres was purchased from Conrad Meir Sr. for a new church. In 1904, the cornerstone was laid and St. Joseph, Klacking Creek Church was built. On April 3, 1931, a fire destroyed the church and, with the help of the community, it was rebuilt by October.

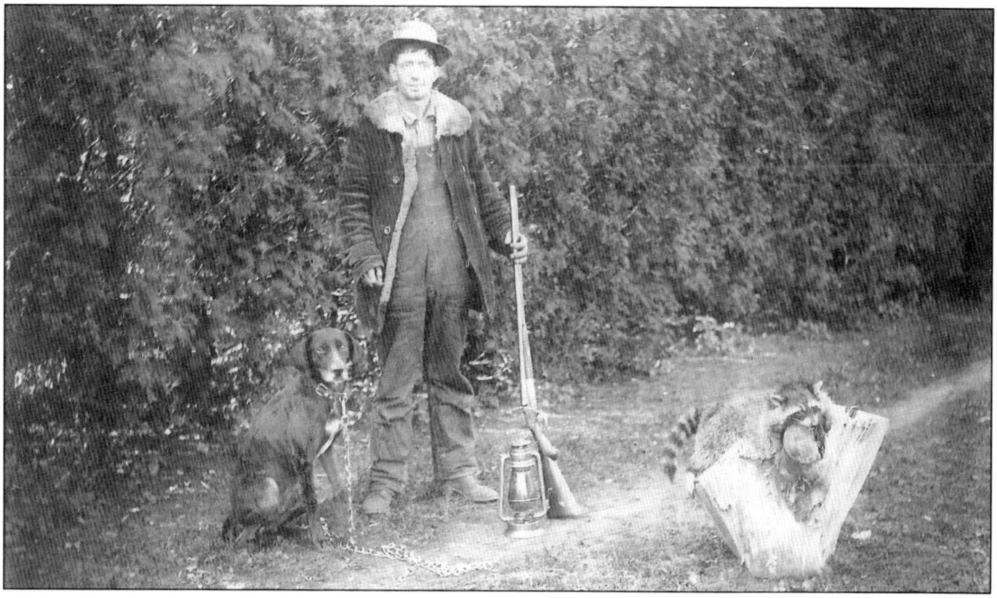

Many men came to Ogemaw County to live off the land. They hunted, fished, and trapped to survive. This unique gentleman appears to have perhaps gotten his dinner as well as a new hat.

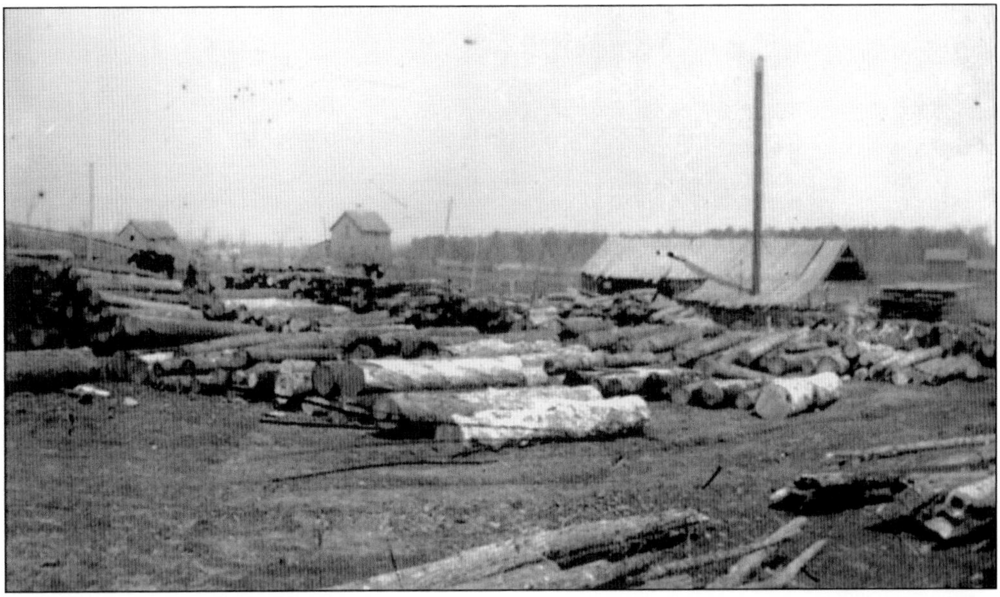

James Campbell (1845–1923) settled in Section 12 of West Branch Township in 1885. Campbell's sawmill and farm were on the northeast corner of Campbell and State Roads. The photograph above, taken 1905, shows the Campbell Mill, with farmhouses in the rear. In 1890, a post office was established at Campbell Corners, and by 1905 the community boasted a population of 145. Campbell Corners, located on the Tawas–Manistique State Road between West Branch and Selkirk, bustled with visitors from all sections of the county. Campbell Corners had a Methodist church, Campbell's sawmill, feed mill, grocery store, school, and a nearby Catholic church. The Campbell Corner School, shown below in 1905, closed when school districts in the county consolidated in the 1960s.

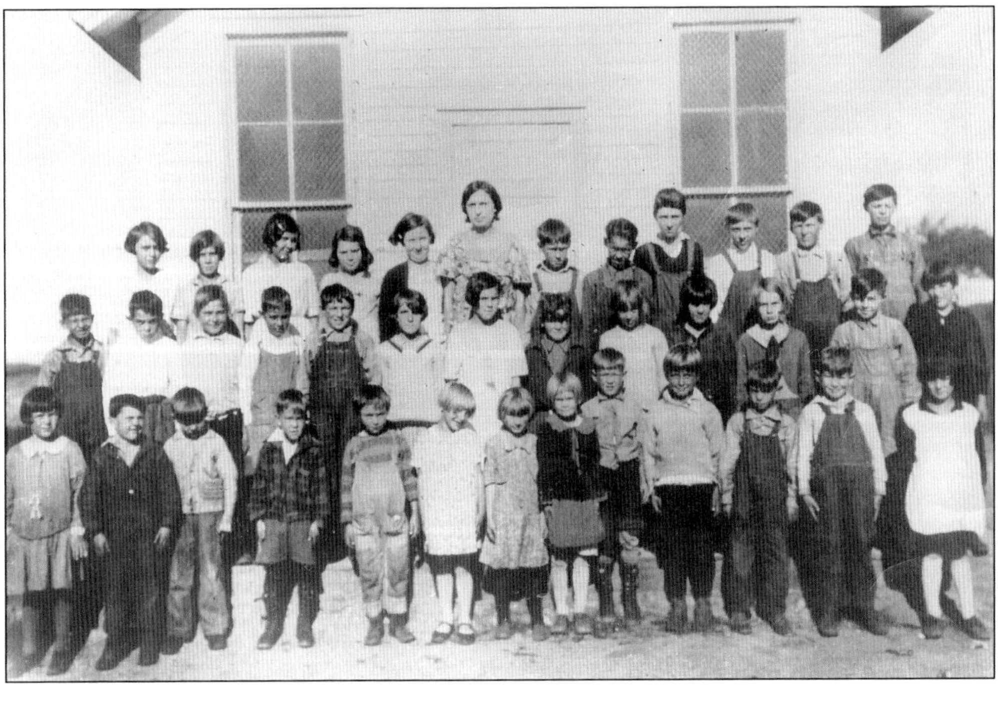

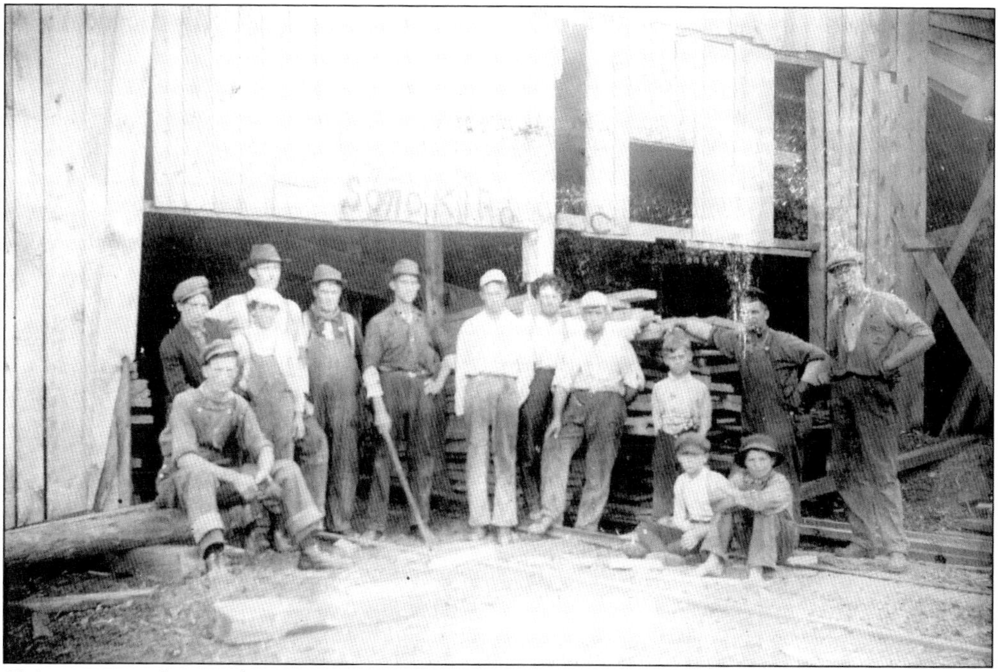

Slabtown, on the northwest corner of M-55 and M-33, was named for all the wood slabs cut there and used to make the roads. The mill and holding pond were on the northwest side of the current corner. Sawdust was carried on an overhead tram south across the road to where the current Wangler farm is.

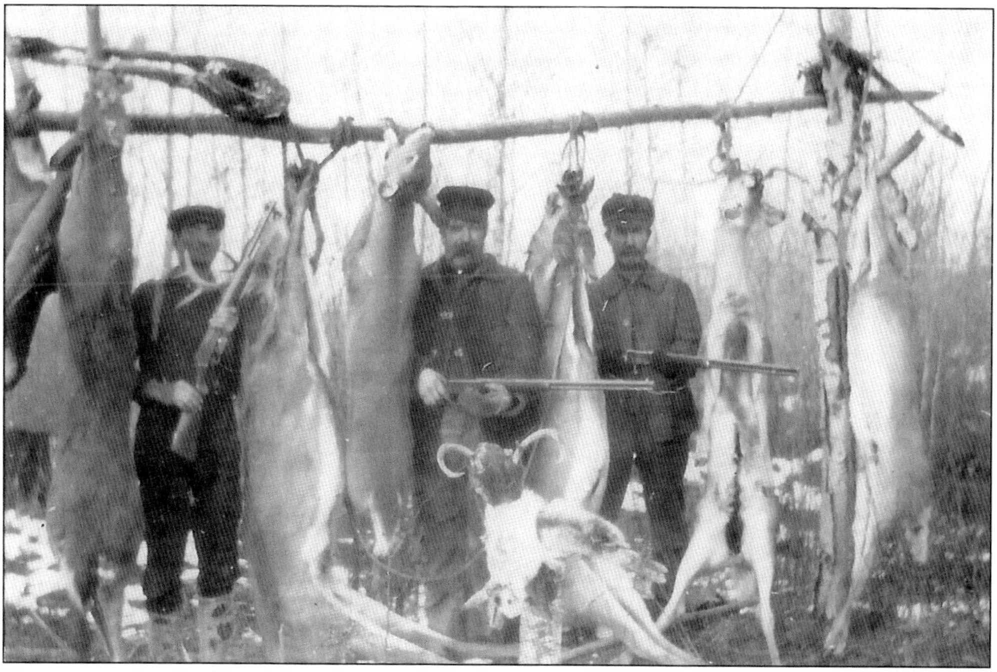

Newspapers in the big cities advertised the hunting, fishing, and camping opportunities in Ogemaw County. Wildlife and fish were plentiful. These deer hunters appear to have had a very successful hunt.

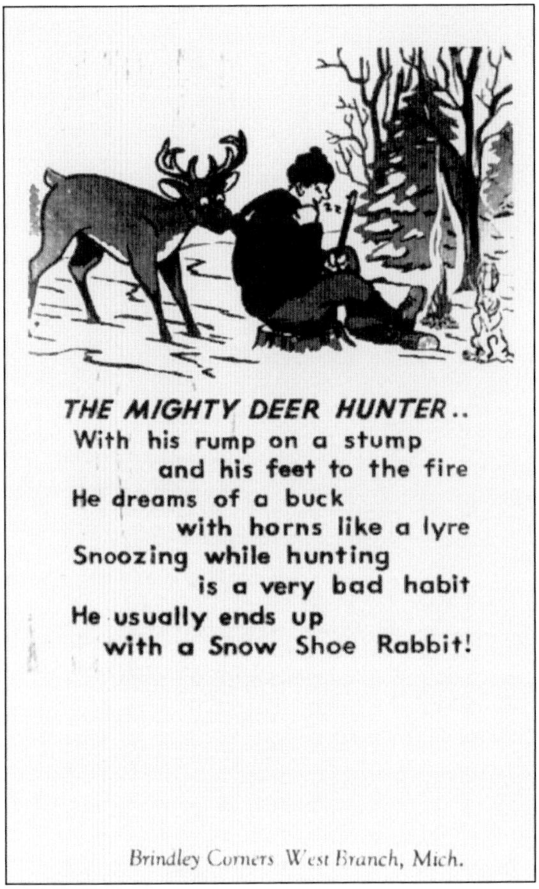

Brindley Corners was located at the intersection of M-33 and State Road. It was often called Brindley Grove because of the beautiful stand of mixed hardwoods there. At one time there was a store with a gas pump located on the southwest corner. Later a small diner and the petting zoo in the photograph below were added.

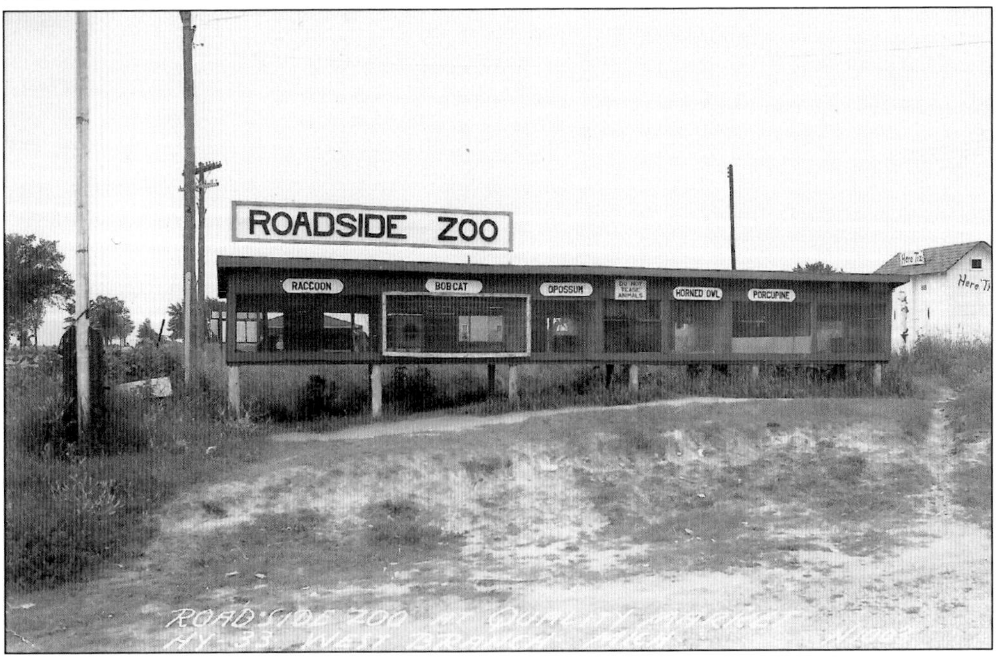

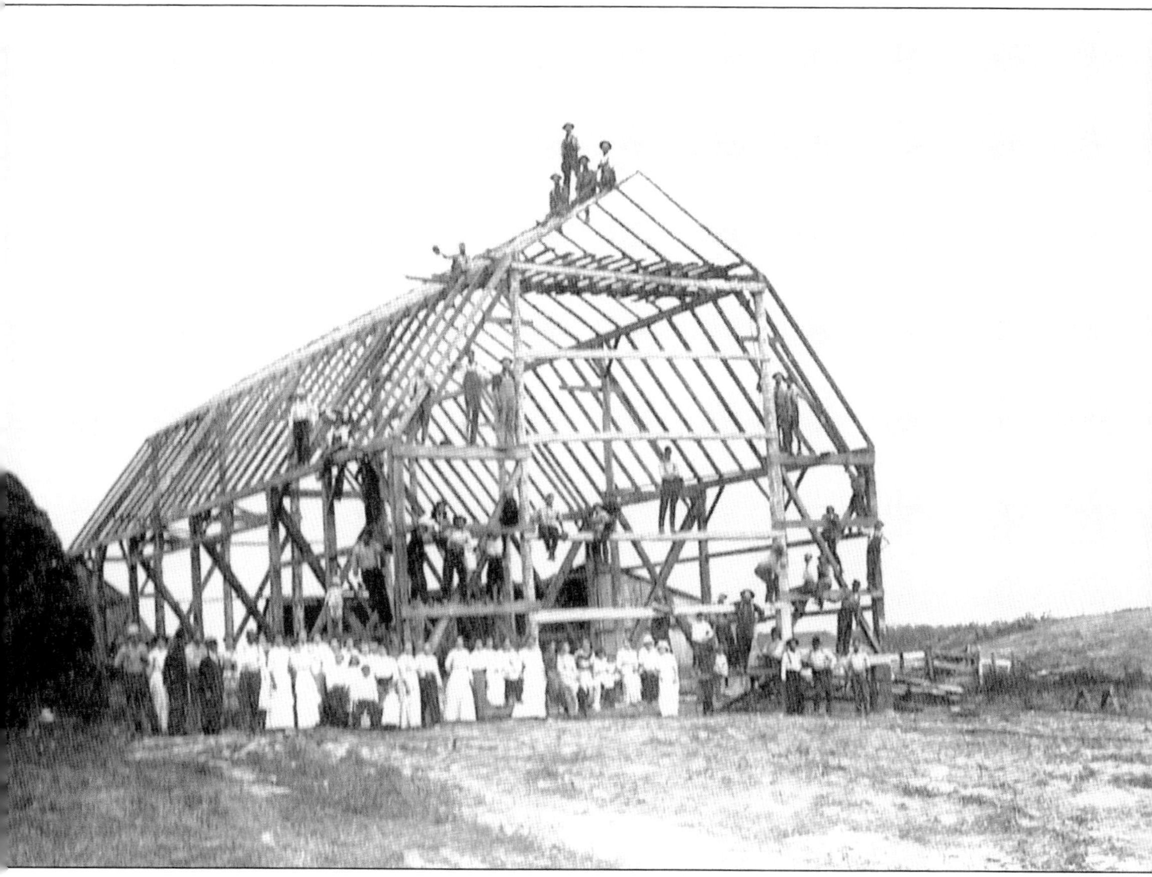

Nester Corners is located at the intersection of M-55 and Sage Lake Road. It was named after Tom Nester, a lumberman in the area. The post office was established in 1901 in the Aldrich Store, Del Rose was the first postmaster. In 1911, a rural route from Prescott was established and the Nester post office was closed. For many years there were two grocery stores there. Nester was known for its celebrations with picnics, baseball games, and horse races.

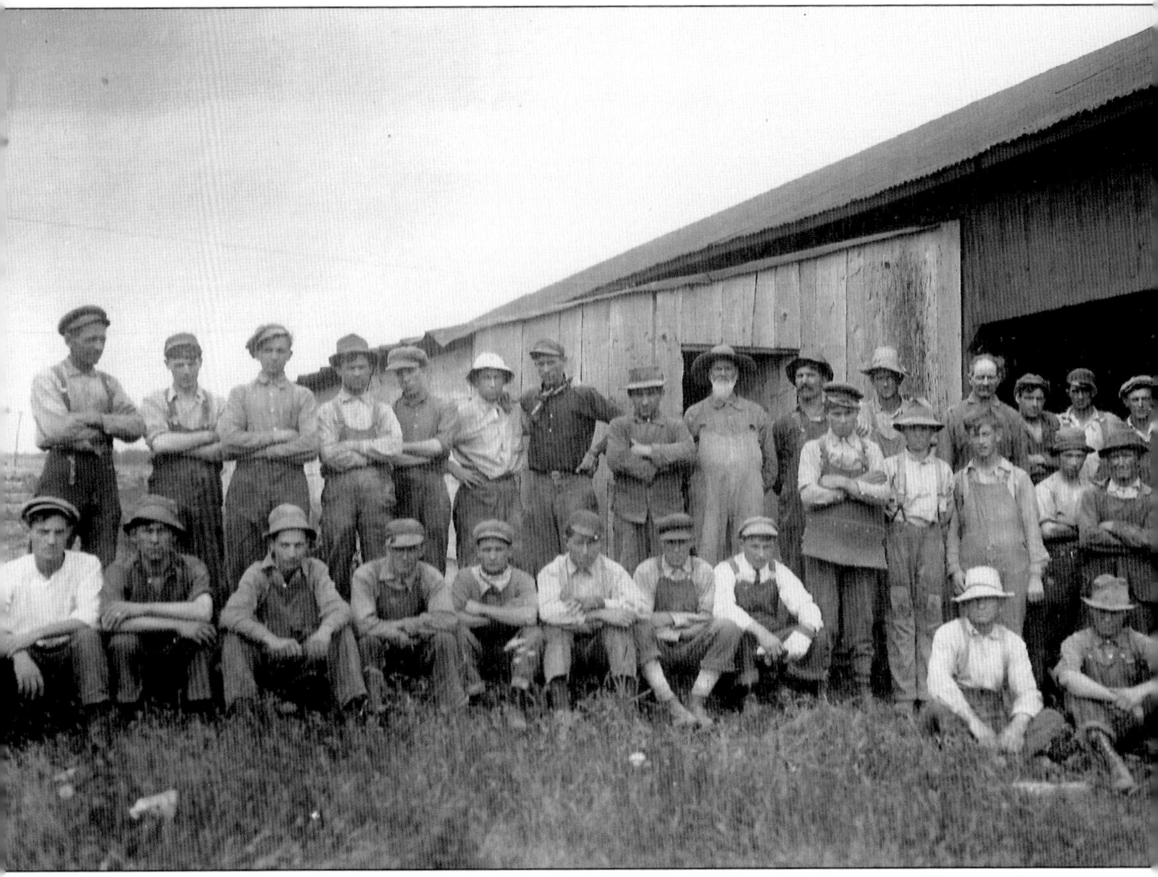

Canfield was located about eight miles west of Hale near Laird Lake. In 1905, it had a post office but mail only ran three days a week. By 1910, the mail ran daily. Canfield consisted of a blacksmith shop, grocery store, sawmill, and a railroad depot with an express agent. Slayton was a small settlement in the northeast corner of Klacking Township, named for Eugene Slayton, a local farmer and lumbering entrepreneur. By 1885, the settlement was no longer large enough for a post office. Deckerville, located in northern Rose Township, grew up around John Decker's mill.

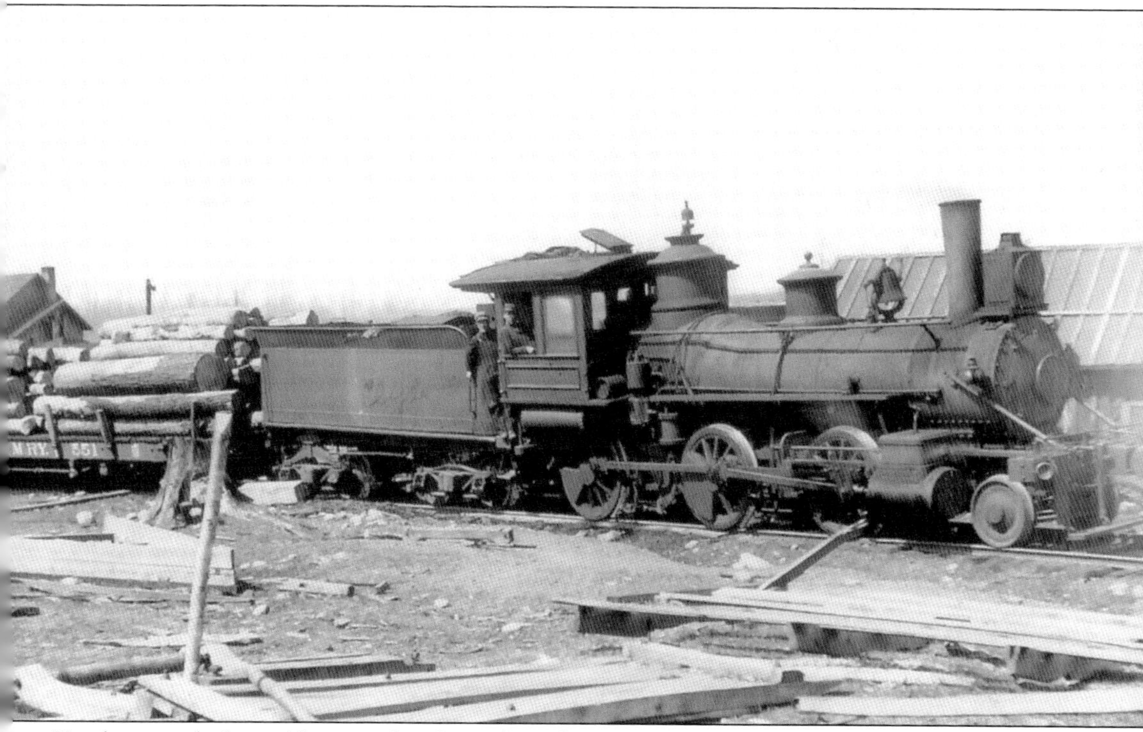

Heading north from Alger on the Central Michigan Railroad, the first stop inside Ogemaw County was Summit Station. Summit boasted a hotel with a post office, saloon, and telegraph office. Next came Greenwood Station, possibly named for its beautiful stands of green timber. There were as many as 30 or 40 camps in the Greenwood Station area. These camps employed up to 2,000 men during the winter months. According to the 1895 *Michigan State Business Directory*, Greenwood was one of the best points on the railroad for sportsmen, with game of all kinds found in abundance here. Continuing north, the next stop was Loranger Station. Loranger had a railroad line that ran west to the Hecla Marl Plant. The Hecla and Portland Cement Company built about eight houses, several outbuildings, and a huge boardinghouse near the plant. Hecla also had a water tower, its own electric-generator plant, and several stores. The Hecla venture lasted less than two years.